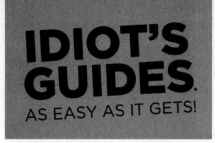

IDIOT'S GUIDES
AS EASY AS IT GETS!

Judaism

by Rabbi Jeffrey Wildstein

A
ALPHA
A member of Penguin Random House LLC

ALPHA BOOKS

Published by Penguin Random House LLC

Penguin Random House LLC, 375 Hudson Street, New York, New York 10014, USA • Penguin Random House LLC (Canada), 90 Eglinton Avenue East, Suite 700, Toronto, Ontario M4P 2Y3, Canada (a division of Pearson Penguin Canada Inc.) • Penguin Books Ltd., 80 Strand, London WC2R 0RL, England • Penguin Ireland, 25 St. Stephen's Green, Dublin 2, Ireland (a division of Penguin Books Ltd.) • Penguin Random House LLC (Australia), 250 Camberwell Road, Camberwell, Victoria 3124, Australia (a division of Pearson Australia Group Pty. Ltd.) • Penguin Books India Pvt. Ltd., 11 Community Centre, Panchsheel Park, New Delhi—110 017, India • Penguin Random House LLC (NZ), 67 Apollo Drive, Rosedale, North Shore, Auckland 1311, New Zealand (a division of Pearson New Zealand Ltd.) • Penguin Books (South Africa) (Pty.) Ltd., 24 Sturdee Avenue, Rosebank, Johannesburg 2196, South Africa • Penguin Books Ltd., Registered Offices: 80 Strand, London WC2R 0RL, England

Copyright © 2015 by Penguin Random House LLC

International Standard Book Number: 978-1-61564-781-1
Library of Congress Catalog Card Number: 2014957362

17   16   15   8   7   6   5   4   3   2   1

Interpretation of the printing code: The rightmost number of the first series of numbers is the year of the book's printing; the rightmost number of the second series of numbers is the number of the book's printing. For example, a printing code of 15-1 shows that the first printing occurred in 2015.

Printed in the United States of America

Note: This publication contains the opinions and ideas of its author. It is intended to provide helpful and informative material on the subject matter covered. It is sold with the understanding that the author and publisher are not engaged in rendering professional services in the book. If the reader requires personal assistance or advice, a competent professional should be consulted. The author and publisher specifically disclaim any responsibility for any liability, loss, or risk, personal or otherwise, which is incurred as a consequence, directly or indirectly, of the use and application of any of the contents of this book.

Most Alpha books are available at special quantity discounts for bulk purchases for sales promotions, premiums, fundraising, or educational use. Special books, or book excerpts, can also be created to fit specific needs. For details, write: Special Markets, Alpha Books, 375 Hudson Street, New York, NY 10014.

Publisher: *Mike Sanders*
Associate Publisher: *Billy Fields*
Acquisitions Editor: *Janette Lynn*
Development Editor: *John Etchison*
Cover Designer: *Laura Merriman*

Book Designer: *William Thomas*
Indexer: *Brad Herriman*
Layout: *Ayanna Lacey*
Proofreader: *Tricia Liebig*

Contents

Appendixes

Introduction

Judaism is both an ancient tradition and a dynamic modern religion. It's ancient in that it was the first to adhere to monotheism, nearly 3,500 years ago. It's modern in that it still thrives today in many forms, with exciting and interesting religious, cultural, and ethnic elements to discover.

By opening this book, you're about to embark on a journey of discovery of this beautiful tradition. The Jewish story is one of triumph and tragedy, spirituality and practicality, experience and eternality, and seriousness and enjoyment. It's rich with meaning, and simply fascinating to learn.

There are many possible reasons you've picked up this book. You might be interested in renewing your heritage as a Jew, reconnecting to the tradition. You might have heard about this amazing people and religion called Jews and Judaism, and want to understand more about them. You might want to learn more about the religion of the person with whom you're falling in love. You might be wondering if Judaism is right for you. You might simply have an interest in learning this wonderful tradition.

Whatever your reason for taking this journey with me, you won't be disappointed. Through stories, sacred texts, and descriptions of unique practices, we'll travel together to gain an understanding of this magnificent faith.

There are a few things you should know before we begin.

Transliteration

Many of the terms used in this book are in Hebrew or Yiddish, two languages closely associated with Judaism. This guide will help with pronunciation of these words.

Vowels

a: Like the "a" in "across"

ai: Like "aye"

e: Like the "e" in "let"

ee: Like the "ee" in "bee"

ei: Like the "ei" in "weigh"

ey: Like the "ay" in "way"

i: Like the "i" in "sit"

o: Like the "o" in "note"

oo: Like the "oo" in "zoo"

u: Like the "oo" in "zoo"

Consonants

Most consonant sounds are the same in Hebrew or Yiddish as in English. There are two not found in English:

ch: A guttural sound a bit like clearing your throat

tz: Like the "ts" in "rats"

Gender usage

Traditionally, Jews mostly have used masculine pronouns to refer to God. However, more and more Jews disagree with favoring one gender or another by identifying God as either masculine or feminine. I agree that assigning a gender to God creates many problems, both for our gender relationships and for our understanding of what God is. I therefore will avoid using any gender pronouns for God, even if this might lead to some awkward sentences.

Dates

Like many scholars, Jews use the terms Before the Common Era (B.C.E.) and Common Era (C.E.) to denote years instead of B.C. and A.D. This is because the latter terms imply the divinity of Jesus, which Jews don't accept. This book will use B.C.E. and C.E. to refer to dates.

How This Book Is Organized

Part 1, Three Defining Moments, tells about the three main concepts you need to know to understand the basis of Judaism. Each is tied to a historical event.

Part 2, Understanding the Basics, develops the basic ideas of Jews and Judaism, describing Jewish history and thought, sacred texts, differences among groups and movements, ethics, and the special connection Jews have with Israel.

Part 3, A Year of Jewish Holy Days, considers the holy days, festivals, and celebrations in the Jewish calendar.

Part 4, Jewish Life Events, speaks about the important milestones in a Jew's life.

Part 5, A Jewish Home, brings you into the Jewish home, exploring Jewish art, food, and family relationships.

Part 6, The Jewish Community, opens the Jewish community to you, welcoming you into the synagogue, prayer, and other aspects of Jewish life.

Part 7, Comparisons and Questions, compares the beliefs of Judaism and Christianity, and presents some commonly asked questions (and answers) not otherwise considered in the book.

Extras

Throughout this book, you'll find sidebars that will guide you in your learning about Judaism. You'll find important information that reveals additional facts and issues to deepen your understanding and appreciation of Judaism.

 DEFINITION

In these sidebars, you'll find definitions to help you understand the Hebrew and Yiddish terms that are part of the fabric of Judaism.

 ASK THE RABBI

These sidebars answer common questions about Jewish spirituality and practice often presented to a rabbi.

 OY VEY!

Pay special attention to these sidebars. They warn you about common mistakes or misconceptions often held about Judaism.

 WORDS OF WISDOM

In these sidebars, you'll find enriching quotes from sacred Scripture, sages, and historical figures.

 WORTH NOTING

These sidebars provide extra facts and important commentaries that explore nuances of the Jewish tradition.

Book Extra

In addition to the material in this book, you'll find a Jewish holiday calendar you can print for your personal use. You'll find it at idiotsguides.com/judaism.

Acknowledgments

Every rabbi relies on the wisdom of his teachers. I'm grateful for my rabbis and those who have taught and guided me: Rabbi Peter Kasdan, Rabbi Hank Zoob, Rabbi Jim Ponet, Rabbi Rosalind Gold, Rabbi Jon Adland, Dr. Michael Cook, Dr. Richard Sarason, Dr. Jonathan Cohen, Dr. Michael Meyer, and Dr. Gary Zola. Any errors are mine, and not a result of their teaching.

I thank the wonderful staff at Alpha Books, particularly editors Janette Lynn and John Etchison, for their help, guidance, and patience throughout the process of writing this volume.

I thank my parents, Richard and Judy, and my in-laws, Barbara and Phil, for their encouragement, love, and support.

Most of all, I thank my wife, Andrea, for reading and advising on every word of this book, and supporting and encouraging me personally and professionally in every aspect of my life and rabbinate. I couldn't hope for a better partner in life.

Trademarks

Three Defining Moments

If you want to understand the primary ideas behind Judaism, you need to know only three stories from Jewish history and their meanings. These three stories describe pivotal moments that define who Jews are and what they believe. Part 1 reveals these three events and their effect upon Judaism.

Chapter 1 discusses the call to Abraham and Sarah, and how that led to the adoption of the Jewish view of God. Chapter 2 relates the story of Moses at Sinai, and how the Covenant made with God there led to the receipt of the sacred Scripture, the Torah, and the acceptance of God's commandments. Chapter 3 speaks about the destruction of the Second Temple and how the aftermath of that tragic event led to the solidification of the Jews as a united people of Israel.

The Call to Abraham: God in Judaism

Judaism began in a world full of gods. People believed in gods that had specific powers or responsibilities. One god would be the god of the sky, another would be the god of the sea, another would be the god of fertility, and so on.

Judaism separated itself from this belief in many gods, called polytheism, to strike a new path. This path introduced the belief that there was only one God, a belief called monotheism. The Bible tells the story of the courageous individuals who first accepted monotheism, which became the core principle of Judaism through the centuries to today.

In This Chapter

- Monotheism: the idea of one God
- The roles of Abraham and Sarah
- What God is and what God does
- One God with many names
- Must a Jew believe in God?

The Story of Abraham and Sarah

According to Judaism's sacred Scripture, the Bible, the first people to accept the idea of only one God were Abraham and his wife, Sarah. Their story of faith, bravery, and separation from other beliefs began the religion we know as Judaism today.

Abraham's Discovery

A story in the Jewish tradition explains how Abraham, then called Avram, realized the truth of monotheism at a young age.

 ASK THE RABBI

How does Avram get the name "Abraham," and why? God gives Avram this new name later in his life. God adds the Hebrew letter *hey* to Avram's name, making it "Avraham," or in English, "Abraham." A commentary says this demonstrates God is always with Abraham, because the primary four-letter name for God in Hebrew has two *heys* in it.

The story tells about Avram's uncle, Nimrod, who owned an idol shop. Idols were statues of the many gods people worshipped. Nimrod sold these idols in his shop, and Avram would help his uncle run the store.

One day, Nimrod needed to leave the store for a while, and decided that Avram was old enough to watch the business on his own. As soon as Nimrod left, Avram took a big stick and smashed all the idols except for the largest statue, which stood in the middle of the store. Avram put the stick into the large idol's arms, and waited for his uncle's return.

When Nimrod entered his store, he saw all his merchandise smashed to bits. Furious, he asked Avram what had happened.

"Uncle, it was the most amazing sight!" Avram said. "All the little idols were teasing that big idol. So the big idol took that stick and smashed all of them to pieces!"

"That's ridiculous!" Nimrod exclaimed. "All these idols are just pieces of stone! They can't really do anything!"

"I see," replied Avram. "But then, Uncle, why do people worship them?"

From this reasoning, Avram understood that the idea of worshipping anything physical as a god made no sense. Also, he realized that there weren't many different gods of various ranks and powers who battled jealously with each other. Avram had grasped the idea of "monotheism," the idea that there is only one God in heaven and Earth.

The Call to Abraham

The Bible first mentions Avram in Genesis 12. God tells Avram to take his wife, Sarai, and leave his father's house and country, and go to a new land that God will show him. God promises Avram that he and his family will be blessed for doing this. He and Sarai will start a new nation with a great name. God promises to bless anyone who treats this nation well, and to curse anyone who treats the nation poorly.

Later, in Genesis 15 and 17, God gives more details about this promise. God says Avram will have children, and he will be seen as the father of many nations. God promises to give the land of Canaan to Avram and his descendants, as long as they always maintain and demonstrate their faith in God. God calls this agreement with Avram a covenant, emphasizing its seriousness.

Judaism sees God's call to Avram and the ritual as Avram's complete acceptance of monotheism. From then until today, we're bound to believe in God if we want the promises God made to Avram to apply to us as well.

 OY VEY!

Although Genesis mostly speaks of Avram, the role of Abraham's wife, Sarai, must not be minimized. Sarai plays a crucial part in the formation of Judaism and the realization of monotheism. We know this because when God calls Avram, he and Sarai take with them all the people they had gathered. This is understood to mean that Avram had spoken to the men about monotheism, and Sarai had spoken to the women, and between them they had begun to form the people who would become Jews. Also, God also changes Sarai's name to Sarah, adding the letter "hey" just as God had done for Abraham.

The journey God calls Avram to take is more than a physical trip. It's a spiritual journey to an understanding and acceptance of a radical new Truth. There is only one God in heaven and on Earth to be worshipped as the all-powerful and all-knowing entity that created and has the ability to control everything.

Describing God

It's very difficult to describe God in Judaism. How do you describe something that has no physical body, and by definition is far beyond anything human beings can know or understand? In fact, one of the most heartfelt stories in the Bible tells how Moses, Judaism's greatest teacher and leader, begs God to let him see God's face. God says no, because no one can see God's face and live. (Exodus 33:18-23) One of the Ten Commandments says that we can't make a "graven image" of God, meaning we can't show God in any picture or statue. Even God sometimes has trouble describing who God is to us in ways we can understand. At one point in the Bible, God says

God is *ehyeh asher ehyeh*, which means, "I will be what I will be." (Exodus 3:14) One might say this description is not very helpful for someone trying to get a first idea about what Judaism means when we talk about God.

We can certainly say some things about God from reading the many stories in the Bible. God is far above and beyond anything in the human experience. God is all-powerful (omnipotent) and all-knowing (omniscient). God exists everywhere, and not just where Jews live. God sometimes can be seen in great displays of awesome power, as in thunder and lightning. (Exodus 20:18) But God also appears in subtler, spiritual forms, like a burning bush that is not consumed (Exodus 3:4) or in a still, small voice heard in our souls. (I Kings 19:12)

Statue of Maimonides in Cordova, Spain.

The great Jewish scholar Maimonides has perhaps the best possible description of God that summarizes the Biblical and traditional views. Maimonides first states that we accept that God exists, echoing the idea in the first of the Ten Commandments: "I am Adonai your God." Maimonides then explains that God causes everything in the universe to exist and happen. God first causes everything in our universe, including all physical things, all energy, and all life.

ASK THE RABBI

Does Judaism offer proof of God's existence? Judaism doesn't offer direct proof of God's existence. By definition, it's impossible to offer direct proof of something beyond our understanding and perception. However, some Jewish teachings see proof of God by inference. One teaching says that just as a palace you see must have had an architect, so too must the world have a designer. Another sees proof of God's power in that when people create coins, each one comes from the press identical to the others. But God made people from one press, Adam and Eve, and by God's power, we all come out differently.

Next, Maimonides explains the unity of God. Simply put, God is One. This means God is unique, different from anything else in the universe. There is no other god besides God, and God is not divided into separate parts or aspects. Any division into parts would lessen God from the all-powerful entity envisioned in the Jewish idea of monotheism.

God is also noncorporeal. This means God has no physical body, but is above and beyond physical form. If God had a body, God could be destroyed or harmed by other physical things in the universe, something that is impossible in the Jewish idea of monotheism. Maimonides therefore concludes that nothing in the physical universe can affect God.

Finally, Maimonides describes God as eternal. God has always existed, and God will always exist.

Together, these qualities combine to describe God as an eternal, omniscient, omnipotent Presence in our universe. Yet God still is involved in our world and our history.

What God Does for Us

Judaism envisions three main roles God plays in our world and our lives.

First, God is our Creator. The Bible begins with the well-known story of God creating the entire universe, our planet, and all life in six days. While God's initial crafting of the universe ended after this first week, Judaism understands that God continues creating every day. Judaism considers the changes in our world, each sunrise and sunset, and the formation of new life all to be the result of God's creative power. One tradition says God creates matches between two people, as we'll see in Chapter 15.

Second, God is our Revealer. God teaches us how to live our lives, and gives us laws and ethics to follow. God guides us on right and worthy paths in our lives.

Third, God is our Redeemer. The greatest example of this is the Biblical story of God's freeing the Israelites from slavery in Egypt in the Book of Exodus. Judaism sees God as redeeming us throughout history from other peoples who hurt us. This redemption continues today. God also redeems us by giving us free will, allowing us to choose what we will do with our lives. God not only redeems us physically. God redeems us spiritually, too.

The Names of God

Judaism gives great meaning to names. We've already seen the importance of the change of Avram and Sarai's names to Abraham and Sarah. God's name has even more power and importance. This is why one of the Ten Commandments prohibits "taking God's name in vain," meaning swearing in, misusing, or destroying God's name in any way.

ASK THE RABBI

Do Jews write God or G-d? Some Jews believe any writing of God in any language falls under the prohibition of taking God's name in vain. Even though the word "god" comes from the German word *"gott"* and has no connection to any Jewish name for God, these Jews still take extra care to not break this commandment. So they write the word "God" as "G-d."

The primary name for God in Judaism is a four-letter word spelled *"yod-hey-vav-hey"* known as the Tetragrammaton. This name was not said in Biblical times except by the High Priest in the most sacred space in the Temple in Jerusalem once a year on the important Holy Day of Yom Kippur. No one knows exactly how this name was pronounced in Biblical times, although most scholars believe it was something like "Yahweh." Today, when reading from our sacred Scriptures in Hebrew, Jews pronounce the Tetragrammaton as "Adonai," meaning "My Lord" to avoid any possible transgression of the commandment about misusing God's name.

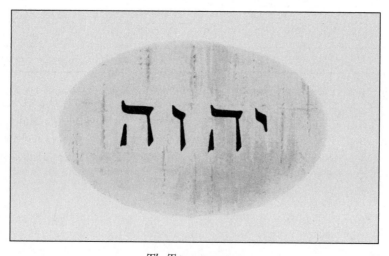

The Tetragrammaton.

There are other names for God in Scripture and in Judaism. Often, the different names are used to emphasize one particular aspect of God in the context in which it's found. Following are some of those names.

Names of God in Judaism

Name in Hebrew	Meaning
Adonai	My Lord
Aveenu	Our Father
Dayan HaEmet	The Judge of Truth
Eil	Simple name for God often combined with other words (i.e., Eil Elyon–The High One)
Ein Sof	The One without End; often used in Kabbalah
HaKadosh Baruch Hu	The Holy Blessed One
HaMakom	The Place
HaShem	The Name
Magen	Shield
Melech; Malkeinu	King; Our King
Ribeinu shel Olam	Master of the World
Shechina	The Close, Holy Presence
Shomer D'latot Yisrael	Guardian of the Gates of Yisrael; abbreviated as "Shaddai"
Tzur Yisrael	Rock of Israel
Ya	Reference to God from the Tetragrammaton

Similarly, Jewish Scripture and liturgy use several metaphors for God. One of the most important prayers of Rosh HaShanah, one of the High Holy Days, calls God Aveenu Malkeinu—"Our Father, Our King." Psalm 23 contains the well-known image of God as a shepherd, caring for us at our darkest times. These and other images help us relate to God and understand God's influence in our lives and our world.

The Sh'mah

The *Sh'mah* is a prayer said in every Jewish worship service expressing our understanding of God. The Sh'mah's first line has been called the "watchword of our faith," meaning if there's anything that is the motto of Judaism, it's this. This line is one verse from the Bible, found at Deuteronomy 6:4:

> Sh'mah Yisrael, Adonai Eloheinu, Adonai echad.
>
> Hear Israel, Adonai is your God, Adonai is One.

The Sh'mah contains three specific points. First, the prayer requires us to listen and pay close attention to what's about to be said. Something extremely important is coming. Second, the Sh'mah states the relationship between God and us. Adonai, and only Adonai, is our God. Third, the prayer affirms the unity and uniqueness of God by stating that God is One.

When written in Hebrew, the Sh'mah looks like this:

שְׁמַע יִשְׂרָאֵל, יי אֱלֹהֵינוּ, יי אֶחָד.

Two letters are written larger than the others. The sages discuss the reason for this in some *midrashim* (interpretations), a technique we will consider in Chapter 5. One is a message to be cautious with this prayer, because if we're not careful, it could be misread or misunderstood. The last letter in the first word, "Sh'mah" is written larger so we don't confuse this letter with another that has the same sound. If we confused these letters, the translation of the verse would be, "Heaven forbid, Israel, that you think Adonai is your God, and Adonai is One." The confusion of these letters changes the entire meaning of the Sh'mah, but we are prevented from making this mistake by the larger letter.

Similarly, the last letter in the last word, "echad," is written larger so that we don't read this letter as another that looks very similar. This change would make the word *"acher,"* which means "another." This simple change of one letter would remove the entire idea of the unity and uniqueness of God, so the letter is written larger to make sure we get it right.

There's another, deeper message in the enlargement of these two letters. Taken together, these two letters form the Hebrew word *eid,* which means "witness." It's our responsibility to speak about the existence and oneness of God, and to offer these ideas to anyone who might be interested in hearing them. This doesn't mean we try to persuade or pressure anyone to believe in God as we do, or to try as much as we can to make others hear our views. Being a witness means we should be proud of our beliefs, and we should present them to others by our example and if someone asks about them.

The Sh'mah is an extremely heartfelt prayer. Traditionally, it's said with the deepest intention and concentration. Many Jews close or cover their eyes while saying this prayer to focus on its meaning. In many congregations, the Sh'mah is sung to a stirring melody composed by Salomon Sulzer, a nineteenth-century Austrian cantor and composer.

Some Modern Views of God

Jewish thought about God continues to this day. We are always searching for new ways to understand God and our relationship to God.

Martin Buber was a philosopher born in Vienna in 1878 who eventually moved to Israel. Buber didn't believe a person could ever truly understand what God is. Instead, he believed that we live our lives through our experiences. Most of our experiences with things in our world are ordinary, which Buber called "I-It" relationships. In contrast, we can open our hearts to having a relationship with something special and important in our universe. Buber called this special relationship "I-Thou," and believed we could experience an "I-Thou" relationship with God.

Another of the great modern Jewish theologians was Rabbi Abraham Joshua Heschel. Rabbi Heschel escaped from Germany in the mid-twentieth century, and came to America. Rabbi Heschel described our relationship with God as if we were walking through a mysterious mist. We can't see far, but we feel that there's something in the mist beyond what our senses can perceive. We are aware that there's something meaningful there. According to Rabbi Heschel, this "meaning beyond the mystery" is God.

The important thing to remember is that Jewish thought goes beyond the portrayal of God as the "old man in the sky" people often see in the Bible. We are constantly exploring and changing our ideas as we try to gain a greater understanding of God that meets our needs and hopes, and can help us find meaning in our lives.

Jewish Atheism?

Is it possible to be a Jew and not believe in God? Yes, this is entirely possible. Once someone is a Jew, whether by birth or by choosing to become a Jew as an adult, that person is always considered Jewish, no matter what he or she believes. Our tradition also recognizes and accepts that people naturally will question the existence of God at one point or another in their lives. Some people question more than others, but most everyone will have at least some moments of doubt.

WORDS OF WISDOM

"The fool has said in his heart, 'There is no God.'"—Psalms 14:1

"Even atheism may be redeemed by charity. If someone seeks your aid, act as if there was no God, as if you alone can help."—Rabbi Moshe Leib of Sasov

However, it's hard to see Judaism as a religion, philosophy, or set of practices without God. God has been at the center of Jewish thought for millennia. God is found everywhere in our sacred Scriptures and other texts. There have been a few attempts to formulate Judaism without God, but they haven't had much of a following. So a Jew can question God or reject the idea of God and still be a Jew, but Judaism without God doesn't really exist.

The Least You Need to Know

- Judaism was the first religion to accept monotheism—the idea that there is one God in heaven and earth.
- As described in the Bible, Abraham and Sarah were the first people to realize the truth about God.
- Judaism sees God as all-powerful, all-knowing, unique, bodiless, indivisible, and existing everywhere in the universe.
- God creates our world, reveals how we should live, and redeems us from physical and spiritual bondage.

Making the Covenant at Sinai: Torah and Mitzvot

The second defining moment of Judaism happens several centuries after the call to Abraham. God has freed the Israelites from slavery in Egypt, and Moses has guided them to a mountain in the desert called Mount Sinai. God gives the Israelites a gift at this mountain: a teaching called the *Torah*. This teaching provides a code of law and ethics that Jews follow to this day. The giving and acceptance of this code also defines how Jews define their relationship with God, and gives them instructions for how we are to live.

The Torah is the central focus of much of Judaism. Jews study the Torah, sing about it, and praise God for giving it to them. Jews call the Torah the "Tree of Life" because they see adherence to it as the source of their longevity and survival as a people. The acceptance of the Torah forms the basis of the Jewish Covenant with God, a critical aspect of Judaism.

In This Chapter

- The importance of the Torah
- Moses and the Ten Commandments
- The idea of mitzvah
- Hiddur mitzvah: making a commandment special

Arriving at the Mountain

When the Israelites reach Mount Sinai, Moses leaves the people and goes up the mountain alone. Eventually, Moses brings two tablets of stone down to the people. These tablets contain the Word of God instructing the people about how God wants them to live their lives. In this way, God becomes the Revealer.

ASK THE RABBI

Where is Mount Sinai? No one really knows, although there are several theories. It could be in the Sinai Peninsula, Jordan, Syria, or Saudi Arabia. There is even confusion about the name of the mountain, as it is called Sinai in the Book of Exodus and Horeb in the Book of Deuteronomy. In the end, the belief that the giving of the Torah happened is much more important in Judaism than where it happened.

Reaffirming the Covenant

Moses offers God's words to the people as part of a deal. If the people accept the rules set forth in this teaching, the Torah, including the acceptance of God as their only God, God will take care of them for as long as they keep their promise. God will not only give them their own land and nation in Canaan, but will send rains and make their crops grow. God will make the people strong and numerous, and will protect them from enemies, disease, and famine. However, if the people don't follow the laws in the teaching, they will suffer. The rains won't come, enemies will harm them, and they won't prosper.

The people accept this agreement, establishing in detail the Covenant between God and the Jewish people. More than the covenants and promises God makes with Abraham and his son and grandson, Isaac and Jacob, this Covenant is detailed and specific. The Torah contains many rules, and the rewards and punishments for following them or not following them are explicitly laid out. You could say the earlier agreements in Genesis were handshake deals, affirming a general under-standing between the parties. The details of the deal are hammered out at Sinai in a much more formal way. The people only realize and accept the scope and meaning of this deal when they accept the Torah at Sinai.

At this crucial moment, the people say, "*Naaseh v'nishmah*—We will do it, and we will hear it." (Exodus 24:7) Jewish sages have pointed out that this is a very strange way to accept the Covenant, because *first* the people say they will do what God says in the Covenant, and *then* they say they will hear what God wants them to do. So they agree to enter the Covenant with God *before* they really know what it says. That's like telling an employer you will work for him or her before you even know what you are being hired to do. But this is an important part of Judaism. We have such faith in God that we will enter into and keep this Covenant, even if we don't initially know or fully understand what it requires of us.

Statue of Moses with the Ten Commandments at Munsterplatz in Bern, Switzerland.
Note the rays of light emanating from Moses' head.

When I say we will enter into and keep this Covenant, I literally mean "we." Jewish tradition teaches that all Jews were present at Sinai and accepted the Covenant, whether they were alive and present at the time, or if they live or lived in another place and time. Some Jews see this teaching as literal, and that all Jews were actually at Sinai at this crucial moment. Others see this teaching as a spiritual or metaphorical statement. Either way, the meaning of this teaching is that the Covenant made at Sinai is accepted and binding upon all Jews for all time.

A Deal We Wouldn't Refuse

On the one hand, it seems like the Israelites eagerly accepted the Covenant at Sinai. But there's evidence in the Scripture and Jewish tradition that this process was not so easy.

The set of tablets the Israelites eventually received was not the first set brought down from the mountain by Moses. When Moses came down the first time, the Israelites had made and were worshipping a golden calf, turning to an idol in the place of God. This betrayal happened because the Israelites were frightened when Moses took such a long time to return to the people. You would think the people would have had a little more faith and patience after God had done many miracles to free them from Egyptian slavery. Moses angrily broke the first tablets, and had to go back up the mountain for another set. (Exodus 32)

There was plenty of drama when the Israelites accepted the Covenant. A thick cloud surrounded the mountain, and there was thunder, lightning, and the extremely loud sound of a horn. The mountain was covered in smoke, God appeared as fire, and the mountain shook as the horn's sound grew louder and louder. The people were very afraid. (Exodus 19:16-19) A story from Jewish tradition even says God held the mountain over the people and said, "If you don't accept the Torah, your grave shall be here." (Talmud Bavli, Shabbat 88a)

Jews understand this all to mean that they had to work hard and grow to be worthy of receiving the Torah. They had to overcome their fears and affirm their faith in God. They also heard the message that accepting the Torah would not be easy, and sometimes would expose them to dangers. Despite all this, they accepted the Torah and committed themselves to their Covenant with God. This demonstrates their firm determination to follow the Torah from the agreement at Mount Sinai until today.

Defining Mitzvah

The Torah contains many important things for Jews. As we are taught, "Turn (the Torah), and turn it, for everything is in it. Reflect on it and grow old and gray with it. Don't turn from it, for nothing is better than it." (Talmud Bavli, Pirkei Avot 5:22) It tells the stories of the creation of the world, our ancestors, and our people's journey to freedom and our homeland. So the Torah is a history book for Jews. The Torah contains genealogies, listing who "begat" whom. So the Torah is partially a kind of family album. The Torah contains majestic poetry that's still used in our worship. So the Torah is the source of some of our oldest pieces of liturgy. Most importantly, the Torah is a guidebook, teaching us the correct way to live.

Commandment or Good Deed?

The way the Torah teaches how to live is by giving a set of *mitzvot*. A *mitzvah* is a commandment, and *mitzvot* is the plural of *mitzvah*. A law found in the Torah isn't just an ordinary rule or statute, like something passed by a legislature or a city council. A law in the Torah is a divine directive, coming from a Source far above and beyond any human governance or authority. It's a commandment, and our obligation as Jews is to follow these commandments.

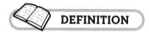

DEFINITION

A **mitzvah** is a commandment given to Jews by God. Sometimes Jews also use the word "mitzvah" to refer to any good deed. **Mitzvot** is the plural of mitzvah.

The mitzvot cover a wide variety of subjects, both large and small. Some mitzvot are ethical commandments, requiring Jews to live according to a set moral code, or instructing them about how to treat other people. Some mitzvot command Jews about how to pray. Other mitzvot describe what a Jew may or may not eat, or how a Jew should dress. The greatest values and the smallest actions are considered by the mitzvot.

Sometimes the word mitzvah is used to describe a good deed. If you help an elderly person, we say you did a mitzvah. If you give to charity, it's a mitzvah. Part of the reason a good deed is called a mitzvah is because the word is used in the Yiddish language in this way. But also, if something is a commandment given by God, by definition it must be a good deed. So you will sometimes hear Jews use the word mitzvah as meaning a good deed, but in the context of talking about the Covenant, it means commandment.

WORDS OF WISDOM

"Doing one mitzvah leads to doing another mitzvah."—Mishnah, Pirkei Avot 4:2

Charting a Way of Life

Rabbis and sages have defined the mitzvot throughout the centuries. They studied the Torah text and sometimes found clear instructions. Sometimes they found mitzvot through implication or clarifying what a particular piece of Scripture meant. Occasionally they found mitzvot in lessons from the stories in Scripture. Through the centuries, the rabbis and sages argued about what each mitzvah required, and challenged each other to consider every possible question that might arise. This led to a very detailed description of the mitzvot.

The sages also wanted to reduce the chances that someone would violate the Torah, so they established more and more restrictive rulings and prohibitions. This became known as "putting a fence around the Torah" as required in the *Talmud* in Pirkei Avot 1:1. It's fair to say one generation of rabbis and sages set up one fence, and then the next generation put a fence around that fence, and so on many times in order to protect the Torah.

The mitzvot found in the actual words of the Torah are called the *Written Law.* The mitzvot, along with their very detailed interpretations, determined by the rabbis and sages over time, are called the *Oral Law.* The Oral Law receives this name because, for a time, it was not written. The rabbis and sages feared that if the Oral Law were put into writing, it would become too inflexible. Students learned the Oral Law through repetition and memorization. After a while, the Oral Law was written down, but it kept its name. The important thing to remember is that traditional Judaism views both the Written Law and the Oral Law as given at Mount Sinai and binding as part of the Covenant between God and the Jewish people.

Together, the *mitzvot* are called the *halachah,* which means "the way" or "the path." Halachah is the general term to describe the obligations of a Jew, and how each of us behaves to fulfill the Covenant with God.

The rabbis and sages didn't always agree with each other about what was halachah, or what each mitzvah required. They discussed and debated their opinions in communities around the world at different times, somewhat like an academic debate today. They adopted some rules to determine what was the correct understanding of the sacred text. Certainly, those rabbis and sages who proposed the more logical and elegant positions were considered more authoritative. The rabbis and sages who gained a higher position in the Rabbinic Court or who headed a more respected school were given higher regard. The rabbis and sages who lived in the earlier time periods generally were considered more convincing because they lived closer to Sinai. The majority opinion on a mitzvah usually outweighed a minority opinion.

Many of the disagreements among the rabbis and sages were preserved in the texts. This showed respect for a differing opinion and teacher even if that opinion was outvoted. The system also recognized it might turn out that the majority was wrong on the issue, or the circumstances of Jewish life might change. They therefore deemed preserving the minority opinions very important.

WORTH NOTING

Two of the greatest sages in Jewish tradition were Hillel and Shammai. They came to prominence about the same time, around the turn to the Common Era. They and their students would argue about the halachah. Hillel is almost always considered correct in his debates with Shammai.

The rabbis maintained the power to determine the proper interpretation of the mitzvot in their communities. (Throughout most of history, and during this time period, only men could be rabbis.) The rabbi would be the judge whenever someone had a question about the halachah. Each rabbi was respected as the final authority in his community, even if he held a minority opinion about a particular rule or practice. This respect for a rabbi's role in his community remains in effect today.

The Ten Commandments

There are 10 directives listed within the story of Moses and the Israelites at Sinai as found in the Book of Exodus in the Torah. These have been called the Ten Commandments for obvious reasons. They are also called the Decalogue.

Inscribed on the Tablets

The Ten Commandments, as contained in Exodus, are:

1. I am Adonai your God who brought you from the land of Egypt, from the house of slavery. You shall have no other gods except for Me.

2. You shall not make for yourself a sculpted image of Me or anything else that is in the heavens above or under the earth, or in the waters under the earth. You shall not bow to them or worship them, because I, Adonai your God, am a jealous God, placing the guilt of parents on the children, the grandchildren, and the great-grandchildren of those who reject Me. However, I will act kindly to the thousandth generation of those who love Me and keep My commandments.

3. You shall not swear falsely by the name of Adonai your God, because Adonai will not absolve anyone who swears falsely by God's name.

4. Remember the Sabbath day and keep it holy. You shall work six days and you shall do all your tasks during them, but the seventh day is a Sabbath for Adonai your God. You shall not do any work—you, your sons and daughters, your male or female servants, your cattle or the strangers who are among you—because for six days Adonai made the heavens and the earth and the sea and all that is in them, and on the seventh day God rested, blessed the story the seventh day, and made it holy.

5. Honor your father and your mother in order that you live for many days on the land that Adonai your God is giving to you.

6. You shall not murder.

7. You shall not commit adultery.

8. You shall not steal.

9. You shall not swear falsely against your neighbor.

10. You shall not covet the house of your neighbor. You shall not covet your neighbor's wife, male or female servants, oxen or donkeys, or anything else your neighbor has.

 WORTH NOTING

Many of the public displays of the Ten Commandments in parks, town halls, and courthouses in the United States were given out as part of the promotional campaign for the Cecil B. DeMille movie of the same name. About 150 of these granite displays were distributed, and Charlton Heston and Yul Brynner, the stars of the movie, personally dedicated some of them. You can find them on the state capitol grounds in Denver and Austin, and the latter became the subject of a United States Supreme Court ruling in 2005.

The tablets Moses brought down from Sinai had the first five commandments on one and the second five on the other. A *midrash* frames the first tablet as having commandments concerning how we act toward God, and the second had commandments concerning how we act toward other people. What about the fifth commandment regarding honoring parents? The sages say our parents are our creators and have a relationship to us like our relationship to God, so being on the first tablet honors them.

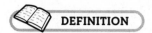 **DEFINITION**

A **midrash** is an interpretation of Scripture, classically written by ancient rabbinic sages, but many continue to be written by rabbis and scholars today. Many *midrashim* (the plural of midrash) compare different texts, examine the grammar or unusual phrasing of Biblical verses, or contain stories or parables. Chapter 5 will discuss midrashim further.

Different Times and Places, Different Ten

Throughout Jewish history, the Ten Commandments have captured the imagination and attention of the Jewish people. The Ten Commandments appear in the story at the critical moment when Moses returns from atop the mountain and the Covenant is formed. Ten is a round number—we have 10 fingers, so we tend to think of 10 as a complete set. We even structured our entire system of mathematics around 10. So having a set of Ten Commandments neatly presented together is an attention grabber. The Ten Commandments draw notice because of their apparent simplicity and ethical logic. God presents this set of mitzvot to us plainly, often giving reasons for them, and they comprise clear moral guidelines that are hard to argue with.

A challenge to this is the fact that there isn't just one set of Ten Commandments in the Torah. Moses repeats the Ten Commandments to the Israelites in his final speech to the people before he dies, as recorded in Deuteronomy. The Ten Commandments found there are slightly different than those found in Exodus. The fourth commandment in Exodus instructs the Israelites to "remember" the Sabbath; in Deuteronomy, the commandment says people shall "guard" the Sabbath.

There have been several interpretations of this difference throughout Jewish history. The sixteenth-century Kabbalistic Rabbi Shlomo HaLevi Alkabetz wrote a beautiful song Jews sing to welcome the Sabbath, called *Lecha Dodi*. In this song, Rabbi Alkabetz writes that "guard" and "remember" were said by God together, so we really should see the words as one commandment requiring one set of practices. On the other hand, other commentators have said that "guard" means observing the Sabbath through our actions or our refraining from action, while "remember" means keeping Shabbat in our thoughts and intentions.

There are other differences between the two sets of Ten Commandments. The fifth commandment as found in Deuteronomy adds an extra reward for honoring your parents, saying that not only will you live long in the land for following it, but also that life will be good for you in those years. The tenth commandment in Deuteronomy switches the order of what you shouldn't covet, placing your neighbor's wife before your neighbor's house. Though some of these differences seem minor, Jews believe these words come from God, so every nuance and difference is considered important, and leads to discussion and interpretation by different rabbis and commentators.

The Ten Commandments also have been translated and understood differently by some of the branches of Christianity. For example, the Anglican Scripture views the first line of the first of the Ten Commandments, "I am Adonai your God," as an introduction, and not really a commandment at all. The Roman Catholic and Lutheran Scriptures merge the first two of the Jewish Ten Commandments into one, and make coveting your neighbor's wife a separate commandment.

More significantly, the Jewish sixth commandment says you can't murder. Some of the Christian versions of the Ten Commandments say you can't kill. There's a significant difference in meaning between the two. Murder is an unjustified or illegal taking of a human life, while killing means any taking of a human life at all. All this means that today there is not just one universally accepted Ten Commandments, but several versions and interpretations.

The Real Number of Mitzvot

Many people believe the Torah contains only Ten Commandments because Exodus lists only these 10 when Moses comes down Mount Sinai with the two stone tablets. However, in Judaism, there are far more commandments than 10. We acknowledge every time the Torah tells us to do something, or tells us we can't do something, as a commandment. Maimonides counted all the commandments, and concluded that there were not just 10 but 613 commandments in the entire Torah. When we think of the Covenant made at Sinai, we don't see our responsibility as following just the 10 statements listed in Exodus. We see the Covenant as requiring us to follow all the commandments within the Torah.

 **OY VEY!**

In Hebrew, the statements of Exodus 20 are not called the Ten Commandments, but *Aseret HaDibrot*, which literally means "The Ten Statements" or "The Ten Words." Some authorities say this is to ensure that we don't see these 10 as the only commandments. Others say these are general categories of commendations that all the other commandments fit into. The Talmudic sages were so worried Jews would ignore all the other commandments and pay attention only to the 10 that they removed their recitation from the liturgy at services.

This seems to be an extremely difficult burden, and practically impossible to do. Our tradition recognizes that no human being can possibly follow all the commandments all the time. Our faith requires us only to do the best we can, understanding that as we live our lives with this intention, we'll be able to do more and more mitzvot, and our task will become easier over time. After all, we're assured in the Torah, "The commandments…are not too hard for you or far from you …. They are in your mouth and in your heart, so that you can do them." (Deuteronomy 30:11-14)

Positive and Negative Mitzvot

Judaism makes a distinction between positive and negative mitzvot. A positive mitzvah is a commandment by which you must do a required action. According to our tradition, there are 248 positive mitzvot, representing one for each bone of the human body as believed at the time they were counted. Examples of positive mitzvot are going to pray, having children, and helping the poor. A negative mitzvah is a commandment by which you must refrain from doing an action. There are 365 negative mitzvot, one for each of the days of the year. Examples of these mitzvot are not murdering and not eating prohibited foods.

The distinction between positive and negative mitzvot is particularly important when comparing the different obligations upon men and women in traditional Judaism. Men are required to do all the mitzvot, whether they are positive or negative. Women are not required to do any positive mitzvot that Jews are called to do at a particular time. These "positive, time-bound mitzvot" include going to synagogue three times a day to pray, any of the rituals concerning a Holy Day, and putting on ritual garments at the required times. There are a few exceptions of positive, time-bound commandments women are required to do, including eating matzah on Passover and saying the blessing over the wine on Shabbat. (Talmud Bavli, Kiddushin 29a)

The tradition determines which mitzvot women must do and which they are not, based on several conditions. If the Torah specifically or implicitly requires everyone to do a particular mitzvah, women are required to follow it. But if performance of the mitzvah interferes with women's responsibilities in traditional Judaism of maintaining the home and raising children, women are not required to do it.

 WORTH NOTING

> Not all Jews today make these distinctions between men and women. Many Jews are influenced by ideas of feminism and gender egalitarianism, and have found ways to depart from these traditional distinctions.

There are numerous opinions in traditional Judaism on whether a woman *may* do a mitzvah she is not *required* to do. This determination often depends upon the rules of a particular community as set by its rabbi and the mitzvah being considered.

Hiddur Mitzvah: Beautifying a Commandment

Judaism praises the performance of a mitzvah whenever and wherever it is done. There is a special merit given when the mitzvah is done in a way that makes it especially notable and beautiful. This concept, called *hiddur mitzvah,* is praiseworthy in the Jewish tradition because beautifying a mitzvah expands the glory of God and encourages other Jews to also perform mitzvot.

An example of this involves saying the blessing over wine or juice, called *Kiddush*. Judaism considers the fruit of the vine to be the symbol of joy, so we are required to say the proper blessing and drink the wine or juice on every Holy Day. We could just quickly mutter the words and take a sip as quickly as possible, but that wouldn't make this important mitzvah into a special act. Instead, we chant the blessing with a beautiful melody. We usually drink the wine from an ornate cup made of precious materials used only for this important ritual. While we can say Kiddush over any fruit of the vine, we usually use a sweet wine or juice on the Holy Day to make the day and act that much more enjoyable and special.

Silver Kiddush cups used on Shabbat and holy days.

The Least You Need to Know

- The Israelites accepted the Torah at Mount Sinai, creating a Covenant with God Jews follow to this day.
- Jews do mitzvot, and in return God commits to taking care of the Jews.
- There are not just 10 commandments, but 613, ranging from great ethical requirements to the smallest minutia of living.
- Traditionally, women are not required to follow positive, time-bound commandments.
- It is especially worthy to do a mitzvah in a beautiful way to increase God's glory.

The Temple Is Destroyed

The third moment in Jewish history happened well after the Israelites received the Torah at Mount Sinai. The Israelites reached the Promised Land and established a nation there. They lived there for about 1,000 years, and during most of that time they more or less maintained their own governance over the land. Ultimately, this possession of the Promised Land ended in 70 C.E. with the second destruction of the Temple in Jerusalem.

This moment had tremendous importance, not only because of what it meant historically and religiously, but also because of how it impacted the Jews' essential identity. The reaction and response to the Temple's destruction and the exile from the Land solidified Jews as a people, and has kept them together through two millennia as they've lived in just about every area in the world. To understand how Jews came to endure as a people, we need to understand exactly what Jerusalem and the Temple meant to the Israelites during this time, and how they persevered when logically they should have disappeared from the earth. So let's start with some history prior to the destruction of the Temple to understand how Jews became a people.

In This Chapter

- The importance of Jerusalem and the Temple
- The destruction of the Temple
- Yochanan ben Zakkai saves Judaism
- The idea of Jewish peoplehood emerges
- What we mean by "The Chosen People"

Jerusalem

After the Israelites entered the Promised Land, they eventually decided to have a king. In approximately 1000 B.C.E., David became the king. David established his capital in a hilly region, in the city known as Jerusalem.

A Special Name

As we have seen, names mean a great deal in Judaism. The name Jerusalem also holds important meaning. There are many stories and interpretations about how Jerusalem got its name. Jerusalem is Yirushalayim in Hebrew. The word *Yirushalayim* itself has been broken down to *Ir HaShalom*, which means "City of Peace."

 WORDS OF WISDOM

"You will find no beauty like the beauty of Jerusalem."–Talmud Bavli, Kiddushin 49b

Another story of the origin of Jerusalem's name connects to the crucial story in Genesis 22 where God told Abraham to sacrifice his beloved son Isaac to God. Abraham agreed to do this, stopping only at the last moment when an angel called to him from heaven to stop. This story of Abraham's faith and dedication is extremely important to Judaism. Abraham named the place where this happened "*Adonai yireh*—God is seen." These words are shortened and combined to form the first part of the city's name, which is then added to the Hebrew word for "peace," *shalom*, to form the name *Yirushalayim*.

A Special Place

Another story from Jewish tradition explains why this area is so special. It happened that two brothers were living on either side of the hill that would become the center of Jerusalem. Both were farmers. One brother had many children, and the other had none.

One year, both brothers' fields yielded abundant crops. The brother without children said, "I have done so well, and have so much extra food. My poor brother has so many mouths to feed. He must need this extra food. But he is proud, and wouldn't accept this gift. I must sneak my extra food into his storeroom at night."

At the same time, the brother with many children looked at his surplus harvest and said, "I have so much more than I need, because my many children have helped me in the field. My poor brother is alone. He has no help, so he must need this extra food. But he is proud, and wouldn't accept this gift. I must sneak my extra food into his storeroom at night."

That night, the brothers each took a large wagon of food to the other. They passed each other, both failing to notice the other in the dark. The next morning, they each were surprised to see they had just as much food in their storerooms as they had the night before. They each decided that they must not have taken enough food to the other brother.

This was repeated night after night, each brother determined to help the other. Finally, after a couple of weeks, they ran into each other at the top of the hill. When each brother saw what the other was doing, they laughed, cried, and hugged, realizing the love and care they had for each other.

The story concludes by teaching that the hill where the brothers met became the center of Jerusalem.

The Temple

Jerusalem became the holiest city in Judaism when King Solomon built the *Temple* there. Unlike his warrior father David, Solomon was a scholar and a man of peace, so God allowed him to have the honor of building the First Temple.

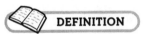 **DEFINITION**

A **temple** is a house of worship, but in Judaism the **Temple** specifically refers to the central site of worship located on Mount Moriah in Jerusalem.

Building the Temple

Solomon built the Temple by enclosing a hill in Jerusalem in the middle of four great retaining walls. The hill was, in effect, in the middle of a box. Solomon then had the open space within the box filled with dirt, creating a mostly flat surface with only the very top of the hill sticking up.

This is what still exists today as the Temple Mount. The Western Wall is the last surviving retaining wall encompassing the hill. As you may have guessed, Jews believe this is the same hill where Abraham went to sacrifice Isaac, and where the two farming brothers finally met on that last night.

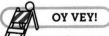 **OY VEY!**

The city walls of the Old City of Jerusalem, though well known, are not part of the Temple as many believe. These walls were actually built much later by the Ottoman Empire's Sultan Suleiman in 1538 C.E.

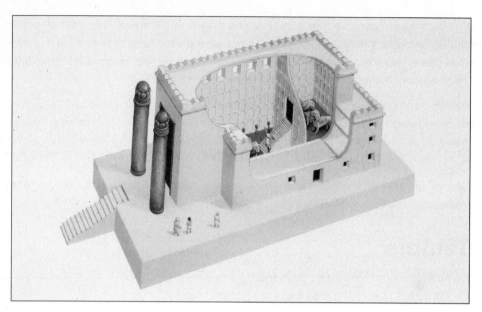

An illustration of Solomon's Temple.

The Importance of the Temple

The Temple was the central location of the Israelites' religion for a thousand years. The Book of Leviticus, the third book of the Torah, outlines many sacrifices the people were obligated to make to God at the Temple. Controlled by a priesthood descended from Aaron, Moses' brother, the Temple came to be seen as the place that had a direct physical connection to God and heaven. You could pray anywhere, and many local places of worship called *synagogues* were established. But if you really wanted to be where the action was, where you could best communicate with and show appreciation to God, and where the highest form of worship took place, you went to the Temple.

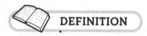 **DEFINITION**

A **synagogue** is a place of meeting or gathering used by Jews for worship.

The Temple was considered the center of the universe. As Jewish tradition teaches, "The Land of Israel is at the world's center. Jerusalem is at the center of Israel. The Temple is at the center of Jerusalem. The Temple sanctuary is at the center of the Temple. The Ark (containing the sacred texts and before which the sacrifices took place) is at the center of the Temple sanctuary. In front of the Temple sanctuary is the stone upon which the entire world was founded." (Tanhuma, Kedoshim section 10)

As the center of the universe, the workplace of a powerful priesthood, the central location of the worship of an entire nation, and the place believed to be connected to heaven and God, you can imagine how important this site was to the Israelites. You can also imagine the effect upon the people when the Temple was finally destroyed.

Rebellion, Destruction, Diaspora

Solomon's Temple lasted until 586 B.C.E., when the Babylonians destroyed it. The Babylonians exiled the leadership of the Israelite community for about 40 years, after which they were allowed to return and rebuild the Temple, which remained the center of Jewish worship into the first century C.E., even as the Jews came to be ruled by the Romans.

There were four primary groups in Israelite society in the first century:

- Sadducees: the wealthy aristocratic class, including the priesthood

- Pharisees: a newer class of scholars who believed in an evolving set of mitzvot and worship practices

- Essenes: a strict and ascetic sect concerned with purity that separated itself from Temple worship

- Zealots: rebels against Roman rule

The approximately 3 million Jews living under Roman rule in Judea in the first century experienced several difficulties. The Romans allowed the people they governed to keep their own gods if they accepted the Roman gods as well. This was actually revolutionary and liberal for the time, and many of the nations conquered by the Romans could live with the situation because of this policy.

The policy worked well with polytheists. What was another few gods to add to the gods you already had, especially when the Roman gods were obviously powerful, as shown by Rome's success? But this policy didn't work so well with monotheists, who wouldn't accept any other god but their God. Much tension resulted in Judea, worsening at times, such as when the Emperor Caligula required a statue of himself to be placed in all synagogues and worshipped. Only Caligula's death prevented a revolt.

The revolt eventually came anyway. The Romans often restricted the Jews' freedoms, and they were corrupt. They levied burdensome taxes on the Jews, appointed the high priests in the Temple, and tended to favor the non-Jews living in Judea. Tensions came to a boil in 66 C.E. when the Roman procurator Flavius took silver from the Temple. Jews joined the Zealots, and they revolted.

The revolution was doomed to fail. The Romans were far too strong, and the Jews were too divided as the sects fought among themselves as much as they fought the Romans. One million Jews died in the revolt.

> **WORTH NOTING**
>
> Traditional Judaism doesn't credit Roman strength for the rebellion's failure and the destruction of the Temple, but blames the loss on the infighting among the Jews. Therefore, baseless hatred *(sinat hinam)* among Jews is considered a great sin.

The revolt ended with the destruction of the center of Judaism, the Temple, in 70 C.E. Most Jews were forced to leave the land, beginning the exile Jews know as the Diaspora. Although a small Jewish presence managed to stay through the centuries in the land the Romans renamed "Palestine," Jews did not govern the land for about 1,900 years. Suddenly, the Jews were without their physical and geographical connection to God, and all the promises made in the Covenant seemed broken. How could they go on?

The Hero: Yochanan ben Zakkai

Yochanan ben Zakkai was a Pharisee leader who was trapped in the Temple as the Romans besieged it at the end of the rebellion. He knew the Israelites' cause was lost, and the Romans would destroy the Temple. He devised a plan in which he was smuggled out of the Temple in a coffin. Once he had escaped, he approached the Roman General Vespasian, who was leading the assault on the Temple. Yochanan addressed the General as the king, which was a surprise to Vespasian because he was only a general. At that moment, a soldier entered Vespasian's tent and told him the Emperor had died, and that he had been elected as the new Emperor. Vespasian decided to grant Yochanan a request because he had been the first to address Vespasian as king.

Yochanan asked to establish a school in the town of Yavneh for him and the scholars of the School of Hillel. Vespasian granted the request, and Yochanan was able to rescue his fellow teachers and students from the Temple and Jerusalem and move them there. Yochanan established a school and Sanhedrin, the rabbinic court, at Yavneh, and set about redesigning a new Judaism that could exist without its central feature, the Temple. Yochanan and his fellows preserved the Temple rules with the idea that one day God would allow it to be rebuilt, but also designed a religion where worship and observance replaced sacrifices.

ASK THE RABBI

What replaced worship at the Temple? A story from the Midrash gives a partial answer. Yochanan was walking in the ruins of the Temple with his disciple, Joshua. Joshua cried, "Woe to us, that we should lose the place where the Israelites received atonement!" Yochanan replied, "Do not worry. We will find atonement now in deeds of loving-kindness." (Avot d'Rabbi Natan 4:21)

Yochanan and his followers did more than reinvent the Israelites' religion at Yavneh. They gave the Israelites something to center their lives around, and something to keep all the Israelites connected as they left their land. Jews were already living in places like Babylonia and Egypt, and the loss of the national center could have caused them to spiral away from each other, becoming separate sects or assimilated groups with no connection to each other. Instead, Yochanan's work preserved a common identity for the Jews, binding them together. They may have been forced into Diaspora, but thanks to what happened at Yavneh, the Jews remained a people.

Remaining a People Against All Odds

The idea of peoplehood is something uncommon, and possibly unique to Jews. Sociologists and other academics debate about what Jews as a group are, and come to different conclusions based upon the definitions they set. However, the term "people" seems to have great meaning and application to the Jews' situation, as shown by considering what terms do not apply to Jews.

Jews are not a race. There are Jews of every skin color. Jews are not an ethnicity. Different Jews hold many different cultural characteristics, from food to music to customs. Jews certainly are not a nationality, as they live in almost every nation in the world, and often identify strongly with the nation in which they live. We can't even say Jews are just a group who subscribe to the religion of Judaism, because many Jews are not religious and not observant at all.

In spite of all this, something holds the Jews together. Jews care about each other, and hold a special affinity for each other. Even in recent times, for Jews living in such places as the Soviet Union or Ethiopia, when a Jew or a Jewish community is threatened, Jews all over the world feel a connection and strive to do anything to help endangered fellow Jews. A Jew might not do anything that could specifically be called Jewish or observe any of the holidays or practices. But try telling that person he or she is not Jewish, and you are very likely to find that person defending his or her Jewishness quite vociferously.

"Am Yisrael chai! Od Aveenu chai!—The people Yisrael lives! Still our God lives!"
—Jewish folk song

The best way to describe this phenomenon of identity, connection, and belonging is to describe Jews as a people. All Jews do not have a common land, a common genetics, a common culture, or a common nation. But they do have a kinship that transcends every other definition, and has endured through the centuries to bind them together as a recognizable and separate group wherever they go.

Peoplehood in the Texts

The sacred texts reinforce the idea of peoplehood. The texts emphasize the importance of staying within the community, and connecting with other Jews.

Traditionally, Jews must pray together within a community. They can say some prayers separately, but other prayers require the presence of 10 worshippers, each at least 13 years old. A group of at least 10 adults gathered to pray is called a *minyon*. In traditional Judaism, the counted participants in a minyon must be male. The understanding that 10 people constitute a community comes from the Book of Genesis, in Chapter 18, when God decides to destroy the cities of Sodom and Gomorrah for their immorality. Abraham argues with God for the few righteous of the city, finally getting God to agree that the cities will not be destroyed if there are 10 righteous people in the city. From this, Jews understand that 10 righteous people together form a community, and maintaining this community is a very important part of Jewish peoplehood.

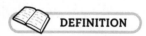

DEFINITION

A **minyon** is a gathering of 10 Jews to pray. A minyon is required to have a complete worship service in traditional Judaism.

Every Jew is a valued and necessary member of the community, and all are required to stay together as a people. As the Talmud says, *"Kol Yisrael averim zeh bazeh"*—"All Jews are responsible for one another." (Talmud Bavli, Shavuot 39a)

Staying together as a people and a community is crucially important to Judaism. If Jews don't each take responsibility for their people, there is no Judaism. This is why Jews are commanded to not separate themselves from the community. In the Torah, one of the most severe punishments for sins is *kareit*, removal from the people and the community.

It's clear that part of being a Jew means connecting with and caring for other Jews. From our tradition's standpoint, you simply can't be a Jew and not be a part of the Jewish people.

The Chosen People

One of the more controversial aspects of Judaism is the term "The Chosen People." Both Jews and non-Jews have used this term, but it's usually not defined. For some, the term supports the idea that Jews are special and favored by God. For others, the term is a statement of conceit and hubris, and even a reason to look down on Jews and Judaism as arrogant and, ironically, unworthy of praise.

The idea of being chosen is really very simple. Jews accept the fact that they were the first to recognize the Oneness of God, and they brought awareness of this to the world. They were chosen to serve God in a particular way through the Torah. In fact, some see the idea not as that Jews were "chosen," but that they always are "choosing" to follow God as they did at Mount Sinai.

WORTH NOTING

The website of Congregation Beth Shalom in Anchorage, Alaska, is www.frozenchosen.org.

Regardless of how the idea of chosenness is defined, Jews generally do not understand it to mean that they are better, more moral, or more intelligent than other people. This is an arrogance forbidden by the sacred texts. Jews learn from the prophet Micah, "What is it that God wants from you? Only to do justly, and love mercy, and *walk humbly with your God."* (Micah 6:8, emphasis added) The Talmud warns Jews away from arrogance, saying that "A name made great is a name destroyed." (Talmud Bavli, Pirkei Avot 1:13)

Moreover, Jewish tradition teaches that the Torah was offered to other nations, but they rejected it because they didn't like some of the commandments contained in it. (Pisikta Rabbatai 21) Furthermore, the Torah was given outside of Israel and in an open, public wilderness to say that anyone who wants to, from any nation, can accept it as their own. (Mekhilta d'Rabbi Ishmael, Bahodesh 1) Far from an expression of vanity, chosenness is a description and definition of how Jews see themselves relating to God and the idea of monotheism. Although some may view the term as arrogant, nothing could be farther from the way it's meant and understood by Jews.

The Least You Need to Know

- The destruction of the Temple in Jerusalem in 70 C.E. marked the beginning of the Diaspora and had the potential of breaking apart the Jewish people until they disappeared from history.

- Yochanan ben Zakkai redefined Judaism without a Temple at Yavneh, which allowed and committed Jews to stay together as a people.

- The idea that all Jews are connected to each other and responsible to one another as a people is an essential part of Judaism.

- Jews call themselves "The Chosen People" because they brought the idea of God's Oneness to the world, and not because they think they're better than other people.

Understanding the Basics

A story is told of a man who comes to see the great scholar Hillel, who lived 2,000 years ago. The man asks Hillel to teach him Judaism while he is standing on one foot. Hillel calmly replies, "Do not do unto others what is hateful to yourself. All the rest is commentary. Now go and study."

Hillel correctly and brilliantly summarized the overriding principle of Judaism by providing the man with the Jewish version of the Golden Rule. However, he also told the man to go and study, because Hillel knew that to truly understand Judaism, you need to know the commentary as well. Part 2 provides that necessary background and basic building blocks of Judaism beyond the primary ideas of God, Torah, and the People of Israel.

Chapter 4 provides a quick history of the Jewish people from Scriptural times to today. Chapter 5 describes the many different holy Jewish texts. Chapter 6 delineates differences among Jews, including the various movements within Judaism. Chapter 7 enumerates some of the ethics and values of the religion. Chapter 8 considers the issue of Zionism and Israel.

A Brief History of the Jewish People

As we've seen in Part 1, history is a tremendously important part of Judaism, and it's impossible to understand Judaism without knowing Jewish history. Jews' lives today are deeply shaped by events that happened, in some cases, thousands of years ago. Jewish rituals and holidays reflect, celebrate, or commemorate happenings of long ago. Our concerns and politics often manifest experiences embedded in our Jewish consciousness.

It's impossible to present all 5,775 years of Jewish history in just one chapter of one book. I'm going to try to present highlights that shape the Jewish story, and provide the background helpful for you to understand Judaism.

In This Chapter

- Biblical beginnings: the creation of the world
- One thousand years of the first Jewish nation
- The Diaspora experience
- The effects of the Enlightenment on Jewish life
- The growth of anti-Semitism and the Holocaust
- The Jewish people today

Biblical Times

Jewish history begins with the creation of the world as described in the Torah. Scripture certainly is not your typical historical source, and not a source that modern historians would consider credible. However, history for the Jewish people is a combination of fact and faith, so they view the stories in the Bible as part of their past.

Creation and Noah

Jewish history, or perhaps more accurately "pre-history," begins with the creation of the universe, our world, and human beings. The Torah tells us at the start of Genesis that God created the world and all life upon it in six days. On the seventh day, God rested.

 ASK THE RABBI

Do Jews really believe the world was created in six days? What about science and evolution? There is a great variety of opinion among Jews on these questions. Some Jews do believe in the literality of the Bible, and that the entire universe was created by God in six days. Others see connections between the order of creation in the Bible and the development of life according to science. They reason that, perhaps, a day in the Bible at the time was not the same as what we call a day today. Still others see the Bible's story as pure metaphor and a teaching of faith, not fact.

The sixth day was the most important day of creation. On that day, God created man and woman from the dust of the earth. God called them Adam and Eve, whose name in Hebrew was *Chava.* God gave the man and woman dominion over the earth and the animals, and told them to be fruitful and multiply in Eden, the paradise in which God placed them. Adam and Eve disobeyed God's commandment to not eat from the Tree of Knowledge, and they were banned from Eden.

Human beings did multiply, but misbehaved. God decided to flood the earth and restart the human race. God chose Noah, because Noah was righteous in his generation, to build an ark to save all the animals from the flood. The flood came, and Noah's family and the animals were saved. The people began to multiply again. They decided to build a tower in Babel to challenge God. Rather than flood the earth, God destroyed the tower of Babel and made the people speak different languages. This was the start of the different nations.

An Italian relief carving of Adam and Eve at the Tree of Knowledge.

The Patriarchs and the Matriarchs

As we learned in Chapter 1, Judaism itself began with Abraham and Sarah's acceptance of monotheism. Abraham had a son with Sarah's handmaiden Hagar when it seemed that Sarah was barren. This son was Ishmael, the forefather of the Islamic people. Abraham did eventually have a son with Sarah named Isaac, who married Rebecca. Isaac and Rebecca had twins named Esau and Jacob. Jacob gained his father's birthright even though he was the younger son. Esau, the more violent son, became the forefather of the Romans. Jacob married two sisters, Leah and Rachel, and had twelve sons with them and their handmaidens. These sons became the forefathers of the twelve tribes of Israel.

These first generations hold an extremely important standing in Judaism as the first to establish our relationship with God and our identity as a people. The men are called the Patriarchs: Abraham, Isaac, and Jacob, and the women are called the Matriarchs: Sarah, Rebecca, Leah, and Rachel. They aren't treated as gods or saints, but they receive a tremendous amount of respect for their courage and achievements. God repeats the initial Covenant and promise of the land to each Patriarch.

Slavery and Redemption from Egypt

Jacob's favored son was Joseph. Through a series of events involving his brothers' jealousy, lies, betrayal, and Joseph's aptitude for dream interpretation, Joseph became a minister in Egypt, assigned to save the country from a famine he had predicted. Joseph eventually invited his brothers and their families to live with him in Egypt.

> **WORTH NOTING**
>
> The name for the Jewish people changes throughout Biblical and immediate post-Biblical times. At the time of Abraham, the people are called *Ivri*, meaning "travellers." The name changes to "Israelites" when we reach the time of Jacob's sons. The name *Israelites* means "those who wrestle with God," reflecting Jacob's experience of wrestling with an angel seen as him grappling with and coming to understand the idea of God. The term *Jew* comes from one of Jacob's sons, Judah, whose tribe becomes the largest, most powerful, and last remaining in the Promised Land at the time of the Second Temple.

Centuries pass, and the descendants of Jacob, now called "Israelites," have grown numerous. The Book of Exodus begins with the ominous warning that "there arose a new king over Egypt who didn't know Joseph." (Exodus 1:8) Fearing that the Israelites were becoming too numerous, the Egyptian king enslaved them. Eventually, God freed the Israelites, employing Moses to be God's representative, along with his brother Aaron. It took the miracles of 10 plagues from God and the parting of the Red Sea, but the Israelites escaped. As we saw in Chapter 2, the Israelites went to Mount Sinai and received the Torah, firmly establishing the Covenant with God.

The Israelites wandered through the desert for 40 years. Despite all his work and greatness, Moses was not permitted to enter the Promised Land because he did not follow God's instructions when providing water to the people at a place called Mamre. As the Israelites approached the Promised Land, they sent a scout from each of the tribes to examine the area and the people who lived there. They returned and said the land was beautiful, "flowing with Milk and Honey," but the people who lived there were giants. Ten of the scouts said the Israelites would not be able to gain control of the land. Two of the scouts, Joshua and Caleb, said God would fulfill the promise God made and they should go forward. Joshua succeeded Moses as leader, and the Israelites moved forward.

The First Jewish State(s)

The Israelites migrated into the Promised Land and began to settle there, sometimes fighting with the Canaanites and Philistines who also lived there. In the beginning, the Israelites selected a leader, called a *shofet*, or judge, only when needed. Eventually, the Israelites determined that they needed a king to secure their position, despite the fact that God had told them never to appoint a king over them. Nevertheless, Saul became king. Around 1000 B.C.E. he was succeeded by David, who solidified a united Israelite nation in the land. David was succeeded by his son Solomon, who built the First Temple.

Following Solomon, the kingdom divided. The 10 Northern tribes formed their own kingdom with their own king, leaving Judah and Benjamin in the southern kingdom. During this time, worship and sacrifice at the Temple became the center of Jewish worship, and a strong priesthood arose to control the Temple. This was also the time of the Prophets, who spoke for God and chastised the kings and people for their misbehavior.

In a war in 586 B.C.E., the Babylonians destroyed the First Temple and exiled the Jewish leadership. This war essentially obliterated the Northern Kingdom. This period lasted only about 40 years, and much of the Jewish leadership returned to Jerusalem and rebuilt the Temple.

For the next few centuries, the Kingdom of Judea maintained a precarious existence among great empires to its east and west. Sometimes these kingdoms gained control over Judea. One of those times occurred around 175 B.C.E., when Assyria, under the rule of King Antiochus, gained control over the Jewish kingdom. King Antiochus tried to eradicate the Jewish religion, but he was successfully defeated by a revolt led by a family called the Maccabees. We will learn more about the Maccabees when we talk about *Chanukkah* in Chapter 12.

The Maccabees, also known as the Hasmoneans, were poor leaders, corrupt and oppressive to even their fellow Jews. Difficulties with the Assyrians continued, until finally a dispute among the Hasmoneans allowed Rome to take over Judea in 63 B.C.E., as described in Chapter 3. Rome ruled Judea through the revolt in 66 C.E., resulting in the destruction of the Second Temple and the Diaspora in 70 C.E.

 ASK THE RABBI

What happened to the Zealots, who affected Jewish history so much by causing the destruction of the Second Temple? They disappeared from history, as their influence waned after their failed rebellion. Some of them fled to a fort near the Dead Sea called Masada, where they committed suicide rather than be captured by the Romans. Consequently, they are remembered for their courage and resistance, not their failure.

Some Jews remained in the Promised Land even after the revolt in 70 C.E., and there has always been some kind of Jewish presence there in the Common Era. However, a last revolt led by Simeon bar Kochba was attempted in 132 to 135 C.E. that failed, and there was no Jewish state in the Promised Land until 1948.

Diaspora and Growth

Following the destruction of the Temple, and during the ensuing centuries, Jews spread throughout the world. At times, they were welcomed and became an accepted part of the broader community, such as in Islamic Spain from the eighth to fifteenth centuries and in Poland from the eleventh through late eighteen centuries. They had economic opportunities and a degree of religious freedom, and their culture and prosperity grew.

At other times they were persecuted, such as under the Almohades in northern Africa, during the Crusades, and as part of the Spanish Inquisition. Jews were expelled from England in 1290, and not allowed to return until the middle of the eighteenth century. Pope Innocent III required all Jews living under Catholic control to wear a noticeable patch on their clothing, most often a yellow circle. They frequently had to leave countries due to violence or threats against them.

For centuries, life for Jews in the Diaspora has been a mixture of successes and sufferings, belonging and separation.

A Separate Life

Throughout the Diaspora, Jews lived separately from other people. Some of this was due to their own needs and desires: Jewish dietary and observance laws required them to remain within their own communities. They needed to live close together to be able to gather a minyon for daily worship. Living close together also offered a degree of safety and protection.

But much of the separation occurred due to the desires of the governments and peoples of the land. They didn't want what they considered to be a strange group of people with different customs to live among them. Especially through the Middle Ages, some communities were concerned that Jews didn't accept the divinity of Jesus, and they didn't want a people they considered blasphemous to reside equally with them.

Jews often were relegated to specific areas of cities, or to their own towns or regions. The Jewish areas in European cities gained a particular name—*ghetto*—named after the Jewish area in Venice established in 1516. Rural Jewish farming towns were called *shtetls*, and were predominantly found in central and eastern Europe. There were hundreds of shtetls in Russia in an area known as the Pale of Settlement, which was the only place in that country where most Jews were allowed to live.

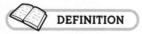 **DEFINITION**

> **Ghetto** means "foundry." The Jewish area in Venice was located next to a foundry, so it and all other restrictive Jewish areas in cities soon were given this name.

Communal separation led to an oftentimes mutually beneficial symbiosis between the secular and Jewish authorities. The secular authorities didn't need to worry about the inner workings of the Jewish areas as long as they protected the areas enough for them to continue to exist. They received taxes from the governing Jewish authorities, who took responsibility for their collection. The Jewish authorities could govern as they wished, and enforced obedience to Jewish law and custom. For centuries, Jews struggled through a precarious existence that allowed them to develop a complex and distinctive way of life and furthered their identity as a people.

Study, Sages, and Scholarship

Part of that way of life was a growing emphasis on study and scholarship. The religion valued knowledge and understanding of sacred texts and ideas. Communities treasured the ability to distinguish between fine points of law and argue positions based on the opinions of great rabbis. It's likely a myth that all Jewish males everywhere were literate and spent hours each day studying sacred texts. However, it's also likely that a larger percentage of Jewish men could read and spent time in study than their non-Jewish contemporaries.

This tradition of learning led to the rise of great scholars who interpreted and reinterpreted Scripture. Teachers, commentators, and philosophers such as the Saadia Gaon, Rashi, and Judah HaLevi wrote great works in the Middle Ages that are still discussed and debated among Jews today. The opinions of scholars and sages were recorded in the Talmud and later works, which formed the basis of the extremely complex system of halachah.

Without a Temple, a homeland, or the ability to participate in general society to the same extent as the non-Jewish population, Jews turned inward. Learning and scholarship became an essential part of Jewish life and values.

Jewish Languages

Many Jews learned the language of the lands in which they lived. However, some languages were adopted as particular Jewish languages, used in prayer, study, and everyday conversation.

The primary Jewish language is Hebrew. Hebrew is called *lashon kodesh*—"the holy language." The Torah is written in Hebrew and preserved in its original form to this day. Hebrew is used in prayer, and scholars wrote many of the original Biblical commentaries in Hebrew.

 ASK THE RABBI

Since Hebrew is written right to left, I am often asked, "Why is Hebrew written backward?" I reply, "Hebrew came before English. So which is backward?"

During the time of the Temple, Jews had already begun to move away from using Hebrew as the common language of society and everyday life. They gravitated to another Semitic language commonly used in the Middle East, Aramaic. Part of the Bible and most of the Talmud is written in Aramaic, along with one of our most important prayers, the *Kaddish.*

As time went on, two major Jewish languages for everyday life emerged. One was Yiddish, a combination of Hebrew and German, used by Eastern European Jews. The other was Ladino, a combination of Spanish and Hebrew, which served the same purpose as Yiddish for Jews living in Spanish lands.

By the time of the formation of the modern state of Israel, most Jews spoke either one of these two languages or the language of the country in which they lived. The people who formed the new State of Israel made a revolutionary decision, reviving Hebrew as the national language. This is perhaps the only time in history that a language that was dead as a spoken and common tongue had been restored and adopted in this way.

Rise of a Merchant and Banking Class

Another characteristic of Jewish life during the Diaspora is the rise of a Jewish merchant and banking class. Like the forces that caused many Jews to live separately from others, this rise was caused by forces both external and internal to Jewish life.

Restrictions placed upon Jews played an important part in compelling many to become merchants. In many areas, Jews could not own their own land, making advancement through farming very difficult. Jews often were not permitted to join a profession, and could not join the craft guilds necessary to become a skilled laborer like a carpenter or blacksmith. This limited the options available for Jews to earn a living.

Jews did have several elements of which they could take advantage. They had their education and attention to detail learned from their studies. They also had a network of connections created by the fact that they were Jewish. A letter of introduction or a simple conversation would prove a kinship to Jews in faraway places. A relationship established by peoplehood could quickly evolve into a trusted business relationship, and Jews were able to trade with each other with greater ease and across national borders than other groups. Starting small, most Jewish merchants were able to build modest businesses. Some Jews were able to develop vast trade networks, and became quite successful and wealthy.

Similar forces brought many Jews into the field of moneylending and banking. Again, Jewish education and literacy gave Jews an advantage in this area. Moreover, collecting interest was illegal as usury under Christian Law, so non-Jews could not engage in this needed field. Often governments, nobility, and non-Jewish businesses had to turn to Jews for this needed service. As with merchants, some Jewish bankers became very wealthy and successful in their professions.

Eventually, a phenomenon called "Court Jews" arose. These were Jews who provided governments in Europe with goods and financial services. They became notable figures, involved at the highest levels of business and politics. Although these Court Jews were still separate from the general populace in some ways, in other ways they became an essential and influential part of society.

WORTH NOTING

One of the most influential Court Jews was Meyer Amschel Rothschild (1744-1812) of Germany. His family became one of the wealthiest and most influential in the world in the following centuries.

Emancipation

A great change came to the Jewish community in Europe with the Enlightenment. Philosophers like John Locke began to write about the value of the individual and the need for toleration of differences in belief and opinion. Naturally, the question arose as to whether this new philosophy applied to the Jews, who had been kept apart and restricted for centuries. The general answer to this question in countries experiencing the Enlightenment became that these new ideas applied equally to Jews as well as Christians. Slowly, restrictions placed upon Jews in Europe eased, and Jews began to integrate more fully and equally within general society.

The Enlightenment had a tremendous effect upon Jews and the Jewish community. They no longer had to live within their own areas, and they could travel wherever they wished. Professions and occupations formerly closed to them became open. Non-Jews' culture had great appeal, and was now available to Jews. The traditional Jewish authorities no longer could enforce obedience as they had before, and Jews found they had choices about how to live. Like the citizens of the general population who no longer had to unquestioningly follow the king, Jews had other options than to automatically obey the rabbis.

The Enlightenment was a shock to Jewish life, and there were varied reactions to it. Some Jews struggled to find a path that maintained their Jewishness but also allowed them to participate in the life of the larger society. One of the early leaders of this movement was a German Jew named Moses Mendelssohn, who propounded that a Jew could fully participate in secular society and still voluntarily remain a Jew inside his home and heart. Mendelssohn's followers and others adopted this reasoning in a movement called the *Haskalah*.

Other Jews responded to the challenges of the Enlightenment by rejecting it. They turned even further inward, turning away from many of the aspects of modern society that were now open to them. They remained in their communities, and held even tighter to traditional Jewish practice. They argued that participation in secular society would lead to assimilation, ignorance of the mitzvot, and eventually the disappearance of the Jewish people. To an extent, they were correct, as society's new openness to Jews led many to lose their connection to Torah study, ritual observance, and the Jewish community, and even to convert to Christianity.

As the mid-twentieth century approached, Jews were a diverse people. They lived in most countries around the world. Some participated in general society and did not connect with Judaism and the Jewish community; some tried to create a new way to be Jewish in the modern world. Others remained in their own communities and enclaves, seeking greater adherence to traditional Jewish ways. Some were economically successful and respected, while others were poor and unknown. There's no one definition that can adequately describe all Jews at this time. However, they would all be tremendously affected by what would happen in World War II.

The Birth and Growth of Anti-Semitism

From the beginning, Jews have always been independent and steadfast in their beliefs. They clung to monotheism when the world around them was polytheistic. They resisted Roman rule even though it meant the destruction of their holiest place of worship. They stubbornly held on to their identity and way of life through centuries of exile. While many today would view this adherence to culture and identity as admirable, as Jews always have, many others through history saw Jewish identity as strange, blasphemous, or wrong. This led many to a hatred called anti-Semitism, and they acted upon that hatred to harm Jewish people.

 WORDS OF WISDOM

"Our emancipation will not be complete until we are free of the fear of being Jews."
–Rabbi Mordechai Kaplan

Some anti-Semitism is connected to a single line in Christian Scripture. According to the New Testament, the Roman leader Pontius Pilate asked the Jews what he should do with Jesus, who had been arrested and tried for treason. The Book of Matthew says "the Jews" three times said that Pilate should kill Jesus. Matthew even relates that the Jews said Jesus' death should be "upon us and upon our children." Pilate literally washed his hands of the matter as he sent Jesus to his death.

Some Christian authorities and other people through history have seen this story as a reason to vilify and persecute Jews. They justified many of the restrictions placed upon Jewish peoples based on both the Jews' refusal to accept Jesus as divine and the belief in the Jews' role in deicide.

Sometimes anti-Semitism led to violence, with anti-Jewish riots called *pogroms* resulting in murder and destruction of property. Some of the ghettos were built with walls not just to keep Jews in their communities, but also to keep those who would harm them out. They suffered persecution throughout the Crusades and endured efforts to convert Jews, including the Inquisition.

The Jewish people's different ways, language, and customs also contributed to anti-Semitism. To a non-Jew, they looked and acted strangely, which caused fear. This also caused misunderstanding, including the myth of the "blood libel," which alleges that Jews used the blood of Christian children as an ingredient in the Passover *matzah.* Jews also had particular washing rituals, which, along with their relative isolation, lowered the occurrence of Bubonic plague in Jewish areas in the Middle Ages. This led some Christians to conclude Jews actually caused the plague, which fueled more hatred.

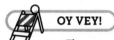 **OY VEY!**

There is a myth that Jews have horns. This comes from a mistranslation of the Hebrew word *keren* in Exodus 34:29. The verse says that "Moses' face shone (keren)" when he came down Mount Sinai. Keren is close to *karan,* which may be translated as "horn." This anti-Semitic myth was exacerbated when Michelangelo placed horns on his famous statue of Moses. You can see the rays shining from Moses's face in the picture in Chapter 2, which also appear like horns.

Jewish involvement as merchants and bankers also contributed to anti-Semitism. After all, it's easy to get angry and dislike the storeowner who charges prices you think are unfair or you can't pay, or the banker to whom you owe money who comes to collect on the loan. Jewish participation in these activities, together with the story of Judas betraying Jesus for thirty pieces of silver, led to the myth of Jews as money-hungry people manipulating the world through their influence. A fictional work titled *The Protocols of the Elders of Zion* is especially noteworthy for promoting these myths early in the twentieth century, and led to dozens of pogroms in Russia and Eastern Europe.

None of this even comes close, though, to the Jewish experience of the Holocaust.

The Holocaust

In the early part of the twentieth century, Jews felt comfortable living in Germany. They had lived there for generations, and it was one of the places where the Enlightenment had taken hold. Many Jews had assimilated, held high positions in business and society, and had fought for Germany in World War I.

The burdens of the Treaty of Versailles and the Great Depression led to an economic and social disaster in Germany. The Germans turned to the fascist Nazi party to lead them out of hard times. The Nazis sought a scapegoat to blame for all of Germany's woes. They found it in the Jews.

A New Form of Anti-Semitism

Much of the anti-Semitism fueling the Nazi hatred of Jews followed traditional stereotypes. They claimed Jews were greedy, and were secretly controlling the German economy, government, and society. The Nazis portrayed Jews as different from the true German, and therefore worthy of persecution and scorn. The Nazis attributed many of Germany's problems to the Jews.

However, there was one aspect of Nazi anti-Semitism that was different from what had been seen previously in the world. The Nazis framed their anti-Semitism on race, presenting pseudo-scientific studies comparing Jews unfavorably with their view of the perfect Aryan–blond hair, blue eyes, light skin, and a pure Northern European bloodline. They decided that a person with only one Jewish grandparent was a Jew in the eyes of the law. This was different from prior anti-Semitic sentiments because, to the Nazis, being a Jew had nothing to do with beliefs or actions. Someone could be a Jew solely because of his or her lineage or genetics, and there was nothing he or she could do to change that. To the Nazis, persecution of Jews was justified based solely on the fact of their existence.

There were other significant differences between Nazism and previous anti-Semitic views. Previously, anti-Semitism resulted in Jews living in separate communities and limiting their actions and freedoms. Though at times anti-Semitism did turn violent and many Jews lost their lives, this happened somewhat sporadically. The Nazis systematized their anti-Semitism, embodying it in their philosophy and governance. They used modern scientific techniques and the power of the nation state to further their persecution.

The Nazis began persecuting Jews with small restrictions, banning them from certain professions and employment in the government and universities. The Nazis boycotted Jewish businesses, and passed law after law that eroded the rights of Jews. The Nuremberg Laws of 1935 went further, including the revocation of German citizenship from all Jews, and the prohibition of intermar-riage. Jews were forced to wear a yellow six-pointed star at all times, reminiscent of the circular patches required in Medieval times.

The Nazis also fostered and organized violence against Jews. There were individual beatings and arrests. There were also pogroms, including the largest in history in 1938—called *Kristallnacht*, The Night of Broken Glass—during which the windows of virtually every Jewish business and synagogue were broken, buildings were burned, and thousands of Jews were arrested.

> **WORTH NOTING**
>
> One of the most remarkable figures of the Holocaust was Anne Frank, a teenage girl who hid from the Nazis in an attic in Amsterdam. Anne kept a diary of her ordeal that captures the emotions of the experience. Notably, she wrote, "I still believe the good in us will win." Anne was captured and died in a concentration camp, but her diary survived and was published.

The Nazis eventually adopted the so-called "Final Solution," in which all the Jews under their jurisdiction would be taken to concentration camps and killed.

Prior to the Holocaust, there were about 9.5 million Jews in Europe. Six million Jews were killed in the Holocaust. Towns that had been centers of Jewish life for centuries suddenly were gone, and cities with significant Jewish populations before the war were emptied. The culture and presence of a people had been largely destroyed.

The Lasting Impact of the Holocaust

Jews today still are greatly affected by the experience of the Holocaust. The Holocaust disputes the proposition that modern life and thought will lead to a time when Jews won't have to worry about persecution. The cry of "Never Again" motivates Jews to be very aware of their position in the world and how others view them.

Anti-Semitism and the Holocaust are realities of Jewish life today. The Jewish people still experience it. It's a fact in their lives, and it causes them to act with caution and concern for their well-being. Many Jews believe their presence in any country is precarious, and while their lives may be good, history teaches that this can easily and quickly change. This is unfortunate and distasteful, but recognition and experience with anti-Semitism and the Holocaust remains an inescapable part of current Jewish life.

The Rise of Two Modern Jewish Centers

Following the Holocaust, the center of world Jewry shifted away from Europe and Northern Africa. Most of the 13 to 15 million Jews in the world today live in either Israel or North America, each with about 6 to 7 million Jews. The remaining Jewish communities are scattered throughout the world.

The Jewish community in the United States dates back to 1654, when a ship of Jews from Recife, Brazil, sought refuge in New Amsterdam (now New York). The governor of the colony, Peter Stuyvesant, wanted to turn them away, but he was forbidden to do so by the Dutch West India Company, which held the colony's charter and had many Jewish investors.

By the American Revolution, there were about 5,000 Jews in the new nation, located primarily in Savannah, Charleston, Philadelphia, New York City, and Newport. A parade in Philadelphia celebrating the ratification of the Constitution famously had a rabbi marching arm in arm with two ministers.

WORDS OF WISDOM

"Proclaim liberty throughout the land unto all the inhabitants thereof."—Leviticus 25:10, engraved on the Liberty Bell

German Jews began immigrating to the United States in the nineteenth century. Jewish immigration hit its highest point from 1880 to 1920, when Jews from Russia and Eastern Europe felt the "push–pull" effect. These people felt pushed out of their home countries by the poor economy and by persecution and pogroms, especially in Russia. They knew they needed to leave *shtetl*, or small community, life for their survival. At the same time, they felt the pull of opportunity of the Industrial Revolution in the United States and freedom of religion embodied in the law. Millions of Jews passed through Ellis Island and eventually became American citizens.

WORTH NOTING

The Broadway show and movie *Fiddler on the Roof,* based on the stories of a Jewish author named Shalom Aleichem, is a well- known and popular musical portraying both the joys and tragedy of shtetl life, leading to immigration to Israel and the United States.

Jews today form only about 2 percent of the American population, but that's still enough people to make the United States one of the two nations in the world with the largest Jewish populations. The other nation is Israel, which we will discuss in Chapter 8. The remainder of the Jewish population lives throughout the world, even in countries most impacted by the Holocaust.

The Least You Need to Know

- Jewish history begins with the stories of the Torah and the Prophets, tracing events from the creation of the world through the establishment of the first Jewish nation in the Promised Land.

- The Jewish nation in the Promised Land lasted for about 1,000 years until the destruction of the Second Temple. The Jews then dispersed in a migration called the Diaspora.

- The Diaspora was a time of growth and study. It was also a time of living as a minority among other peoples, and sometimes suffering from anti-Semitic acts.

- The Enlightenment ended much of the separation of Jews from other peoples, and radically changed the position of Jews in the world.

- The Holocaust destroyed most of the Jewish community in Europe. This tragedy still greatly affects Jewish perspectives today.

- Today, there are two large Jewish communities in Israel and North America, with the remaining Jews scattered throughout the world.

People of the Book(s)

Jews have long been known as the "People of the Book." The Book referred to in this name is the Bible. It makes sense to call them the People of the Book because they were the first to accept this Scripture, at Mount Sinai. Other religions later accepted the Jewish Bible as their own and added to it, but the name People of the Book stuck with the Jews.

There's a limitation that comes with this name. Even if you view all the books in the Bible as one book, the Bible is far from the only book that has great importance in Judaism. There are centuries of important authoritative writings that came after the Bible—volume upon volume of interpretation that has affected Judaism so much that it would be unrecognizable to anyone who only studied the Bible. One of the most difficult questions I have to answer is when a non-Jew asks, "How do Jews observe this chapter in Leviticus today?" because, so often, later writings have dramatically impacted Jewish practice. To answer the question, I have to convince the asker that the Bible doesn't give the whole story, and I'm met either with resistance or a lack of comprehension. "But you're Jews," the questioner says. "It's your Bible. You *have* to be following it!"

In This Chapter

- A Scripture called the Tanach
- Interpretations in the Midrashim
- The great body of Jewish law: the Talmud
- Commentaries, responsa, and codes

To really understand Judaism, it's important to know and appreciate the many important books of the people and the religion.

The Tanach (Bible)

The Jewish Bible is composed of three large parts: *Torah, Nivi'im* (Prophets), and *Ketuvim* (Writings). They're written mostly in Hebrew, although a few of the later books contain Aramaic. There are translations of the Jewish Bible into just about every language, which Jews use for worship and prayer. But since every translation is at least partly an interpretation and diverges from the original meaning, rabbis and Jewish scholars use the original Hebrew for their work.

The Jewish Bible is called the *Tanach,* which is an anagram of the first letters of the names of the Bible's parts. The final sound becomes a *"ch"* (pronounced as a guttural, a bit like clearing your throat, not like "ch" in English) instead of a *"k"* because of Hebrew pronunciation rules, so it's pronounced 'ta-**nach**'.

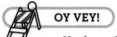 **OY VEY!**

Until now, I've been using the word "Bible." Now that you know the Hebrew term "Tanach," which is the true designation of Jewish Scripture, I'm going to use "Tanach" instead of "Bible" for the rest of this book.

There's evidence that over time there were variations in the text of the Tanach. You can see some of these variations through study and comparison of today's text with the famous Dead Sea Scrolls found at Qumran. A group of respected scribes called the Masoretes operating in Israel in the seventh through eleventh centuries determined what was the single authoritative text. This Masoretic text is the only version Jews deem to be the Tanach.

Torah

The Torah is the first part of the Tanach. It's known as "The Five Books of Moses" because Moses is the dominant figure in four of the books, and because Moses received the Torah on Mount Sinai. Sometimes the Torah is called *Chumash,* after the Hebrew word for "five." More importantly, the Torah is called *Eitz Chayyim,* "the Tree of Life," because we see adherence to the Torah as part of our Covenant with God that ensures our continued existence.

The Torah contains several types of writing. There are narratives telling the story of the world and people from creation to Moses' death right before the Israelites enter the Promised Land. The Torah contains many laws ranging from details of personal conduct to ethical rules applicable both to individuals and to the entire people. There are details about the construction and ritual of the Temple, and much about purity and holiness that both traditional and liberal Jewish authorities view applicable only to Temple times. There is also poetry in the Torah that's still used in Jewish worship today.

The following chart lists the books of the Torah and a general description of what is found in them:

The Books of the Torah

English Name	Hebrew Name	Content Highlights
Genesis	Beresheet	Creation to the Israelites living in Egypt
Exodus	Shemot	Slavery in Egypt and the Exodus; the Ten Commandments and other laws
Leviticus	Vayikra	Temple sacrificial and ritual laws for the building and priest; purity laws
Numbers	Bemidbar	Stories of the Israelites wandering in the desert; additional laws
Deuteronomy	Devarim	Moses' final address to the Israelites

The Hebrew names of the books come from the first uncommon word in the text. So "Moses" would not be the name of a book because this name occurs many times in the Torah.

Nivi'im (Prophets)

The second part of the Tanach is *Nivi'im,* or Prophets. A prophet in Jewish tradition is not what is commonly defined as a prophet in English. In English, a prophet is someone who tells or predicts the future. In Judaism, a prophet might do a little of that, but more often fills the role of being God's spokesman to the people. A prophet chastises the people when they stray from God's commandments or act unjustly or unethically. The prophet warns the people that God will punish them if they don't repent and change their behavior, which they almost always do.

The first six books in the Prophets are not really the writings of specific prophets at all, but are the continuation of the narrative story of the Israelites. These are called the "First Prophets" or the "Former Prophets." Prophets appear as figures in some of the books, but these six books are more historical accounts than words attributed to actual prophets.

The Books of the First Prophets

English Name	Hebrew Name	Content Highlights
Joshua	Yehoshua	The entrance of the Israelites into the Promised Land and conflict with Canaanites
Judges	Shoftim	Conflicts with Canaanites as the Israelites are led by temporary leaders (Judges)
First Samuel	Shmuel Aleph	Stories of the prophet Samuel, King Saul, and the rise of King David
Second Samuel	Shmuel Beit	The reign of King David
First Kings	Melachim Aleph	The death of King David, the split into Northern and Southern Kingdoms, and events to about 850 B.C.E.
Second Kings	Melachim Beit	Events from about 850 B.C.E. to the destruction of the First Temple

ASK THE RABBI

Why are Samuel and Kings in two parts? These books were probably split because they were too large to fit on one scroll, which was customary in ancient days before printing. In some Hebrew versions of the Tanach the books are not divided.

The Second or Latter Prophets contain writings attributed to God's spokesmen filling this particular role. They contain some of the strongest words in the Tanach about caring for the poor, and create an imperative for social justice embedded within Judaism.

The first three Latter Prophets, Yesha'yahu (Isaiah), Yirmeyahu (Jeremiah), and Yechezkel (Ezekiel) are sometimes separated simply because the books are longer. The remaining 12 books are sometimes called the "Minor Prophets" not because they're less important or authoritative, but because they're shorter. They include:

- Hoshea (Hosea)
- Yoel (Joel)
- Amos (Amos)
- Ovadyah (Obediah)
- Yonah (Jonah)

- Mikah (Micah)

- Nachum (Nahum)

- Chavakook (Habakkuk)

- Tzefanyah (Zephaniah)

- Chaggai (Haggai)

- Zecharyah (Zechariah)

- Malaki (Malachi)

Ketuvim (Writings)

The final part of the Tanach is *Ketuvim*, or "Writings." This is the most eclectic part of the Tanach, as the books vary in length and style. The only real commonality among these books is that they were written or describe events following the destruction of the First Temple and were considered worthy of inclusion in the Tanach.

The process of determining which books were included in the Tanach, and particularly in Ketuvim, is called *canonization*. It's unclear exactly who made these decisions and when they were made, although canonization probably happened in stages, fixing the Torah, Nivi'im, and Ketuvim at different times. However, it seems certain that canonization was completed by the time of the rabbis in the two centuries prior to the start of the Common Era.

Some questions remain about why some books were included. Why did *Shir HaShirim* (The Song of Songs) make it into the Tanach, considering its explicit romantic content? Why was Daniel included, considering its apocalyptic content is so different than the rest of the Tanach? Why was Maccabees not included, since it's the basis of the holiday of Chanukkah? Scholars continue to debate these and similar questions to this day, and call books known at the time but not included in the Tanach, *Apocrypha*.

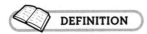 **DEFINITION**

> **Apocrypha** are the books known to have existed at the time of canonization with similar content and style of writing as books in the Tanach, but ultimately were not included in the Tanach. Notable Apocrypha include Maccabees, The Wisdom of Ben Sira, Tobit, and Judith.

The following table lists the books of Ketuvim and a general description of what is found in them:

The Books of Ketuvim (Writings)

English Name	Hebrew Name	Content Highlights
Psalms	Tehillim	Liturgical poems mostly attributed to King David and possibly used in Temple worship
Proverbs	Mishlei	Wisdom sayings attributed to King Solomon
Job	Iyyov	The story of a pious man whose faith is tested by God
Song of Songs	Shir HaShirim	A poem attributed to King Solomon seen as a metaphor for the love between God and the Jewish people
Ruth	Rut	The story of a woman who converted to Judaism and was David's great-grandmother
Lamentations	Eikah	Poems of sorrow for the exile and the destruction of the First Temple
Ecclesiastes	Kohelet	A philosophical book promoting wisdom and simple pleasures over vain pursuits
Esther	Ester	The story of Esther saving the Jews of Persia; the basis of the holiday *Purim*
Daniel	Daniel	The story of upper-class Jews exiled in Babylon
Ezra	Ezra	The story of the return of Jews to Jerusalem under Cyrus the Great and the dedication of the Second Temple
Nehemiah	Nechemyah	The continuation of the rebuilding of Jerusalem in Ezra
Chronicles	Divrei HaYamim	A separate history of the Jewish people attributed to Ezra, sometimes separated into two books

Midrash

A *Midrash* is a text that expands on the meaning of the Tanach's text, fills in a gap in a Biblical story, adds detail, or otherwise expands upon the Scriptural text or its ideas. *Midrashim* (the plural of Midrash) may be divided into two categories: classical and modern.

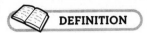 **DEFINITION**

A **Midrash** is an interpretation of the Scriptural text of the ideas contained within it. It may include a story otherwise absent from the text, laws, commentary, or folklore.

Classical Midrashim

Classical Midrashim are interpretations composed or compiled by the rabbis and sages of Judaism. They date back to the first century C.E. or earlier, although sometimes they weren't compiled or published until much later. There is no single collection of classical Midrashim. Instead, there are several bodies of work attributed to many authors in a variety of time periods.

Midrashim are quite imaginative and clever. Some may have been sermons, and others shrewdly connect seemingly unrelated verses from different parts of the Tanach. Some are parables, especially those in which an analogy is made between an earthly king and God. Midrashim use wordplay and puns to make their points. They examine the Hebrew text of the Tanach, and use similar-sounding or similar-appearing letters or words to make connections and reveal hidden meanings. Every word, letter, and space in the Torah has multiple divine implications, and the midrashist's role is to expand on and explain these for the Jewish people.

 **OY VEY!**

Many Midrashim rely on fine points of Hebrew, so if you read a Midrash in translation, you might not be able to see exactly how the writer made his interpretation.

Midrashim may use the traditional reading method of Scriptural text called *pardes*, an anagram for four stages of interpretation:

1. *Pshat:* the plain meaning of the text

2. *Remez:* hints about what the text might mean

3. *Drash:* creative interpretations and understanding of the text

4. *Sod:* secrets found in the text only through skill after intense study and understanding

The word *pardes* in Hebrew means "paradise," reflecting the rabbinic idea that a full and complete analysis and comprehension of all levels of Scripture lead to wisdom and fulfillment.

There are two primary types of classical Midrashim. The first is *aggadic* midrashim, which tells a legend or story or answers a question concerning the narrative sections of the Tanach. The second is *halachic* midrashim, which uses the same techniques as aggadic midrashim but focuses upon explaining or developing a point of Jewish law.

Let's look at the beginning of a very important story for Jews in *Bereisheet* (Genesis) to see the imagination of the classical rabbinic midrashists at work. The story is the *Akeidah*—the binding of Isaac—which is both a proof of Abraham's commitment to God that is imputed to us, and a rejection of brutal pagan rites such as child sacrifice. The beginning of the first verses of the story reads:

> "After these things God tested Abraham ...." (Genesis 22:1)

The midrashist often seeks to answer a question about the text, even if he doesn't always explicitly state the question. The first question in this verse comes right at the very beginning. The text says, "After these things ...." After what things? It could be after the events of the previous chapter, but that seems to be an insufficient explanation. The Tanach usually just goes from one event to another, and doesn't ordinarily use a phrase like this. Why, then, does this phrase appear here? The midrashist concludes something else must have happened. Likely reaching into Jewish folklore, the midrashist presents a conversation between God and one of the angels. The angel doesn't believe Abraham is truly faithful, so God devises this test to prove Abraham's commitment. Thanks to the Midrash, a question about a strange part of the Tanach text is resolved, and we learn that this difficult request was not God's whim, but was meant to prove an important point to the Heavenly Court.

Modern Midrash

The Midrashim process continues today, with many rabbis and scholars providing new interpretations of the Tanach. There have been journals of modern Midrash, and the internet provides a way for any rabbi to offer a new Midrash instantaneously. Modern Midrash certainly doesn't have the time-tested authority of classical Midrash, but if a modern Midrash uses the same cleverness and techniques, it has the potential to add a new understanding or depth to our understanding of Scripture. Modern Midrash is also extremely important in that it offers an opportunity for new interpretive voices to be heard.

The Talmud

An even larger body of Jewish discourse is the *Talmud,* which means "instruction." The Talmud is a huge compilation of Oral Law, discussion and debate among rabbis, midrashim, and commentary that became the basis of Jewish practice for most of the past 2,000 years.

There are actually two versions of the Talmud. The Talmud Yirushalmi (Jerusalem or Palestinian Talmud) was written in the land of Israel and attained its final form in the middle of the fifth century C.E. At that time, Christianity had become the official religion of the Roman Empire and Jews in Israel were persecuted, stopping further additions and development of the Talmud Yirushalmi. The Talmud Bavli (Babylonian Talmud) was written in Babylonia and was completed in the sixth or seventh century C.E. The Talmud Bavli contains most of the material in the Talmud Yirushalmi and much more. It's better organized and more elaborate, so when Jews say Talmud, they almost always mean the Talmud Bavli.

The Talmud Bavli is comprised of 63 major parts, each called a *maseket* or "Tractate." The standard text is called the *Vilna shas* and was printed in Lithuania in the 1880s.

Mishnah

The starting text of the Talmud is called the *Mishnah*. The Mishnah is the first compilation of Jewish law after the Torah. The Mishnah began with the work of Rabbi Yochanan ben Zakkai and his contemporaries at Yavneh following the destruction of the Second Temple. As described in Chapter 3, these scholars adapted Jewish law to meet the new realities of Jewish life. A great scholar named Rabbi Akiva began to gather and organize these teachings in the second century C.E., and this was completed by Rabbi Judah HaNasi in the third century.

WORTH NOTING

The work of Judah HaNasi in completing the Mishnah is so important that he is identified in the text simply as "Rabbi."

The Mishnah organizes the Law into six large parts called "orders," and each order is divided into tractates. The language of the Mishnah is terse, but does include midrashim and preserves opinions of rabbis even if these opinions are contrary to the determination of the Law.

One special tractate of the Mishnah is *Pirkei Avot,* or "Sayings of the Fathers." Pirkei Avot contains special and noteworthy proverbs, especially some attributed to the great Rabbi Hillel. Pirkei Avot holds special stature as a distinct nonlegal part of the Mishnah filled with ethical teachings.

Another text worthy of note with the Mishnah is the *Tosefta. Tosefta* is Aramaic for "supplement," and it contains texts, opinions, and teachings contemporaneous to those in the Mishnah but not included for unknown reasons. It's still recognized as having some persuasive authority, even though it's not in the main collection of Jewish law.

Gemara

Following the completion of the Mishnah, the Mishnah itself was analyzed by the ensuing generations of rabbis and sages. The terseness of the earlier work was ripe for further explanation. Changing times and circumstances demanded more law and commentary, and the rabbis became concerned with specific details and questions. These commentaries through the sixth century C.E. are collected in a part of the Talmud called the *Gemara*.

Gemara is Aramaic for "study" or "learning." The Gemara is composed of legal opinions, midrashim, stories of the rabbis, and ethical and philosophical discourses. Much of it is arranged as a conversation among the rabbis. This is an editorial technique, as the rabbis cited often didn't live in the same times or places. It sometimes contains opinions or teachings from rabbis of the time of the Mishnah or earlier that are not included in the earlier work. Each of these is called a *baraita*.

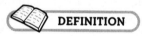 **DEFINITION**

A **baraita** is a teaching from a sage from the time of the Mishnah found in the later text of the Gemara.

The Gemara is very difficult to read. It's set up as a commentary on the Mishnah, with a paragraph of the Mishnah appearing first, followed by the associated Gemara. However, the Gemara often rambles, and switches from one topic to another for pages and pages seemingly at random, and then turns back to the original subject. Like the Mishnah, the Gemara assumes the reader has significant knowledge, citing verses from the Scripture only in part, and often not the part upon which the Gemara relies to make its point. The Gemara also doesn't tell you where in the Tanach the verse is found; you are expected to know.

The Law in the Gemara is determined by the opinion of the majority of the rabbis. Sometimes the text specifically states that a given point is the Law. Other times, the text simply state the Law, and you have to assume this is the majority opinion. If an opinion is specifically attributed to a rabbi, you know this is a minority opinion that's being preserved but is not the final rule, unless the text specifically says it's the rule. Moreover, it's understood that the majority opinion of the rabbis overrules any single rabbi, or even what God seems to command in the Tanach.

Nowhere is this seen more than in the Talmudic story of Rabbi Eliezer. The rabbis were discussing a fine point of law about whether an impure oven could be purified. The rabbis said yes, but Rabbi Eliezer said no. Rabbi Eliezer, who was well known for his wisdom, started to prove his position by saying, "If I am right, let this miracle happen." His words made a tree move its location, a stream run backward, and the stone walls of a House of Study begin to collapse. Finally,

Rabbi Eliezer called upon heaven to tell the others that he was correct. A voice from heaven told this to the rabbis, but the rabbis stuck to their opinion. They said the matter was not for heaven to decide, but was left to the authority of the rabbis according to the Tanach. God laughed and said, "My children have defeated Me!" Rabbi Eliezer was excommunicated. The primacy of the Talmudic rabbis was assured. (Talmud Bavli, Baba Metzia 59b)

 ASK THE RABBI

> How can the rabbis of the Talmud overrule something stated in the Tanach? The rabbis use reasoning and comparisons between multiple texts to determine the Law. For example, the Torah says, "eye for an eye" in several texts. The rabbis in the Talmud reason that there is no assurance that an eye of one person is equal to the eye of another, and compare the usage of the word "for" to how it's used in another place in the Tanach. From this, they conclude that "eye for an eye" is not meant literally, but rather means monetary compensation for an injury. They totally change the plain meaning of the text, but their opinion is still considered the Law given at Sinai.

Other Parts of the Talmud

If you look at a page of the Vilna shas, you will see the slightly larger Hebrew or Aramaic text of the Mishnah and Gemara in the center. This is surrounded on all sides by other important texts necessary for Talmud study.

The text appearing to the side of the Mishnah/Gemara near the binding of the volume is a commentary by a great rabbi of the Middle Ages, Rashi. Rashi is an anagram for Rabbi Shmuel ben Yitzchak, who lived from 1040 to 1105 C.E. and founded a school in Troyes, France. His commentary on the Talmud is considered brilliant and worthy of this special placement on the page. Rashi is so revered that his commentary is printed in a special font styled after his handwriting called "Rashi script."

On the opposite side of the page, you'll find the commentary of Rashi's students called the *Tosefot*, meaning "additions." The Tosefot considers both the text of the Mishnah/Gemara and Rashi's commentary. It's also printed in Rashi script.

Other commentaries appear at the bottom of the page, and citations and other notes appear in the margins. So to fully read a page of Talmud, you have to start from the inside and read outward, understanding Hebrew and Aramaic without punctuation, working through two distinct but related typefaces, unraveling a confusing text that jumps from one subject to another and cites incomplete verses from the Tanach as proof. It's no wonder Talmud study takes years to master.

Commentaries

The great age of commentaries occurred in the Middle Ages after the completion of the Gemara. Some of these commentaries were written on the Talmud, as we've seen with Rashi's commentary and the Tosefot included on the Vilna shas.

Other commentaries were written on the text of the Tanach itself. These classical Biblical commentaries are verse-by-verse companions to the Tanach text, and you can read them together. Many of the commentators have a particular style or point of view. Rashi's commentaries tend to rely on classical midrashim. Rabbi Moshe ben Nachman was a commentator who lived from 1194 to 1270 c.e. in Spain. He was also known as Ramban, an anagram of his name, or Nachmanides. Ramban's commentary on the Torah is very concerned with criticizing Rashi's commentary and providing alternative explanations. Abraham ibn Ezra, a commentator from Navarre who lived from 1089 to 1164 c.e., relies on grammar and the plain meaning of the text, or *pshat*. These commentaries are collected in volumes called the *"Mikra'ot Gedolot."*

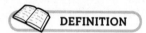 **DEFINITION**

> A **Mikra'ot Gedolot,** or "Great Scripture" contains the text of the Tanach along with various commentaries. Similar in structure to the Talmud, the Tanach text appears in the middle or at the top of the page, and the commentaries appear below or surrounding it. Most of these volumes are in Hebrew. However there is now an excellent version in English with the commentaries of Rashi, Ramban, Ibn Ezra, Rashbam and others being published by the Jewish Publication Society.

There are many modern commentaries, as the tradition of writing running annotations of the text continues throughout Jewish history. It's important to know who wrote a particular commentary when you read it, and to understand the author's knowledge, perspective, and biases to determine the value of the work.

Responsa

Even with the detailed discussions of Talmud, or perhaps because of them, individual rabbis sometimes could not resolve difficult questions about the Law. These rabbis would write a *she'eilah,* or question, to the more learned scholars, posing the problem and any relevant texts and conflicts the asking rabbi had found or considered. The scholar would then write an answer, called a *"Teshuvah"* or *responsum,* resolving the question according to his opinion. Responsa provide informative opinions about the Law, but they don't provide authoritative halachah themselves. They're not binding precedent like a Supreme Court ruling, but they do give important insight into what the halachah should be.

Like commentaries, responsa are still produced today by leading rabbis and the rabbinical organizations of the various Jewish movements.

Codes

Eventually, the mass of Talmud, commentaries, and responsa became extremely difficult to manage. There was no index or any other method of organizing all the sources and information that existed. It was almost impossible to absorb all of it to determine what the halachah should be on any particular topic. After a while, some great scholars began to try to solve this problem by writing codes. Codes take the various sources and restate the halachah in clear language. They often remove the reasoning behind the decision, simply stating the Law for the easy understanding of the reader. They are organized by subject, making the code even easier to use and helpful.

Maimonides wrote the first great code. The code is called the *Mishneh Torah*, and considered all subjects and many opinions in Jewish law, including rules about the Temple that had not existed for about a thousand years.

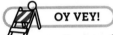 **OY VEY!**

Don't confuse the Mishnah with the Mishneh Torah. Their names are similar, but they're entirely different works from different eras.

An equally influential code, or perhaps even more influential, is the *Shulchan Aruch*, which means "Set Table." Rabbi Joseph Caro, a legalist who lived in Safed in the sixteenth century, wrote this code. Published in 1565, the Shulchan Aruch is actually an abbreviated version of a more elaborate code Caro wrote called the *Beit Yosef.* The Shulchan Aruch only considered issues relevant to the times, did not include some citations, and only contained opinions with which Caro agreed.

The Shulchan Aruch considered the halachah applicable to Sephardic Jews. There were differences in the halachah applicable to Ashkenazic Jews. (We will consider the groupings of Sephardic and Ashkenazic Jews in the next chapter.) Fortunately, a German Rabbi names Moses Isserles, also known as the Rama, was writing a similar code for Ashkenazic Jews. He adapted his code to the Shulchan Aruch, organizing it along the same lines so that it highlighted the differences between the Sephardic Laws summarized by Caro and the Ashkenazic Laws familiar to Isserles.

Appropriately, Isserles named his code *"HaMapa,"* or "The Tablecloth." These two codes are often published together, forming a complete body of work that many Jews throughout the world accepted as the final summary of the halachah for all time. Eventually, this determination would contribute to later divisions among the Jewish people, as we will see in the next chapter.

The Least You Need to Know

- The Jewish Bible is called the Tanach, an anagram for its three parts, Torah, Nivi'im (Prophets), and Ketuvim (Writings).

- Midrashim are interpretations of the text that tell legends, give some Jewish Law, and explain interpretations of the Tanach. The midrashic tradition began thousands of years ago, and continues today.

- The Talmud is a large collection of Jewish Law that provides the traditional halachah. It was developed over centuries, and contains the Mishnah, the Gemara, and several commentaries.

- Commentaries are line-by-line notations about the Talmud or the Tanach, and provide further understanding of Jewish Law and Scripture.

- Responsa are questions posed by rabbis to greater scholars on confusing points of the halachah. Codes are summaries of the halachah from all these sources organized into a readable and easier-to-use form.

One People, Many Views

Like any large group of people, Jews have found themselves with some divisions and sub-groupings. Some of the differences are based on ethnic or cultural factors, while others are based on religious ideas and perspectives. Some divisions are an accident of history, caused simply by living in different places and being influenced by different factors.

It's important to understand these differences to completely understand Judaism. But it's also important to realize that, despite these differences, Jews see themselves as one people. They may argue about one religious or philosophical point or another. They may have some different customs. They may have some really strong disagreements. None of this goes so far as to call into question their vision of themselves as one people. They simply have many different views.

In This Chapter

- Two main groups of Jews: Sephardic and Ashkenazic
- The development of movements in Judaism
- How it's determined who is Jewish
- The Beta Israel community of Ethiopia
- Kabbalah, the core of Jewish mysticism

Sephardic and Ashkenazic Jews

There are two main groups of Jews in the world: Ashkenazic Jews and Sephardic Jews. This division is based on several elements. There's a difference in history, culture, and even religious law, which necessitates both a Sephardic and Ashkenazic Chief Rabbi of Israel. The separation occurred over time during the Middle Ages following the start of the Diaspora.

Sephardic Jews come from areas that were governed at one time by Muslims, including Spain, Portugal, Northern Africa, and part of the Middle East. As you might imagine, Sephardic food and traditional dress share some similarities with Islamic culture. The history of Sephardic Jews is intertwined with Islamic history, as Sephardic Jews thrived during Muslim rule in Spain, but then suffered under the Inquisition, which required many of them to flee, convert, or pretend to convert. Sephardic intellectualism is notable for its poetry and philosophy.

 WORTH NOTING

Marrano Jews converted or pretended to convert due to the threat of the Inquisition. Over generations, much of the Marranos' knowledge of Judaism, and even their awareness that they or their ancestors were Jewish, dissipated. Many families continued to follow Jewish traditions for generations, such as lighting two candles on Friday nights, without knowing why.

Ashkenazic Jews come from Germany, France, England, Eastern Europe, and Russia. Just as Sephardic culture resembles that of the Islamic people among whom they lived, Ashkenazic food and traditional dress share similarities with those found in northern and Eastern European nations.

Ashkenazic and Sephardic Jews at one time had slightly different ways of pronouncing Hebrew. Israel followed the Sephardic method after adopting Hebrew as its national language, so most Israelis and many Americans use Sephardic pronunciation even if they're Ashkenazic. You'll still hear Ashkenazic pronunciation in some places, especially among the older generations and in some Conservative and Orthodox communities.

The difference between Sephardic and Ashkenazic Jews has become less important in some ways. There's much more interaction between the two groups, and the separation between synagogues and biases that used to exist are gone in many places, especially in America. Still, there are some places where the distinction is still important, such as in certain communities in Israel. Cultural differences also persevere, as you will hear Yiddish and see Ashkenazic food in some families, and hear Ladino and see Sephardic food in others.

Movements in Judaism

Judaism today is divided into "movements," sometimes called "streams" or "branches," especially in North America. All these different views result in one way or another from the effects of the Enlightenment. Enlightenment ideas and the openness of secular society to Jews was welcomed by some and seen as threatening by others. The differing reactions to this great historical force led to the movements' development.

The movements have had a tremendous impact on Jewish life. They formed significant organizations of rabbis, congregations, and laypeople. They built great *yeshivot* (schools of Jewish learning) and seminaries. They produced summer camps for kids, programs, prayer books, publications, music, responsa, and so much more, while offering support for Jewish communities seeking to form synagogues or struggling to continue. Sometimes the movements are criticized for their bureaucracy, failure to achieve more, and all too frequent infighting, but certainly the movements have enriched and advanced Jewish life.

WORTH NOTING

Although movements exist in Israel, Israelis are more likely to divide themselves as either *dati* or *chiloni*. Dati are observers of traditional halachah, often to quite an extreme. Chiloni are more secular Jews who observe Jewish law and custom similarly to the way a Christian observes his or her religion in the United States.

Movements are not the same as different forms of Christianity. There's not the same sense of being in a separate religion. However, there are parallels you might see, as the spectrum of belief and observance in Judaism is similar to the spectrum you'll find in Christianity.

Orthodox

Responding to the Enlightenment, Orthodox Judaism reinforced even more the idea of the receipt of both the Oral and Written Law at Mount Sinai. Orthodox Jews believe the Torah was literally given by God at this holy place and time, and they're strictly obligated to follow the 613 mitzvot as outlined and detailed by the sages. To Orthodox Jews, the halachah is God's will—unquestionable and inviolate. For most, the Talmud as summarized by the Shulchan Aruch/HaMapa is the guide they follow.

Orthodox Jews are notable for their firm observance of traditional Jewish rituals and ideas. Their manner of dress is distinctive, as they're concerned with the value of *tzni'ut*, or modesty, which we will discuss more in Chapter 21. Sometimes this requires Orthodox Jews to resist or reject secular culture or ideas they see as conflicting with the halachah. Orthodox Jews also have a very high regard for the leader of their community, in some communities called the "Rebbe." The

Rebbe has the final word on all decisions of halachah and appropriate conduct for members of the community, and therefore holds a position of great respect, authority, and influence.

It's very important to understand that Orthodox Judaism is not monolithic. Many people believe Orthodox communities are virtually identical and all hold the same extremely strict views. This is not true. There are great variations among Orthodox communities. They're probably less united in many ways than Jews in other movements. Some, called "modern Orthodox," are much more open to interaction with secular culture and the secular world. Some have allowed for greater participation of women in leadership roles while still keeping to the traditional halachah. Even in the most traditional communities, different groups have different Rebbes, and this leads to differences in behavior and requirements based on fine points of halachah.

One of the more notable and visible sections of Orthodox Judaism, due to their customs and dress, is the *Chassidism*. Chassidism began in the early eighteenth century, primarily in Eastern Europe. It was founded by a spiritual leader named the Baal Shem Tov, which means "Master of the Good Name." He is also referred to as the *Besht*. The Baal Shem Tov favored emotionalism over intellectualism, and taught that faith and devotion were at least equal in importance to knowledge. To the Besht, singing and dancing with joy in worship was just as significant as saying the correct words of prayer and knowing why they were being said. There are many stories of the Baal Shem Tov urging the worship of God in nature.

WORDS OF WISDOM

"A man needs no fixed places to say his prayers, no synagogues; among the trees of the forest, everyone can pray."—Baal Shem Tov

"The important thing is not how many separate commandments we obey, but the spirit in which we obey them."—Baal Shem Tov

In Chassidism, every man could become a *tzadik*—a righteous individual—even if he was not knowledgeable about the fine points of Jewish Law. This was a radical change from previous traditional thought, which favored learning above all else. Emotional and mystical experience, including Kabbalistic encounters, replaced book learning in priority. Additionally, because every Jew who pursued this lifestyle was a tzadik, the highest level in the community a Jew could attain, they started to dress like those noblemen in the highest ranks of secular Eastern Europe at the time. This explains the distinctive black suits and wide-brimmed hats, sometimes with fur, male Chassidism still wear today.

Different branches of Chassidism arose in different towns or areas in Eastern Europe, explaining the variations in practice, dress, and rabbinic authority. The Holocaust was particularly devastating to Chassidic communities. Many reformed in the United States or Israel after the end of

World War II, transplanting the people and practices in their entirety. Over the past few decades, many of these communities have experienced rapid growth.

Somewhat ironically, Chassidism today are some of the strongest proponents of strict religious observance and practice, and the most resistant to change and the influence of secular culture. This leads to a greater emphasis on halachic learning and knowledge of the fine points of Jewish Law, even while maintaining the value of mystical and emotional experience. Some branches of Chassidism also believe it's important for them to convince less traditionally observant Jews to become more Orthodox, and spend a significant amount of effort trying to make this happen.

Reform

Other Jews had an opposite response to the Enlightenment than those who became Orthodox. They found the offerings and opportunities presented by secular culture quite enticing. They also began to consider what traditional Judaism offered in comparison to secular culture, and found the former archaic and unappealing. They began to move away from the philosophies, values, and practices of Talmudic Judaism.

These Jews were very much influenced by the democratic elements in Enlightenment philosophy. Previously, the rabbis and communal authorities had control over the details of their lives. Now they had new freedoms, and like their new friends in the general society, they rejected the idea that authority could be placed in a sovereign without their consent. With the ability of these Jews to leave their communities, the traditional Jewish authorities lost power over them.

These Jews also looked at the fixed nature of Jewish Law following the publication of the Shulchan Aruch, and saw a system that had become too rigid. They believed that through the centuries Judaism had been in a constant state of change, even influenced by outside culture.

Additionally, and most controversially, these Jews became influenced by scholars like Julius Wellhausen. These scholars applied modern literary and linguistic techniques to Scripture, and argued that the Torah had developed over time from various sources, and that the Oral Law also was the product of people. No longer did these Jews totally believe the Torah was literally and completely given at Sinai.

 WORTH NOTING

The problems with seeing the Torah as completely given at Sinai were recognized earlier in traditional Judaism. The commentator Ibn Ezra noted a problem in that the Torah, in speaking about Moses' death, said no one knew where he was buried "to this day." (Deuteronomy 34:6) Ibn Ezra attributed these words to Joshua, but didn't comment on their implications. It took the Reform Movement to actually act upon these ideas.

The development of these ideas took many years, and became accepted more in some places and less in others. However, over time these Jews began to see their religion as something open to change, and they could change it intentionally if they had reason to do so. They believed true Judaism, at its core, was "ethical monotheism," which required them only to be good and moral people and believe in one God. Everything else, including all the detailed rituals and practices required by the sages and rabbis, not only was unnecessary, but also could even become a barrier to what was really important in Judaism due to the complexity and focus upon minutia in the halachah. They consequently sought to reform Judaism, even if it meant that they would no longer consider the halachah binding upon them.

The early Reformers began in Germany in the nineteenth century, and largely focused on ritual change. They shortened the service by removing repeated prayers and prayers they no longer found relevant, like those about the restoration of the Temple. They sought to mimic the type of edifying worship they found in Christian churches, adding musical instruments—especially the organ—using vernacular language, and seating men and women together.

Reform Judaism became outward looking, and emphasized social justice, a concern that remains at the center of Reform Judaism today. Reform is also influenced by feminism and gender egalitarianism, becoming the first movement to allow women to become rabbis. Recently, Reform Judaism has departed from its original rejection of ritual laws, and has become more open to traditional practices. Reform also has sought to be open in ways contrary to traditional law, welcoming those who have intermarried or are GLBT.

Reform Judaism's largest contingency is in the United States and Canada, where it's the largest Jewish movement. It exists in other locations, including Israel, but remains a smaller segment of the overall world Jewish community outside of North America.

Conservative

Conservative Judaism seeks a middle ground between Orthodox and Reform. Conservative Jews hold to the halachah and see great value in keeping as many of the traditional rituals and practices as possible. They also realize modern life requires that the halachah evolve and change. Because it's a halachic movement, the rabbis have the authority to determine what changes are appropriate, in contrast to Reform, in which the authority is placed in each individual. The rabbis can make changes in the halachah, but only when these changes are based upon necessity and sound reasoning.

For example, the traditional halachah doesn't allow fires to be lit on *Shabbat*. A car's ignition creates a spark, which the Law deemed the same as lighting a fire, so Orthodox Jews couldn't drive a car on the Sabbath. The Conservative movement recognized that people were living in different places and climates than previously, and it wasn't always practical to prohibit people from using their cars to get to Shabbat services. The rabbis concluded that driving a car on Shabbat was acceptable in the halachah—but only if you were driving it to synagogue.

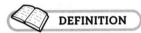

> **DEFINITION**
>
> **Shabbat** is the Jewish Sabbath, a day of rest occurring each week that begins on Friday at sunset and ends on Saturday at sunset. We'll look closely at Shabbat in Chapter 9.

The Conservative Movement, like the Reform, was born in Germany. It gained its greatest strength in the United States, breaking away from the Reform Movement, which practitioners began to see as too liberal and rejecting of traditional practices.

> **ASK THE RABBI**
>
> How did the split between the Reform and Conservative movements happen? At first, there was just one non-Orthodox movement in the United States. There were tensions between the more and less traditional minded. Legend says the final split happened after nonkosher food was served at the first ordination of the rabbinic seminary intended to be for all non-Orthodox Americans. This dinner is now called the *Treife* (nonkosher) Banquet.

There are a variety of practices among Conservative Jews, as some communities are more traditional and others are more liberal. Some maintain the traditional separation of men and women during prayer, while others do not. The practice of the congregation depends upon the opinion of the rabbi and congregants, but almost always remains within boundaries set forth by the governing rabbinical body of the movement.

Reconstructionist

The Reconstructionist Movement is the newest of the formal movements in Judaism. It traces its origin to an early twentieth-century rabbi and philosopher named Rabbi Mordechai Kaplan. Rabbi Kaplan believed Judaism was more than just a religion, and was better described as a civilization. This civilization rested equally on three values—God, Torah, and the People of Israel. While Kaplan greatly influenced all the non-Orthodox movements, some people who followed Kaplan felt a new branch of Judaism was necessary to reflect his ideas, and the Reconstructionist Movement was born.

Reconstructionist Jews broke away from the Conservative Movement because they desired a greater openness to Jews who favored one of the three elements of the Jewish civilization over another. They sought to "reconstruct" the very definition of Judaism away from merely people who were religious. They were equally open to those who were religious and those who were not but who wanted to connect with other Jews and experience Jewish celebrations and culture.

The Reconstructionist Movement is the smallest of the formal movements of Judaism in the United States, with about 100 affiliated congregations.

Renewal

Through the 1960s and 1970s, many young Jews were greatly affected by the countercultural elements in American society. They yearned for a spiritual and meaningful Judaism they didn't find in the established synagogues, which they viewed as staid and bureaucratic, rigid and restricting. Renewal Judaism was formed out of these concerns.

Renewal Judaism isn't a formal movement itself, but a description of smaller spiritual groups that creatively express their Judaism and craft Jewish experiences. They're open to all forms of Jewish expression, traditional and nontraditional, and even adapt non-Jewish forms of worship and practice like Eastern meditation and mantras to Judaism.

Much of Renewal Judaism sprang from the creation of *chaverot*—small groups of Jews who gathered to worship and observe outside any formal synagogue. Often these groups have less of a hierarchical structure, and don't have their own buildings or rabbis, but are led by laypeople and meet in homes. Over time, some of the chaverot joined the Reconstructionist movement, and some have continued on their own. Some have grown quite large, particularly in cities with significant Jewish populations, attracting young Jews who desire a more spiritual and informal Jewish experience.

Unaffiliated

It's important to recognize that many Jews do not belong to any synagogue, movement, or group. These Jews are generally referred to as "unaffiliated," and in the United States their numbers are growing. Many describe themselves as "spiritual but not religious." Others have no religious or spiritual practices, but maintain a very strong Jewish identity. While the unaffiliated are not a movement or a defined group in Judaism, they are a growing factor in American Jewish life.

Who Is a Jew?

It may seem strange that we haven't yet defined who is a Jew. You might think that would be a question answered at the very beginning of a book about understanding Judaism. I haven't addressed this topic until now because we've had to build our understanding of the basics of Judaism and the different movements before we could talk about this question. The challenge is that the traditional movements have a different definition of who is a Jew than the Reform Movement.

Traditional View

According to the halachah, a person is a Jew if he or she was born of a Jewish mother, or if he or she converts under the guidance of a rabbi. We'll talk about conversion in Chapter 16. For now, we need to take a look at the implications of the halachic law.

There are some theories as to why the traditional Law says a person must be born of a Jewish mother to be a Jew. While not really a race, as we've discussed, the idea of belonging to the Jewish people is connected with family and communal ties, physically, educationally, and through activity. It consequently makes sense that Judaism is passed through a familial connection. Some people hypothesize that the mother was chosen as the defining parent because the mother has the primary responsibility for the care of the child under traditional Law. Even though the father traditionally has the responsibility of educating his son, the sages chose the mother to define Jewish status.

Others believe the mother was chosen because a time came when Jews were being kidnapped and ransomed, as shown by the large amount of attention and the high value given for redeeming captives in the Talmud. The Talmud calls the redemption of captives "*pidyon shvuim,*" and describes this act as a "great mitzvah" because the sages considered captivity worse than death. (Talmud Bavli, Baba Batra 8b) The practice of kidnapping Jews continued for centuries, as criminals, Crusaders, and even slavers took Jewish men and women, vulnerable as a minority, for their own gain. The Talmud has many stories about Jews redeeming their relatives from captivity, the Cairo geniza had hundreds of documents concerning redemption of Jews from the Alexandria slave market in the Middle Ages, and Maimonides himself was involved with the redemption of captives from the Crusaders.

When the captive was a woman, pregnancies could have resulted from interactions occurring during captivity. Without certain evidence of male parentage, it became logical to rely upon the status of the mother to determine the status of the child. Jewish Law, which is very concerned about categorization and personal status, became settled and certain by defining a born Jew as someone born of a Jewish mother.

A New View—Patrilineal Descent

Matrilineal descent was the halachic rule for centuries. The Reform Movement began to question this rule in the 1970s, and changed the rule for their movement in 1983. The Reform rabbis determined that a person would be considered a born Jew if *either* that person's mother *or* father was Jewish *and* the child was being raised as a Jew as demonstrated by positive Jewish actions such as education and holiday celebrations.

The Reform Movement made this change based on several concerns and observations. They were concerned about the rising rate of intermarriage in North America, and reasoned that they would lose many good people from the religion by insisting on the traditional Law. They saw a basic unfairness in the halachah. Why should a child whose mother (but not father) was Jewish enjoy Jewish status, while a child who behaves and believes the same yet whose father (and not mother) is Jewish is not considered Jewish?

This conclusion also seemed unfair to Jewish men who married non-Jewish women when compared to Jewish women who married non-Jewish men, contravening the Reform Movement's concern about gender egalitarianism. The Reform rabbis saw that the concerns about uncertain patrimony were less pressing in modern times due to blood and genetic testing and lack of concern about widespread captivity. Finally, they noted that the sons of Jacob all took non-Jewish wives, and their children were considered Jewish.

 **OY VEY!**

> It may seem that the Reform Movement made the rule of who is a Jew more liberal, and in most cases, it does. However, when you read closely, you'll see that an Orthodox rabbi will find any child born of a Jewish mother to be a Jew, regardless of the child's father's religion or how that child is raised. But the patrilineal descent decision technically doesn't recognize a person with a Jewish mother and a non-Jewish father as a Jew *unless* the child is raised as a Jew.

The change in this personal status rule has increased the number of people who may be considered Jews, at least by Reform authorities. However, it has also caused great disagreements between the Orthodox and Reform, as the Orthodox now can't be sure if a person who claims to be Jewish meets their definition of who is a Jew. This remains one of the more serious disputes within the Jewish world.

Other Groupings

There are two other segments of the Jewish people worth considering separately. They don't fall into the category of a movement or the traditional Sephardic/Ashkenazic differentiation, but are notable for their uniqueness.

Ethiopian Jewry

Through the centuries, an isolated community of Jews lived in northern Ethiopia. These Jews lived in a manner closer to Biblical teachings, as they had not experienced the entire development of the Oral Law. As you would expect from a people living in Africa, these Jews had black skin, and had some cultural aspects similar to their surrounding people, just like every group of Jews in the world throughout history. At first, the outside world called these people "Falasha," but when it was realized that some Ethiopians saw this name as an insult, they were called Beta Yisrael.

It's unclear exactly how this group came to exist. Some guess that they're descendants of King Solomon and Queen Sheba, while others believe they're from a lost tribe of Israelites or exiles that went south instead of north. Some in the outside world throughout history knew of their existence, and there are references to them scattered in documents over the centuries. However, the main Jewish community was oblivious to their existence until late in the twentieth century.

As the Jewish world became aware of Beta Israel, their political circumstances caused them to become endangered. Ethiopia came to be governed by a Communist government that was hostile to them, especially in the aftermath of the Yom Kippur War. Israel decided to rescue Beta Israel, and thousands were relocated to Israel in operations over several years. More than 100,000 natives of Beta Israel have immigrated to the Jewish state.

WORDS OF WISDOM

"Among all the fragments, the flotsam and jetsam of Jewish history, none have had a more baffling fate than [Beta Israel] …. To the rest of us, the supreme vindication of the scholar's view [of them] lies in their invincible allegiance to the Jewish heritage—a steadfastness that has been matched only by that of their rescuers."—Henrietta Szold

The transition hasn't always been easy. Some Orthodox authorities have wrestled with the question of whether these people are really Jewish, or if they require conversion before enjoying the same status as other Jews. There also have been difficulties absorbing this community into Israeli society, with continued problems of poverty and, some feel, discrimination. However, Beta Israel today remains an accepted and unique branch of the Jewish people.

Kabbalah and Jewish Mysticism

Jewish mysticism, called "Kabbalah," has existed for centuries, yet has experienced intense growth in popular culture and awareness over the last few years. Kabbalah is not a separate movement—Jews from the Chassidism to those in Renewal communities have adopted some of its elements. It's somewhat separate and distinct in its outlook, so it merits a discussion as a separate group in Judaism.

Kabbalah means "received teaching." The primary text of the Kabbalah is called the *Zohar,* which means "radiance." A Spanish Jew named Moshe de Leon wrote the Zohar in the thirteenth century. De Leon presented the work as written by Rabbi Simeon bar Yohai, a well-known sage of the second century. The Zohar is difficult to decipher and is said to contain many mystical and spiritual secrets. Rabbi Isaac Luria, also known by the acronym *Ari,* which means "lion," further developed Kabbalah in the mid-sixteenth century in Tzfat.

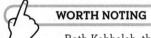

WORTH NOTING

Both Kabbalah, the epitome of Jewish mysticism, and the Shulchan Aruch, the epitome of Jewish legalism, were developed in Tzfatat at exactly the same time.

Kabbalah states that at the beginning of creation there was only God. God encompassed the entire universe and, fittingly, the name the Kabbalists used to describe God was *Ein Sof*—the One without End. God withdrew the Divine Presence from part of the universe to allow the rest of creation, as part of God's essence flowed outward into 10 vessels called *sefirot*. One level of the sefirot was higher than the others, and together they formed a sort of body for God. Part of the goal of Kabbalah is to understand each of the sephirot, attaining higher wisdom and knowledge of God.

According to the Kabbalah, a problem occurred in creation because the vessels of the sephirot were unable to hold God's radiance. The vessels shattered, so the world needs repair, otherwise known as *tikkun olam*. Kabbalists believe that performing mitzvot repairs the world.

Kabbalah involves many mystical and emotional practices and images. Meditation and singing jubilantly are an important part of Kabbalistic practice. Someone practicing Kabbalah attempts to feel close to God at all times, even in the performance of ordinary acts. There are many wonderful images in Kabbalah, especially the picture of Shabbat as a queen or bride to be welcomed with honor and joy each week.

ASK THE RABBI

Can anyone study Kabbalah? Lots of people study Kabbalah, and there are many books written about it. Some celebrities, both Jewish and non-Jewish, have adopted parts of the Kabbalah. However, Kabbalah requires a great amount of knowledge to understand the texts and references in the Zohar, and a great amount of experience to comprehend and appreciate its power. This is why no one is supposed to study Kabbalah until age 40.

There has been much resistance to Kabbalah throughout Jewish history. Legalists in the Middle Ages disliked it due to its mystical nature. Reformers didn't like it because it was not modern and rational. The popularity of the Kabbalah has waxed and waned over time but it perseveres and, in some places, thrives today.

The Least You Need to Know

- Jews are not uniform. They have many differences in practice and belief, even as they see themselves as one religion and one people.

- The largest cultural division between Jews is Ashkenazic and Sephardic. Ashkenazic Jews come from Russia and Central, Northern, and Eastern Europe. Sephardic Jews come from Spain, Northern Africa, and the Middle East.

- There are several different movements in Judaism, ranging from the most traditional (Orthodox) to the most liberal (Reform). Other movements include Conservative and Reconstructionist. Some Jews don't affiliate with any movement.

- Some Jews practice a Jewish mysticism called Kabbalah, which offers a spiritual path to knowing God and understanding the world.

Ethics and Values in Jewish Life

When many people think of Judaism, they think of one of the world's great religions in which its adherents follow particular rules and customs. They focus on the rituals and the unique way of life many Jews follow. However, Judaism is far more than theology and practices. Judaism requires Jews to live in an ethical and moral manner as outlined by the Tanach and Jewish sages through the centuries.

Jewish ethics are both universal and particular. They're universal in that Judaism shares many values with other great religions. When you see a Jew and a non-Jew side by side feeding the hungry at a soup kitchen, on many levels there's no difference between the two. Both care about helping their fellow human beings, and believe providing sustenance for the less fortunate is a worthy act. However, the Jew likely is performing this good deed for a different reason or based on a different theology or worldview than the non-Jew. This demonstrates the particularistic nature of Jewish ethics.

In This Chapter

- A Jew's ethical obligations to God to care for the world
- The ways Judaism values life
- Equality and respect for all people
- The requirement to seek peace, pursue justice, and act honestly

Ethics and God

The first category of ethics in Judaism involves the relationship between the Jewish people and God. The Covenant made at Mount Sinai requires Jews to fulfill certain obligations to God. These ethical requirements don't necessarily involve how Jews relate to one another or to non-Jews. They may have a secondary effect of defining appropriate human relations, but these are primarily ethical rules and ideas that arise from the Jewish acknowledgment of God as their Creator, Revealer, and Redeemer.

The Importance of Learning

The guidebook of the relationship between God and the Jewish people is the Torah. The Torah contains all the moral rules God expects Jews to follow. The Torah states some of these rules clearly. However, others are derived only through inference.

Learning the Torah, therefore, is more to Jews than just an academic act. The study of the Torah is an ethical act in itself. In one section, the Talmud lists many important ethical behaviors— honoring parents, performing acts of love and kindness, welcoming strangers, making peace, and more. However, the Talmud also concludes that the study of the Torah is greater than any of these, because it leads to all of them. (Talmud Bavli, Shabbat 127a)

 WORDS OF WISDOM

"If you learn and do not act, it would be better if you had not been born."—Leviticus Rabbah 35:7

The Talmud says learning is so important it transcends other important aspects of Judaism. It teaches that learning is even more important than the sacrifices performed in the Temple. (Talmud Bavli, Eruvin 63b) One may destroy a synagogue used for prayer and gathering in order to build a house of study. (Talmud Bavli, Megillah 27a) By learning the Torah, Jews act and become the ethical people God wants them to be.

Caretakers of the World

One of the most important concepts of Judaism is that God created the world, and therefore the world is God's property. As Psalms 24:1 says, "The earth and all it contains belongs to God."

God gave human beings the right to use and enjoy the world. God told the first human beings, Adam and Eve, they were to master the Earth, and have dominion over the fish, birds, animals, and plants. However, along with the privilege of enjoying and using God's world came the responsibility to care for it. Humans may subdue the world, but they also must replenish it. (Genesis 1:28)

This means Jews have an ethical obligation to God to protect and conserve the world even as they enjoy and use its resources. This is encompassed in the term *baal tashchit*—the requirement that Jews don't needlessly destroy or waste any of the world's resources. For example, the Torah forbids Jews to destroy fruit trees of their enemies while at war unless there's absolutely no other option. The fruit trees are an important resource, and it would be unethical to ruin them even if they belong to an enemy, or even if they would be helpful or more convenient to use for their wood against the enemy. The value of the trees outweighs almost all other concerns, so their destruction in war is forbidden as a waste of God's resources. (Deuteronomy 20:19-20)

Another aspect of caring for the world is the idea of *tza'ar baalei chayyim*—the prohibition against cruelty to animals. God obligates Jews to show kindness to animals. Jews must feed their animals before they themselves eat. (Talmud Bavli, Berachot 40a) Animals receive a day of rest on Shabbat. (Deuteronomy 5:14) They must not be muzzled while working in the field so that they can't eat (Deuteronomy 25:4), and must not be harnessed to a plow with another type of animal because it might cause both the larger and smaller animal to suffer injury. (Deuteronomy 22:10) As Scripture says, God shows mercy to all creations. (Psalms 145:9) Likewise, Jews must be kind and strive to care for their animals. (Proverbs 12:10)

ASK THE RABBI

Can Jews eat animals? The requirement of kindness to animals doesn't mean Jews must be vegetarian. God allows people to use the world for their needs, and specifically says in the Torah that animals may be used as food. (Genesis 9:3) On the other hand, some Jews are vegetarian, and understand the requirement of tza'ar baalei chayyim is to mean refraining from eating animals.

The ethical balance of using and caring for the world may be seen in the Jewish attitude toward hunting. Most Jewish authorities allow hunting if the animal is to be used for food. However, these authorities disapprove of hunting for sport, noting that the only two figures identified as hunters in the Torah, Nimrod and Esau, are also immoral and unsavory characters. The potential cruelty and wastefulness of hunting for sport also contradict Jewish values of proper caretaking of the world, furthering the arguments in Judaism against this practice.

Tikkun Olam—Repair of the World

A midrash tells of a non-Jew who asked a rabbi why God required Jews to circumcise their sons. After all, the non-Jew reasoned, if God made human beings in that particular way, it seemed unreasonable for people to alter what God had made. The rabbi disagreed with the reasoning, observing that almost everything God made in the world required man's actions to finish the creation. The rabbi cited examples, noting that mustard needs sweetening and wheat needs grinding. (Genesis Rabbah 11:6)

While this midrash is intended to justify the Jewish rite of circumcision, it also raises an important aspect of the Jewish view of the world. The fact that God created the world doesn't mean the world is perfect. On the contrary, the only part of the Earth that was perfect was the Garden of Eden, which people left long ago. Instead, we are partners with God in continuing to create the world, and repairing the imperfections of the world where necessary. This idea of repairing the world's imperfections is called *tikkun olam.*

Jews vary in their perceptions of how to engage in tikkun olam. Some see their keeping the ritual mitzvot and their prayers as the proper way to engage in tikkun olam. The devout acts bring holiness into the world and effectuate repair. Other Jews see the obligation of tikkun olam to require them to act to solve social ills such as poverty, injustice, and environmental damage. Jews who particularly become active in promoting causes are rooted in the philosophy of tikkun olam.

 **OY VEY!**

Tikkun olam is not a political position. Although the majority of Jews in the United States are liberal and often cite tikkun olam as part of their religious beliefs that lead them to their opinions, conservative positions are equally consistent with the idea of tikkun olam.

Tikkun olam may seem like an overwhelming challenge. The problems of the world run so deep that it isn't feasible to imagine a person can solve them in his or her lifetime. A statement from Pirkei Avot in the Mishnah helps Jews cope with this frustration, teaching that "it is not your obligation to complete the work, but neither are you free to desist from it." (Pirkei Avot 2:21) This means that God requires Jews to engage in tikkun olam, but only as much as they reasonably can do. The world is better with every step taken forward toward its repair, even if the repair is never completed.

B'tzelem Elohim—In God's Image

The Torah specifies in the story of Creation that God created man and woman *b'tzelem Elohim*— in God's image. (Genesis 1:27) This is a somewhat confusing statement because Judaism doesn't picture God as having a physical form in the same way as people or animals. How can humans be made in the image of God if God doesn't have an image?

The idea of b'tzelem Elohim means something more than a physical resemblance. B'tzelem Elohim means that not only does the human physical form somehow resemble whatever God is, but also that all human beings share a spiritual kinship with God. Everyone is endowed with an aspect of divinity and a capability to act in a holy manner. We can reason, make decisions, and understand the difference between right and wrong. Humans are not gods, but we are significantly like God in that we are created in God's image, and we can act accordingly.

An example of the meaning of b'tzelem Elohim is found in a midrash concerning the Israelites' escape from Egyptian slavery. The Israelites had been slaves in Egypt for 400 years until God sent Moses to tell the Egyptian king, the Pharaoh, to let the Israelites go. After God inflicted 10 horrible plagues upon the Egyptians, the Pharaoh agreed to let the Israelites go. But as the Israelites were leaving Egypt, the Pharaoh changed his mind, and sent his chariots after the fleeing former slaves.

God parted the Red Sea so the Israelites could escape. After they were on the other side, the sea returned to normal, and the soldiers who were following the Israelites drowned. The midrash says the angels rejoiced at the Egyptians' deaths, but God rebuked them, expressing sorrow that God's creations were dying. (Talmud Bavli, Sanhedrin 39b) This is understood to mean that everyone is created in God's image and has intrinsic worth and potential, no matter who we are or what we do.

WORTH NOTING

Jews remove one drop of wine from their cups for each of the 10 plagues at the Passover festival meal. This shows the diminution of joy caused by the harm that God had to inflict on those created b'tzelem Elohim to secure the Israelites' freedom.

The concept of b'tzelem Elohim also applies to interactions between people. A midrash teaches that when one person needlessly embarrasses another, God is diminished because the embarrassed person was created in God's image. (Genesis Rabbah 24:7) This also demonstrates the close relationship between the Jewish view of ethics with God and ethics with people. Considerations of how Jews need to behave toward God easily lead to ideas about how Jews must act toward other people as creatures created b'tzelem Elohim.

Ethics with People

Judaism and Jewish teachings are very concerned with everyday lives. There is commentary and mitzvot on great ideas as well as the small details of living. The Jewish Covenant with God and the fact that all people are created b'tzelem Elohim requires every Jew to act with a great deal of care and concern for the lives of other people. Judaism establishes a firm ethic of moral behavior governing our relationships with fellow human beings.

Pekuach Nefesh—Primacy of Life

The highest mitzvah in Judaism is *pekuach nefesh,* which literally means "saving a life." Judaism considers human life to be the most special and unique gift given by God, and Jews must do everything possible to preserve and save lives. The sages derive this idea from Leviticus 18:5, which says "You shall keep my statutes and my ordinances and live by them." They see those last few words—"live by them"—as a command that the entire purpose of all the mitzvot is to improve human life, and that Jews should live by the mitzvot, but not die because of them. (Talmud Bavli, Yoma 85b) As a result, a Jew must *not* do a mitzvah if doing it would imperil a life, including his or her own. The only exceptions to this where a Jew must follow the mitzvah, even at the risk of his or her own life, are murder, idolatry, and sexual immorality.

> **WORDS OF WISDOM**
>
> "If you save a single life, it is as if you have saved an entire world. But if you destroy a single life, it is as if you have destroyed an entire world."—Mishnah, Sanhedrin 4:5

The priority of saving a life overrides laws concerning Shabbat, the most important holy day on the Jewish calendar. On Shabbat, Jews traditionally are prohibited from working, lighting a fire, and carrying anything outside the home, as we'll see in Chapter 9. However, if a life is in danger, a Jew must act to save that life, even if this means doing an act normally prohibited on Shabbat. Similarly, Leviticus 19:16 explicitly prohibits Jews from "standing by idly while a neighbor bleeds." This requires a Jew to do everything reasonable to save a life. A Jew must take every reasonable action to help someone who is drowning, attacked by animals, or assaulted by robbers. (Talmud Bavli, Sanhedrin 73a) Some legal systems don't impose a duty on people to help strangers who are in danger. Judaism demands that a Jew act to help others.

Equality of People

Judaism accepts that all people are equal in God's eyes. A midrash explains that God created all of humanity from one man and woman, Adam and Eve, to teach that no one can say their family is superior to anyone else's. (Mishnah, Sanhedrin 4:5) Judaism especially emphasizes equality between the rich and poor, teaching that one economic class doesn't have greater intrinsic merit than the other. In the time of the Temple, God accepted all the sacrifices people could afford, whether a valuable animal or less expensive grain, so long as each gave the sacrifice with a whole heart. (Leviticus 5:1-13) Every human being has equal dignity, and a Jew may violate a mitzvah to preserve that treasure for another. (Talmud Bavli, Berachot 19b)

A story from the Talmud illustrates Judaism's concern for the equality of people. The Talmud permits a person to act in self-defense, even to kill an attacker if the attacker comes to kill that person. (Talmud Bavli, Sanhedrin 72a) The story tells how a man came to the great scholar, Rava, for advice. The man explained that the governor was going to kill him unless he killed an innocent third person. The man asked if he was allowed to kill the third person in self-defense. Rava answered that the man was not permitted to kill the third person, even if it meant the governor would kill him. Rava stressed that the man and the person the governor wanted him to kill were equal, and that the man could not give his life a higher priority than that of another innocent person. As Rava directly explained to the man, "Who says your blood is redder than his?" (Talmud Bavli, Pesachim 72a)

Love Your Neighbor as Yourself

Leviticus 19:34 contains the famous injunction for Jews to love their neighbors as themselves. The Torah repeats several times that Jews should not oppress the strangers in their communities or wrong them. (Exodus 22:20, Deuteronomy 10:19, and Deuteronomy 24:17-18) The Torah insists that there should be one law for both Jews and the strangers within the community. (Exodus 12:49, Leviticus 24:22)

Together, these ethical laws demand that Jews construct a society in which everyone is treated with care, respect, and dignity. It doesn't matter if others are Jewish, related to Jews, or people who just happen to live alongside Jews. Everyone deserves the same love and compassion as Jews expect for themselves.

The Torah provides a very specific reason for this requirement. The text reminds Jews that they were slaves in Egypt, and they didn't receive care or concern. Jews know how it feels to try to live among people who don't care about them, or who treat them badly or with disregard because they're different. Judaism rejects this sort of cold, unfeeling society.

Jewish ethics also rejects hatred of others. The Talmud teaches that the Second Temple was destroyed because Jews held unreasoned hatred for one another, a concept called *sinat chinam*. They didn't merely disagree with, but hated those who held differing perspectives. Consequently, they divided the people and incurred God's anger, and lost the Temple. (Talmud Bavli, Yoma 9b) The Mishnah teaches that hatred removes a person from the world, meaning that hatred causes someone to be unable to live with other people. (Mishnah, Pirkei Avot 2:11)

Do Not Do to Others What You Hate

As noted in the beginning of this part, Hillel said that the basic rule of Judaism is "Do not do unto others what is hateful to yourself." (Talmud Bavli, Shabbat 31a) The formulation of this negative version of the Golden Rule is very important. Hillel's rule states that if you wouldn't like something done to you, you shouldn't do the same thing to someone else. For example, no one likes being punched in the nose for no reason. Hillel's rule thereby prohibits Jews from taking such unreasonable and disrespectful actions, and allows everyone to live together without fear of harm while respecting everyone's freedom to live as they deem appropriate.

ASK THE RABBI

What's the difference between Hillel's formulation of the Golden Rule and the rule stated in the positive—do unto others as you would have others do unto you? There's a lot of overlap between the two formulations. However, Hillel's rule only prevents someone from doing something that person judges as harmful. The positive formulation may require someone to judge what others would like, and then do it to them without necessarily knowing if they in fact want what the judger is offering. While such an action sometimes can be beneficial and appreciated, Hillel's formulation avoids the potential misunderstandings arising from doing something for someone that the latter really doesn't want.

The Torah contains several specific examples of the application of this rule. It commands Jews to refrain from taking revenge or bearing a grudge. (Leviticus 19:18) Similarly, Jews may not "put a stumbling block before the blind." (Leviticus 19:14) The sages closely examine this verse, asking who would actually do something so cruel as to try to make a blind person trip. They reason that the Torah really is saying we all are blind at times because we don't know all the facts concerning a given situation. In such a case, a Jew is prohibited from taking unfair advantage of someone else.

Lashon Hara—Evil Speech

There's a story about a man who had committed the sin of *lashon hara,* meaning "evil speech." He had said things about others that weren't true, and that had hurt others.

He came to the rabbi and said, "Rabbi, I have said things that I regret, and that have hurt other people. I wish to make amends for what I did. How do I undo the hurt I have caused?"

The rabbi said, "Go home, and get the biggest feather pillow you own, and bring it to the center of town, where I will meet you."

The man was confused, but he did as the rabbi said. He went home and got his biggest feather pillow. He took it to the center of town, where he saw the rabbi waiting. The rabbi was holding a large knife.

"Now take this knife," said the rabbi, "and cut open the pillow, and shake out all the feathers."

The man did so, and the wind caught the cascade of feathers and spread them in every direction. Soon, there were feathers all over the town, as the wind carried them farther and farther from the man and the rabbi.

"Now," said the rabbi, "Go and collect all the feathers."

"But that's impossible!" cried the man.

"Yes, it is," said the rabbi. "And, like the feathers, once words are uttered and scattered, they cannot be retrieved."

Judaism values the great power of speech. After all, God began the work of creating the world through speech, saying, "Let there be light!" (Genesis 1:3) Judaism recognizes that people may use speech for pure and noble purposes, expressing words of love, care, and comfort to each other, as well as prayers to God. But Judaism also knows that speech can be used in a way that harms other people, or lashon hara.

Lashon hara may come in many forms. The most common is gossip when people say something about others that they don't know is true. Gossip also includes statements that are true but are hurtful to another, and that the speaker might say for his or her own enjoyment or entertainment without regard for the feelings of the other. The Tanach admonishes Jews to not go about telling tales about others (Leviticus 19:16) and to guard their tongues from speaking evil. (Psalms 34:13-14) The Talmud teaches that destroying someone's good name is like committing murder. (Talmud Bavli, Arachim 15b) Gossip is an unbridled uncontrollable harm. Accordingly, the Talmud says, a gossiper stands in Rome and kills in Syria. (Talmud Yirushalmi, Peah 1:1)

The Midrashim further illustrate the power and potential harm of lashon hara. The prophet Jeremiah likens speech to an arrow, not a sword. (Jeremiah 9:7) The Midrash explains this verse to mean that if someone swings a sword, he or she may alter its course or stop the swing at the last second to avoid hurting the target. In contrast, an arrow can't be stopped once it is launched. Lashon hara is like the arrow and not like the sword—it can't be stopped once spoken. (Midrash Tehillim 120:4) Another midrash says the tongue is so powerful that it's the only part of our bodies trapped behind a cage (our teeth) and hidden from view (by our cheeks) to prevent its misuse. (Talmud Bavli, Arachim 15b)

Jewish ethics therefore requires Jews to take care with even the most casual conversations. This ethic is so strong that there is an entire book on what does and doesn't constitute lashon hara named after its author, the *Chafetz Chaim*, also known as Rabbi Yisroel Meir Kagan, a nineteenth-century Polish rabbi.

Shalom—Peace and Completeness

Judaism places a high value on peace, but sees peace as something greater than the absence of war or conflict. In Hebrew, the word *shalom* means "peace." The three-letter root of the word, *shin-lamed-mem*, means "wholeness" or "completeness." Shalom is a sense of satisfaction, contentment, and comfort in life that causes a person's soul to feel at ease. Shalom is so important that one of the great sages of the Mishnah, Rabban Shimon, names it as one of the three foundations of the world. (Mishnah, Pirkei Avot 1:18)

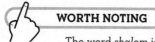

> **WORTH NOTING**
>
> The word *shalom* is also used to say "hello" and "goodbye," expressing the hope that people find peace and completeness when they meet and when they depart from each other.

According to Psalm 34:14, Jews must "seek peace and pursue it." Some of the most vivid and beautiful images in the Tanach concern peace, detailing how one day "the lion will lie down with the lamb" (Isaiah 11:6) and every nation will "beat their swords into plowshares and their spears into pruning hooks. Nation will not raise sword against nation, and none will learn war anymore." (Isaiah 2:4)

The care for peace affected the events described in the Tanach in unexpected ways. King David is highly respected for uniting the Israelites and establishing the strength of the first Jewish nation so that it lasted in various forms for 1,000 years. Yet God didn't permit David to build the Temple, because David was a soldier who shed blood and not a man of peace. (I Chronicles 22:7-8) In another story, the evil people of Babel challenged God, but God didn't destroy them like all the people except Noah and his family in the Flood. The Midrash explains that God made this distinction because, despite their evil ways, the people of Babel worked together in peace, so God knew they could redeem themselves. (Bamidbar Rabbah 11:7) This demonstrates that the ethic of peace is so strong in Judaism it can override other concerns.

Justice

Another important ethic in Judaism is justice. The Torah commands "Justice, justice shall you pursue." (Deuteronomy 16:20) The sages deem the repetition of the word "justice" in this verse as extremely significant. For some, the repetition indicates that both the means one uses to attain justice and the end result must be just. Jews can't use unfair methods to bring about justice. For others, the repetition means justice is an unending pursuit. Once a Jew has obtained a just result, he or she can't stop, but must move to the next injustice and work to rectify it.

Justice requires that society doesn't hold either parents or their children responsible for the sins of the other. (Deuteronomy 24:16) The Torah also requires that Jews and non-Jews in the community receive the same standard of justice, and that there is no favoritism toward one or the other. (Leviticus 19:34, Numbers 15:15) The Talmud contains specific requirements for establishing just courts, insisting that judges not prejudge litigants based on their wealth or poverty, and ensuring that all parties in a dispute be present in the court before hearing a case. (Talmud Bavli, Shavuot 30b-31a)

Honesty in Business

A section of the Talmud speculates about the questions God will ask a person about his or her life after death. The first question is somewhat surprising. God asks, "Were you honest in your business dealings?" (Talmud Bavli, Shabbat 31a)

Honesty in business is an important ethic in Judaism. Judaism doesn't place a greater value either in being poor or being wealthy. Instead, Judaism focuses on how a person behaves, and how a person attains his or her possessions. A Jew can't sustain himself, or acquire wealth, by unfair or immoral means.

The injunction for honesty in business applies to how business owners treat their customers. The Torah requires them to use fair and accurate weights and measures. A Jew is strictly and explicitly forbidden to "skim off the top" or otherwise fail to give customers exactly what they purchased. Such conduct is beyond immoral—it is abhorrent to God. (Leviticus 19:36, Deuteronomy 25:13-16) The prohibition against placing a stumbling block before the blind applies to a business owner, because trickery or use of unfairly acquired information in effect makes the customer blind. Stealing is prohibited, as the Talmud attributes the destruction of humanity in the story of Noah to the sin of theft. (Talmud Bavli, Sanhedrin 108b)

Business owners also must treat their employees fairly and with respect. They must pay their employees' wages on time, which in Biblical times meant daily. (Deuteronomy 24:14-15) The Talmud ties this requirement to the mitzvah of *pekuach nefesh*, explaining that the worker places his life in the employer's hands, trusting the employer to treat him fairly and honestly. It's immoral for the employer to betray that trust. (Talmud Bavli, Baba Metzia 112a) Employers also must treat employees according to the prevailing standard of the community. The employer can't gain an advantage by depriving employees of a benefit or practice customarily offered, such as meals or periods of rest. (Talmud Bavli, Baba Metzia 83a)

When people operate their businesses fairly and honestly, they not only make a living, but they increase peace in the world. A dishonest business destroys trust. Nearly one quarter of the Shulchan Aruch provides rules for the workplace and business, demonstrating how important Judaism considers honesty in business.

Tzedakah—Acts of Righteousness

Traditionally, Jews give 10 percent of their income to the needy. This mitzvah is not called charity, but *tzedakah*, an act of righteousness or justice. Jewish thought acknowledges that God is the ruler of the Earth, and the Earth and all its resources belong to God as its Creator. (Psalms 24:1) People are allowed to use and enjoy these resources as God told Adam and Eve in the Garden of Eden. However, one of the responsibilities that come with the privilege of the enjoyment of God's Earth is the obligation to share and help other people who are also created b'tzelem Elohim.

The Torah places many of the original laws about aiding the needy in an agrarian context. A farmer must leave fallen crops—gleanings—for the poor to come and use. A farmer also must leave the corners of his field unharvested, allowing the needy to come and take what they need. The requirement that the corners provide for the poor allows them to easily find the sections designated for them when they're able to collect the food, preventing the farmer from hiding what he sets aside for them and then taking it for his own profit. The designation of the corners also prevents the needy from having to travel far into the farmer's land so they are seen and potentially embarrassed. The preservation of the dignity of the poor is an important aspect of the justice and righteousness of tzedakah. (Leviticus 19:9-11, Mishnah, Kedoshim 1:10)

WORTH NOTING

A legend says that Solomon's Temple provided a room for tzedakah that preserved the dignity of the poor. Everyone would enter the room alone. Some would leave tzedakah and some would take what they needed. No one ever knew who gave and who took, and the room always had enough resources for the poor.

Maimonides said there are eight levels of giving tzedakah, in ascending order of merit:

1. Giving grudgingly, reluctantly, or with regret.

2. Giving less than one should, but pleasantly.

3. Giving what one should, but only on request.

4. Giving before one is asked.

5. Giving without knowing the recipient, although the recipient knows who you are.

6. Giving without making known that you are the giver.

7. Giving when neither you nor the recipient know each other's identities.

8. Helping someone to become self-supporting through a gift, loan, or finding employment.

The Least You Need to Know

- The study of Torah leads to ethical behavior.
- The world belongs to God because God created it. According to Judaism, God allows people to use the world, but they also must care for it.
- Everyone is created b'tzelem Elohim—in God's image—and therefore merits respect, equality, and justice.
- The highest mitzvah in Judaism is pekuach nefesh—the saving and preservation of life.
- Jews must refrain from lashon hara—evil speech—act to bring about justice and peace, behave honestly in business, and assist the needy.

The Hard Road Home: Zionism and Israel

The destruction of the Second Temple and the Diaspora didn't lessen the Jewish people's affinity for the land of Israel. Jews remembered the promise of the land given by God to Abraham, Isaac, and Jacob. They remembered that the Babylonians had exiled them before, but they had been able to return and establish a nation. They concluded that there was no reason why this couldn't happen again.

The longing to return to Israel became a central focus in post-Temple Judaism. The sages of the Mishnah and Talmud preserved the laws applicable to life in the Holy Land and the Temple, even as it became apparent that, with the recent abolishment of a Jewish nation, a return to Israel wouldn't happen in their lifetimes or in the foreseeable future. A prayer to God asking for a return to Israel became a fixture in the traditional *amidah* prayers, and Jews prayed for such deliverance every morning for century after century. This longing became especially poignant at times when Jews were persecuted.

In This Chapter

- Returning to the Jewish homeland
- The development of Zionism
- Many years of war and terrorism
- An incredible nation for the Jewish people

A classic Jewish folktale expresses this hope for a return to Israel. The story tells of a young goat herder in Eastern Europe who loses a goat each day during a cold winter. He always finds the goat at nightfall, but the goat has in its horns flowers that do not grow in the middle of winter. Curious as to where the goat goes during the day, the young goat herder fastens a bell to the goat's neck and follows it. The goat goes into a cave, and the herder follows through the darkness by listening to the bell. They finally emerge in the land of Israel, which is lush and green, and where they live happily ever after.

Eighteen centuries after the destruction of the Second Temple and the start of the Diaspora, practical efforts to build a modern Jewish nation in the Promised Land began. The State of Israel came into existence in 1948, causing tremendous changes in Judaism and how the world perceives Jews. The issues involving Israel are complex, open to debate, and overall far beyond what we can consider in this book. Even Jews disagree about issues relating to Israel, especially when it comes to politics and interpreting history.

My purpose in this chapter is to present the mainstream Jewish view of Israel, because Israel has become so much a part of Judaism and Jewish life. I recognize that others have a different view of much in this chapter. But to understand Judaism today, it's essential to understand the Jewish perspective and the value of this tiny nation in the Middle East.

The Beginning of the Return

The nineteenth century saw the beginnings of formal attempts to enable Jews to return to Israel. Often, wealthy Jews organized these efforts for poorer Jews in dire economic or political circumstances. The benefactors sought to buy land and gain permission for their brethren to settle in the Holy Land. Moses Montefiore, a financier from London, established some small communities in Jaffa and Jerusalem, overcoming restrictions on Jewish purchase of land by the governing Ottoman Turks. A windmill built with funds from Montefiore still stands in Israel. The Baron Edmund de Rothschild of France donated millions to build other Jewish communities.

 WORDS OF WISDOM

"My heart is in the East, and I am in the depths of the West. My food has no taste. How can it be sweet? How can I fulfill my pledges and my vows when Zion is in the power of Edom? And I in the fetters of Arabia? It will be nothing to me to leave all the goodness of Spain. So rich will it be to see the dust of the ruined sanctuary."–Judah Halevi

As a result of these and other efforts, a significant Jewish presence grew in the Holy Land. Between 1882 and 1903, 25,000 Jews emigrated there. This is known as the First *Aliyah*.

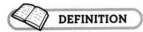 **DEFINITION**

Aliyah literally means "going up"; it's a Jew's immigration in Israel. It's called Aliyah because it's equated to Moses' going up to Mount Sinai to receive the Torah.

The new Jewish communities resulted from an ancient yearning to return to the land and the desire of some Jews to help others. There was no modern political philosophy or justification for the return. This rationale came from an unlikely source—an Austro-Hungarian journalist.

Herzl, Dreyfus, and Zionism

Theodore Herzl was a journalist from Budapest who lived in Paris during the trial of Captain Alfred Dreyfus. Dreyfus was a Jew and a captain in the French army who was convicted of treason and sentenced to life imprisonment in 1894-1895. Two years later, evidence came to light that showed someone else was the true traitor. Other officers attempted to suppress the evidence, and a debate ensued. Dreyfus was retried, and found guilty again despite the evidence. A military commission finally cleared him in 1906.

Herzl Creates Modern Zionism

Herzl covered the initial trial and concluded that the charges against Dreyfus were false. He heard the chants in the streets of "Death to the Jews," and realized that Dreyfus had been targeted because he was Jewish. Herzl concluded that the emancipation of the Jews in secular society would fail. He began to believe that the only way Jews could be safe and could reach their potential was for them to return to their ancient homeland and form their own nation.

 WORDS OF WISDOM

"We (Jews) have sincerely tried everywhere to merge with the national communities in which we live, seeking only to preserve the faith of our fathers. It is not permitted us."—Theodore Herzl

Herzl began to meet with Jewish leaders, and wrote articles outlining the rationale for creating a Jewish state. One of his most influential publications was *Der Judenstaat* (*The Jew-State*), deliberately titled to mock anti-Semites. He also wrote *Altneuland* (*Old-New Land*), a utopian novel describing what the Jewish state would be like.

Herzl successfully organized several conferences discussing every aspect of a possible Jewish state. Ultimately, he died without seeing his dream fulfilled. However, the idea of a Jewish state, and the questions of whether a Jewish state was necessary and what it would be like, had now become an active part of the modern discourse about Jews and Judaism, both within Jewish communities and in the larger world. Herzl is credited as the Father of Modern *Zionism*.

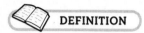

> **DEFINITION**
>
> **Zionism** is the aspiration to create and sustain a Jewish state in the Holy Land. There are several different types of Zionism, including political Zionism, which focuses on the legal establishment of the nation and relations with other peoples; religious Zionism, which focuses on fulfilling the promise of the land God made in the Tanach; and cultural Zionism, which focuses on the potential achievements the Jewish people can reach in their own nation.

Not all Jews became Zionists. The early Reform Jews wanted acceptance in the countries in which they lived, and feared Zionism would cause suspicion among their non-Jewish neighbors. They openly rejected Zionism. Ultra-Orthodox Jews disapproved of Zionism as premature. Only God could re-establish the Jewish nation. Any effort by men to do it was presumptuous. Zionism was far from a universal Jewish value at the beginning of the twentieth century.

The Balfour Declaration

World War I changed the landscape of the Middle East. After the dust from the war settled, Great Britain held control over the Holy Land in place of the defeated Ottoman Turks in what was called the British Mandate. A document issued by Britain's Foreign Secretary Lord Alfred James Balfour supported the establishment of a national home for the Jews in the lands they controlled. This document, known as the Balfour Declaration, promised British help in reaching this goal, while also asserting that other peoples living in these lands would maintain their civil and political rights.

The Arab communities in these areas did not approve of the Balfour Declaration. About 30,000 Jews arrived prior to World War I in a migration known as the Second Aliyah as Jews fled from pogroms and sought to create Socialist communities there. They formed utopian farming communities called *kibbutzim* throughout the region.

A Third Aliyah of 37,000 Jews fleeing persecution arrived in the early 1920s. They believed in the imminent founding of a Jewish state following the Balfour Declaration. Tensions rose between the Arab and Jewish communities, often breaking into violence. Nevertheless, Jews continued to immigrate to the area, and a Fourth Aliyah of 70,000 Jews arrived in the mid to late 1920s. In the 1930s, an even larger immigration from Central Europe took place and was known as the Fifth Aliyah.

Recognizing the building tension, the British amended their position, saying the land of the Mandate would eventually divide into two states: a Jewish state west of the Jordan River, and an Arab state east of the river in what we know today as the country of Jordan. They later pulled back even farther, indicating that they would create one state for both Arabs and Jews. They then restricted Jewish immigration. The violence continued, and the entire situation changed with the events of the Second World War.

Partition and the Formation of Israel

World War II and the Holocaust left European Jewry in shambles. Thousands of Jews remained in concentration camps, and many didn't want to return to the countries where they had lived before the war. They feared going back to a place where their freedom had been taken or where the general population had assisted the Nazis in identifying and persecuting them, as had happened in Germany and several other nations. Simultaneously, Britain had been devastated by the war, and could no longer afford to maintain their governance over their territories throughout the world. They particularly had grown frustrated with the Holy Land and with trying to manage the animosity and violence between Jews and Arabs.

The United Nations Vote

Britain decided to transfer the decision of what to do with this troubled region to the new international organization called the United Nations. This body decided to partition the land, creating a Jewish state and an Arab state, with Jerusalem left as an international city.

 ASK THE RABBI

Why did both the United States and the Soviet Union support the partition plan? This rare occurrence of postwar agreement likely resulted from both new superpowers expecting the new Jewish state would support them. There were many Jews in Israel formerly from Russia who still had relatives there or who shared socialist or communist ideology. The United States expected that a democratic Jewish state would support America. If either side had not seen an advantage for them, it's likely the partition plan would not have passed.

Neither the Jews nor the Arabs particularly liked the partition plan, because neither side got as much as they wanted or felt they deserved. Jews noted that there was already an Arab state east of the Jordan River from the original British Mandate, and felt that dividing what remained was unfair. They also didn't like the situation with Jerusalem, as their centuries-old yearning for the city would remain unfulfilled. Despite all this, the Jews accepted the plan, figuring that the need was so great, any state would be better than none.

Principles of the State

The Jews would call their new state "Israel" after the ancient name Jacob received, which defined their united people for so many centuries.

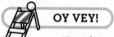 **OY VEY!**

"Israel" may refer to either the people of Israel, meaning Jews living throughout the world, or the State of Israel. The context in which the name is used always must be considered to determine whether it denotes the Jews in general or the Middle Eastern state in particular.

Israel's Declaration of Independence was signed on May 14, 1948, the date the British Mandate expired. It recounted the history of the Jews, their connection to this land, and their years of Diaspora and yearning to return. It referenced the Balfour Declaration and the Holocaust. It also enunciated principles for Israel, including:

- The natural right of Jews to govern themselves and their fate, just like other nations

- The openness of Israel to any Jew who desires to immigrate

- Freedom, justice, and peace as described by the Prophets in the Tanach

- Complete equality of social and political rights for all inhabitants regardless of religion, race, or sex

- Freedom of religion, conscience, language, education, and culture

- Safeguarding the holy sites of all religions

The declaration specifically extended citizenship to the Arab residents within its borders, urging them to help the Jews build a prosperous nation for everyone.

The War of Independence

The surrounding Arab states didn't accept the partition plan. The Arab League, consisting of Egypt, Iraq, Transjordan, Syria, Saudi Arabia, and Yemen, attacked when Israel declared its independence. Common wisdom said the new state of Israel would lose this war, as it was newly organized and outgunned and outmanned by its neighbors. Israel managed to survive, and fighting that began in May of 1948 continued through the beginning of 1949 until an armistice was signed.

The war left Israel in possession of land along the Mediterranean coast to Lebanon, along the Jordan River in Syria, and in the Negev desert, separated from Arab-controlled lands by a division called the *Green Line*. The cities of Tel Aviv, Haifa, Safed (Tzfat), Ashkelon, and Beersheba fell under Israeli territory. A section of Jerusalem also became part of Israel. Egypt controlled a strip of land along the coast called Gaza, and Jordan controlled territory on the west side of the Jordan River called the West Bank. Jordan also controlled part of Jerusalem, including the Old City and the Western Wall of the Temple Mount.

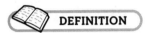 **DEFINITION**

> The **Green Line** was the line establishing territorial possessions following the 1949 armistice between Israel and its neighbors. It's supposedly called the Green Line because an officer used a pen with green ink to denote the positions of the armies on a map at the time.

The Arabs living within the new state of Israel's borders became citizens. However, many of them left their homes, either to flee the fighting in general, in response to threats from the Israelis, or at the request of the invading Arab armies to allow their passage. Different people have very different opinions about exactly what happened and why these people left. However it happened, the people became refugees, which would become very significant later in Israel's history.

Wars and Peace

The Nation of Israel has been in a constant state of war since its founding. Several of Israel's neighbors have never accepted Israel's existence, and fighting has flared between them many times. As a result, Israel is constantly concerned about its security, and has universal military service for almost all of its citizens. The history of Israel's wars has had a great effect on its citizens' perception of belonging to a nation constantly threatened, fighting for survival.

The War of 1956

Even after the armistice ending the War of Independence, Israel and its neighbors regularly exchanged mortar fire. The Arab nations executed raids into Israeli territory. Convinced that the Arab states intended to break the armistice, and concerned about Egypt's nationalization of the Suez Canal, Israel joined forces with England and France to attack Egypt. During this campaign, Israel captured Gaza, which was returned to Egypt as part of the ceasefire agreement.

The Six Day War (1967)

Hostility and sporadic raids and fighting continued between Israel and her neighbors following the 1956 conflict. Tensions again rose to a high peak in 1967, as Egypt requested the removal of United Nations troops in Sinai, which had been stationed there as part of the ceasefire, and closed Israeli access to the Gulf of Aqaba. The Arab nations threatened to attack Israel again, and Arab leaders made radio broadcasts calling for the destruction of Israel.

Israel decided not to wait to be attacked, and launched a strike particularly aimed at the Arab air forces. With air superiority established, Israel quickly gained the upper hand. In six days, Israel captured the West Bank, the Sinai Peninsula, the Gaza Strip, the Golan Heights, and, most importantly, all of Jerusalem. For the first time in 1,800 years, Jews had control over their holiest site, the Temple Mount, and Jews were able to visit and pray there for the first time since the establishment of the State of Israel.

The acquisition of this land had major implications for Israel. Israel now controlled territory with non-Jewish residents who were not citizens of Israel. Many of these residents considered themselves refugees or the descendants of refugees from the War of Independence. An organization calling for the destruction of the "Zionist entity," and rejecting the legitimacy of the Balfour Declaration and the United Nations partition, had been formed in 1964. This organization called itself the Palestine Liberation Organization (PLO).

> **WORTH NOTING**
>
> The word "Palestine" originated from the Roman name for the area. Both Jews and Arabs used this name for various purposes until the creation of the State of Israel. Jews had a newspaper called *The Palestine Post*, which became *The Jerusalem Post*, and the charitable organization the United Palestine Appeal reformed as the United Jewish Appeal. Jews stopped using the word Palestine with the formation of Israel.

The Six Day War had a major effect on Jews throughout the world. Israel's quick victory became a source of pride. Many non-Jews admired Israel's determination and success against a larger opponent.

The Yom Kippur War (1973)

Israel found itself at war again just a few years later. Egypt and Syria coordinated a surprise attack on Israel on Yom Kippur, the holiest day of the Jewish year with the exception of Shabbat. The war lasted only a few weeks, as Israel again persevered.

Peace with Egypt and Jordan

After so many wars and years of animosity, Egyptian President Anwar Sadat stunned Israel by making peace overtures in 1977. After months of negotiations, Egypt and Israel signed an accord at Camp David in 1979 with help and aid from the United States. Israel returned the Sinai

Peninsula to Egypt for the promise of peace. The accord with Egypt has held through today, and raised great hopes in Israel and among Jews throughout the world that peace in this area could be attained.

Unfortunately, the only other formerly belligerent nation that has made peace with Israel is Jordan. The two nations signed a peace treaty in 1994, normalizing relations and pledging not to act militarily against each other. This agreement also has lasted through today.

The Lebanon Wars (1982, 1986)

In 1982, Israel invaded Southern Lebanon after a group that had split from the PLO attempted to assassinate Israel's ambassador to the United Kingdom. Israel hoped to install a Christian government in Lebanon with which it could make peace. This plan ultimately failed, as Israel occupied Southern Lebanon for months while Palestinians in refugee camps were attacked and killed. A resistance group called Hezbollah formed. The United States and other western nations eventually labeled Hezbollah a terrorist organization after it attacked or planned attacks against both Israeli and Lebanese civilians and nonmilitary infrastructure.

The Lebanon Wars caused a great amount of questioning by Israelis and throughout the world about Israel's actions. Some Jews felt Israel had gone too far in its use of armed force and attempts to influence another nation's internal affairs. They felt Israel was at least partially responsible for the deaths of refugees and the creation of Hezbollah. Some have called these conflicts "Israel's Vietnam." The conflicts changed the image of Israel for some from righteous and successful underdog fighting for survival to regional power seeking to impose its will.

Terrorism and Territories

Part of the reason Israel took action in Lebanon may have been its frustration from coping with decades of terrorism. Arab groups like the PLO would raid and attack Israeli civilians and nonmilitary installations in Israel and elsewhere throughout the world. Some of these attacks were cross-border raids. Others were bombings or kidnappings. Israelis felt constantly in danger, now not only from hostile nations, but also from irregular paramilitary groups they called terrorists who might attack at any time.

 WORTH NOTING

Israelis are so concerned about attacks that no school groups may go on a trip without an armed guard. You can't go into a movie theater or shopping mall without having your bags searched. Armed soldiers are also stationed in busy streets and other civilian areas.

Some notable attacks particularly have affected Israelis. In 1972, a Palestinian group took 11 members of the Israeli Olympic team hostage and eventually killed them. In 1976, a Palestinian group hijacked an Air France flight originating in Israel and flew it to Entebbe Airport in Uganda. The hijackers released all the non-Israeli and non-Jewish hostages. Israeli commandos raided the airport and saved almost all the hostages.

In the 1990s, the Palestinians engaged in *intifada,* meaning "shaking off," demonstrating and throwing rocks at Israelis and Israeli soldiers, and implementing a campaign of suicide bombings in civilian areas. One attack during an intifadah occurred in 2002 when a suicide bomber attacked a Passover Seder being held in a hotel. More recently, Israel has sustained rocket attacks directed at civilian areas in Gaza.

Israel still possesses the West Bank and Gaza following the Six Day War, as Egypt and Jordan have both given up any claims on these areas. The Palestinians desire their own state in the area. Israel has perceived some of the motivation behind attacks on its territory, soldiers, and civilians to be motivated by this desire for statehood. However, Israelis and Jews throughout the world also fear that some Palestinian military groups and the Arab nations supporting them desire to destroy the State of Israel.

The Palestinians have received some rights of governance and freedoms through negotiation during more peaceful times. Israel has also contributed to the health-care system, infrastructure, and other resources in these areas. On the other hand, the Palestinians have been frustrated by their lack of complete self-governance, and steps Israel has taken to prevent both military equipment from entering the West Bank and Gaza and attackers from entering Israel. Further taxing the situation, Israel has founded Jewish settlements in areas Palestinians consider their own. It's an extremely complicated political situation, and opinion about it is strong on all sides.

Israel Today

While it's important to know Israel's history of conflict and struggle for survival to understand Jews and Judaism today, it's equally important to know that Jews see Israel as more than a country in difficult political circumstances. Israel is a source of pride for many Jews who celebrate the achievements of this relatively young nation.

A Jewish Homeland Open to All

One of the founding principles of the State of Israel is that it's a Jewish homeland that will accept any Jew and his or her family who wants to live there. This is called the "Law of Return." Israel has opened its doors and welcomed Jews throughout its history. Holocaust survivors found a home in Israel. In the 1950s, as many as 1,000,000 Jews from Middle Eastern countries found the nations in which they were living unfriendly to them. They made Aliyah en masse to Israel.

The Soviet Union allowed the Jews within its borders that they had persecuted and restricted for decades to leave, and large numbers of them found a home in Israel. Israel rescued Ethiopian Jews and brought them to the Holy Land. Israel is a place of refuge and opportunity for any Jew who seeks a new and better life free from second-class citizenship or persecution.

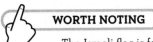

WORTH NOTING

The Israeli flag is fashioned after the *tallit*, the Jewish prayer shawl.

Israel is also the only nation on Earth where the dominant religious and cultural practice is Jewish. It's not difficult to find *kosher* food in Israel as it is in almost the entire remainder of the world—almost all the restaurants and markets are kosher. The public and school calendars follow the Jewish calendar. December 25, for the most part, is just another day in Israel. There is something special and unique for a people who have spent centuries as a minority to finally live in a nation where being Jewish is normal and easy.

DEFINITION

Kosher is the term for the set of Jewish dietary laws traditional Jews follow. These laws permit traditional Jews to eat only animals that have split hoofs and chew their cud, and prohibit the mixing of milk and meat. We'll consider these and other elements of keeping kosher in Chapter 20.

A Stable Democracy

Israel is a source of pride for Jews as perhaps the only stable democracy in the Middle East. Israel is governed by a parliamentary system in which citizens vote for a party to represent them in the legislature, which is called the *Knesset*. There are 120 seats in the Knesset, and the party with the most votes has the first opportunity to form a coalition with other parties to reach the necessary 61 or more votes required to form a government. While this system gives great and perhaps disproportionately large influence to smaller, more specialized parties, it's a democratic system that allows all to be heard.

It's crucial to know that Israel prides itself on universal suffrage, an uncommon occurrence in the Middle East. Women have full political rights in Israel. Citizens have full rights to vote and participate in Israeli society and governance regardless of religion. Although Israel sees itself as a Jewish state, Christians and Muslims have full rights in Israel, and have served in the Knesset. Additionally, Israel guarantees freedom of religion, assembly, and a free press to all.

An Economic Powerhouse

When Jews first arrived in Israel in large numbers in the modern era, they found a land that was swampy and undeveloped. The common image of an early Israeli is a pioneer working the land and struggling to make it usable. Through decades of hard work and innovations such as new irrigation methods, Israel has become a leading producer of food in the Middle East.

Israel's economic development has gone much farther than agriculture. Israel is a world leader in computer and biomedical technologies. Computer chips, cell phones, MRI machines, medicines, and alternative energy technologies have been developed in Israel. Israel has gained the nickname the "Start-Up Nation" from the number of entrepreneurial and innovative Israeli companies that have succeeded.

A Mix of the Old and the New

Israel is home to holy sites from each of the Abrahamic religions. In Jerusalem alone, Jews pray at the Western Wall, the last remaining structure of the Temple. Muslims pray at the Al-Aqsa Mosque atop the Western Wall, the third holiest site in Islam. A bit farther away but still in Jerusalem's Old City, Christians pray at the Church of the Holy Sepulchre, where it is believed Jesus was crucified and buried. These and other ancient religious sites are open to visitors and worshippers as permitted by the various religions, including the Baha'i World Center in Haifa. The Israeli government protects them all.

Israel is also full of significant archeological sites. It's said that you can't go more than 10 meters in Israel without finding an ancient treasure. While this is surely an exaggeration, there's hardly an area in Israel you can go where there isn't an interesting and significant ancient site within an easy drive.

Among all these ancient treasures, Israel also stands as a modern nation with a vibrant culture. The theater and music in Israel are among the best in the world. Haifa is a shining city on the hills of the coast that has been compared to San Francisco. Tel Aviv is quite metropolitan with an exciting nightlife. The spas at the Dead Sea are unique due to the resources of this body of water at the lowest point on land in the world. Eilat in the south provides amazing sea resorts with scuba diving and water skiing.

Israel is a nation with a wide diversity of people, culture, and history. It's a nation with tensions, to be sure, but it's also a place highly treasured by Jews throughout the world.

The Least You Need to Know

- Although a small number of Jews have always lived in Israel following the Diaspora, and there have always been many who hoped to return to the land, Jews started to return to Israel in larger numbers at the end of the nineteenth century.

- Zionism is the longing of Jews to return to their historic homeland and create a Jewish nation there. But not all Jews are Zionists, and not all Zionists have the same vision for the country.

- The end of the British Mandate, the circumstances of Jewish refugees following the Holocaust, and post-World War II superpower dynamics all led to the establishment of the State of Israel in 1948.

- Israeli history has been marked by conflict with its neighboring nations and with the Palestinians living on land captured by Israel in the Six Day War. War and terrorism have greatly affected Israel and Jews throughout the world.

- Israel is a dynamic nation with a strong economy, vibrant culture, and incredible archeological treasures. Most of all, for Jews, Israel is a homeland where Jewish religion and customs are the norm, and where all Jews can find refuge.

A Year of Jewish Holy Days

Much of the spirit of Judaism comes from the cycle of the year. At times Jews celebrate; at other times they're serious and solemn. The year brings them through a gamut of emotions from delirious happiness to the greatest sadness at losses they've sustained. The holy days mix their religion and culture into experiences that shape their lives.

Part 3 examines these special days in the Jewish calendar. Chapter 9 describes how the calendar works and focuses upon the most important holiday, Shabbat. Chapter 10 explains the values and practices of the High Holy Days. Chapter 11 discusses the Pilgrimage Festivals. Chapter 12 shares the joy of the fun holidays of Chanukkah and Purim. Chapter 13 illustrates other holidays in the Jewish calendar.

The Jewish Calendar—
It's Luni-Solar!

As a congregational rabbi, barely a year goes by when I don't hear a comment about the holidays. One year it's, "Wow! The holidays are really early this year!" Another year it's, "Wow! The holidays are really late this year!"

I have to remind my congregants that the holidays are neither early nor late. They are always right on time. The reason they seem to change is that the Jewish calendaring system is different than the Gregorian system adopted by most of the world.

This chapter introduces the Jewish calendar, explaining the reasoning behind the calendaring system and how it works. I also describe the most important holiday in the Jewish calendar, which arrives every week—*Shabbat*.

In This Chapter

- The construction of the Jewish calendar
- The holiness of Shabbat
- Refraining from work on Shabbat
- A traditional Shabbat observance

The Jewish Calendar System

It's helpful to start by describing the calendaring system with which we're all familiar. The Gregorian calendar is based on the revolution of Earth around the sun, which takes 365.24 days. That fraction of a day means that we need to add one day every four years to make sure that, over time, the calendar and the seasons always properly align. We want February to fall in the winter in the northern hemisphere, and July to fall in the summer, and so on. That fraction of a day would cause a lot of problems if we didn't add a leap day—February 29—every four years.

WORTH NOTING

Every 400 years, we skip the leap day because the fraction is a little less than a full quarter of a day. This is how precise the Gregorian calendar needs to be to ensure it remains constant through the centuries.

If you're comfortable with the idea of adding February 29 every four years, then it's easy to understand the Jewish calendar once you accept one difference. The Gregorian calendar is a solar calendar, meaning it's based on the time the Earth takes to go around the sun. The Jewish calendar is "luni-solar," meaning it's based on both the moon and the sun.

A Mix of the Moon and the Sun

The Jewish calendar is primarily based on the revolution of the moon around Earth. This takes about 29.5 days, so a Jewish month may have either 29 or 30 days. There are 12 months in the standard Jewish year, which is a total of 354 days.

Here's the problem. Like the Gregorian calendar, the Jewish calendar has to keep its months in line with the seasons. Many of the Jewish holidays have agricultural meanings, and it wouldn't make sense to have the planting festival in autumn, or the harvest festival in winter. If a full turn of the seasons takes about 365 days, as the Gregorian calendar measures, then the Jewish calendar will "lose" 11 days a year, and the seasons and calendar will quickly misalign unless something is done.

The Jewish calendar solves this problem by adding a "leap month" every two or three years. This is the exact same practice and reasoning as adding a leap day every four years—it's just more days, and more often, so it makes a more noticeable difference.

The added month is called "Adar II." There is always a month of Adar in the calendar, so when it's a leap year, a second Adar is added after the first. *Adar* means "happy," so the calendar can be said to be increasing happiness in the year when there is an extra month.

What Year Is It?

The Gregorian calendar bases the years on the amount of time since Jesus' birth. This book is first being published in the year 2015 A.D., meaning we're living in the 2015th year since Jesus was born according to the calculations of those who established this calendar.

The counting of the years in Judaism predates the establishment of the Gregorian calendar. The sages looked to the Tanach to provide their gauge as to when to start counting the years. The logical starting point was the creation of the world. The sages looked at the number of years each king ruled and each life span the Tanach listed. Their calculations lead the Jewish calendar to say that, as of the first publication of this book in mid-2015 A.D., the Jewish year is 5775.

The easiest way to calculate the Jewish year is to follow these steps:

1. Determine when Rosh HaShanah, the Jewish New Year (discussed in Chapter 10), falls on the Gregorian calendar.

2. If Rosh HaShanah has not yet occurred in the Gregorian year, add 3760 to the Gregorian year.

3. If Rosh HaShanah has occurred in the Gregorian year, add 3761.

When a Day Begins

The Tanach also provided the necessary information for the sages to determine when a day began. The source again was the story of the creation of the world. Genesis Chapter 1 describes exactly what God created on each day. At the end of each description, the text reads, "There was an evening, there was a morning …." The sages concluded from this that evening came first, so in Judaism, a day actually begins at sundown.

 **OY VEY!**

When reading most Jewish calendars, a holiday begins at sundown the day before the day listed. In such a calendar, if Rosh HaShanah is listed on the Gregorian calendar as beginning on September 25, the holiday actually begins at sundown on September 24. On some calendars, the start of the holiday is noted as *erev*, meaning "evening."

Traditional vs. Reform Calendars

The basing of the Jewish calendar on the revolution of the moon around Earth created other difficulties in ancient times. People had to observe the moon to determine if it had completed a cycle, and a Jewish court called the *Sanhedrin,* or the appropriate sages, had to assess and announce correct dates for the beginning of a month or a holiday. This observation had to be made in Israel because that was the central location of Judaism and the basis for the calculation of the entire calendar. Sometimes they needed to adjust the calendar to match their observations.

This created significant problems for anyone living away from the authorities who ruled on the calendar. People residing miles away couldn't communicate with the authorities on time, and there could be great uncertainty or miscommunication as to the correct date. To ensure that everyone observed the holidays at the right time as they occurred in Israel, the traditional calendar added an extra day to most major holidays. Yom Kippur, discussed in Chapter 10, is a notable exception to this due to the mitzvah of fasting, which would be too difficult to do on two consecutive days.

The Reform Movement changed this practice. The early Reformers decided that advancements in astronomy and communication had removed the uncertainty, and they could know the correct day for the observance even if they were oceans and continents away from Israel. Most Reform Jews therefore do not add the extra day. Jewish calendars usually follow the traditional system, so you may find a Reform Jew who considers a holiday to have ended on the same day as an Orthodox Jew is still observing.

The Calendar in Israel

Israel presents a special case for the calendaring system and determination of the holidays. The Israeli holiday calendar doesn't add the additional days, because Israeli Jews are in the land and have no need to add another day. The one exception to this is Rosh HaShanah, which tradition-ally occurs over two days even in Israel. Jews celebrated Rosh HaShanah over two days even in the times of the early Prophets to guard against the possibility that the proper witnesses of the moon would not appear to testify on time. The Israeli calendar maintains this tradition of two days for Rosh HaShanah today. Additionally, some traditional Jews in Israel still observe the traditional calendar even though they live in Israel, matching what had been done for centuries and what was done during the Diaspora.

Shabbat: The Most Important Holy Day

I sometimes play a game with my younger students. I tell them I'm going to ask them a question, but warn them that it's a little bit of a trick question. I ask them, "What is the most important Jewish holy day?" Some say Yom Kippur. Some say Pesach. Some say, "None, because they're all important!" A few get the correct answer, especially after a hint or two. It's the Sabbath, in Hebrew called *Shabbat*.

People don't usually think about Shabbat because they think of a holiday happening once a year. Shabbat happens every week from a little before sundown on Friday to a little after sundown on

Saturday. Despite its frequency, Shabbat is the most important holy day in the Jewish calendar. It originates at the beginning of the world, as God ended the work of Creation on the seventh day, blessing and sanctifying it. Shabbat is the only holy day mentioned in the Ten Commandments, and Jews are commanded multiple times throughout the Torah to observe this day. Shabbat observance has been a central, essential focus of Judaism for centuries.

The Meaning and Purpose of Shabbat

Why is Shabbat observance so important? Why is it important that we take one day out of the week and make it different and special?

 WORDS OF WISDOM

"More than the Jewish people have kept Shabbat, Shabbat has kept the Jewish people."—Ahad Ha-Am

The answer to these questions begins with an observation about the first Shabbat. When God creates the world, God stops working and rests on the seventh day. (Genesis 2:2-3) Why? Surely God had no need to rest. In Jewish understanding, God is omnipotent. Why are we told that an unlimited source of power took a day to rest? Why are we told to do the same?

Part of the answer is in recognizing God's majesty over the world. By behaving as God did at creation, we honor God and acknowledge God's blessings and beneficence. After all, the best way to show respect to a Sovereign and Parent is to do what they do. The first version of the Ten Commandments implies this reason by emphasizing God's creation of the world. (Exodus 20:8-11)

The second recitation of the Ten Commandments implies a different motivation for Shabbat observance. Like the first recitation, the second says that not only you, but all members of the household, servants, strangers living among the Israelites, and animals all must observe Shabbat. Moses reminds the people that they were slaves in Egypt, and they enjoy freedom only because God redeemed them. Shabbat ensures that everyone shares that freedom by making sure that, unlike slaves, everyone gets a day free from ordinary work. Shabbat is social justice enacted.

The purpose of Shabbat goes even deeper, especially for those of us today who enjoy plenty of leisure time and holidays. Rabbi Abraham Joshua Heschel noted this when he identified one of the most important aspects of Judaism as the sanctification of time. In Judaism, we don't bless objects or venerate things. Instead, we create holy time, and more than anything else, no matter how many physical possessions we have, that sacred time rejuvenates us and gives life meaning.

Think about your favorite memory of a treasured object from your childhood. Is it the actual object or possession that created the good memory, or is it the *time* when you enjoyed the object? Aren't the most treasured parts of our lives the time we get to spend with our friends and loved ones, and the experiences we have with them? Sacred time is what makes our lives sweet, and Judaism seeks to create this sacred time with Shabbat.

On Shabbat, we seek to distinguish one day from the ordinary and make it special. Six days a week we concern ourselves with matters of the physical world—our work, our homes, and our tangible needs. Shabbat is a day for us to focus on the spiritual, which allows us to better handle the challenges of the week once Shabbat ends.

What Does It Mean to Rest?

The Torah commands us that on Shabbat, *"lo ta'aseh chol melachah atah*—no work shall you do." (Deuteronomy 5:14) However, the Torah does not describe exactly what it means when it uses the word *melachah*—"work." There's no complete definition of this word in the Torah, and therefore no clear definition from the Torah alone of what it means to rest.

WORTH NOTING

The three main goals of Shabbat are *menuchah* (rest), *oneg* (joy), and *kedushah* (holiness).

The Torah does provide some guidance by explicitly and implicitly proscribing four activities. The Torah explicitly prohibits lighting a fire (Exodus 35:2-3) and field work such as plowing and harvesting (Exodus 34:20) on Shabbat. Scripture implies that travel should not be done on Shabbat by saying that "no man should go from his place on the seventh day." (Exodus 16:29) The Torah makes an even stronger implication prohibiting wood gathering on Shabbat by telling a story about how a man was punished by death after doing this. (Numbers 15:32-36)

The rabbis of the Talmud couldn't be satisfied with the open question of what constituted prohibited work on Shabbat, and sought an answer through interpretation. They found it in the story of the building of the Tabernacle, the portable center of worship used by the Israelites during their 40 years of wandering through the wilderness before entering the Promised Land.

The Israelites were very excited to build the Tabernacle. Artisans had been chosen, and the people brought their most valuable possessions and riches for its construction. They brought so much that the builders had more than they needed, and had to ask the people to stop bringing contributions. (Exodus 36:5-7) Moses met their enthusiasm by gathering the people before the building began … and first reminding them that, no matter what, they had to remember not to do any work on Shabbat. This is not exactly the start of a pep talk you would expect to hear from Moses if you were excited about building a place to worship God.

The sages noted this discrepancy as well, so they logically concluded that this must mean the actions used in constructing the Tabernacle must be the work prohibited on Shabbat. They found this work to be 39 actions, which they memorialized in the Mishnah: sowing, plowing, reaping, binding sheaves, threshing, winnowing, cleansing crops, grinding, sifting, kneading, baking, shearing wool, cleaning wool, combing wool, dyeing fabric, spinning thread, weaving, making two loops, weaving two threads, separating two threads, tying a knot, loosening a knot, sewing two stitches, tearing, hunting a gazelle, slaughtering, flaying, salting meat, curing skin, scraping skin, cutting skin, writing two letters, erasing to allow two letters to be written, building, pulling down, extinguishing a fire, lighting a fire, striking with a hammer, and taking anything from one place to another.

Over time the rabbis elaborated on this extensive list, and expanded the definition of prohibited work even further. As much as anywhere, the sages employed the concept of setting fences around the Torah to ensure the Jews didn't transgress Shabbat. This meant Jews couldn't carry the keys to their home on Shabbat when they went to the synagogue. They couldn't light a fire to cook. In the modern age, they couldn't use electricity because this was creating a spark, which the rabbis deemed the same as lighting a fire.

After a while, the restrictions imposed on Shabbat became onerous, so rabbis and communities found ways to comply with the letter of the law while offering some relief. Since Jews always were allowed to carry items within one type of area like a home, they found a way to make large areas the equivalent of a single type of area by enclosing an entire community in an *eiruv*. Fires lit before Shabbat could continue to burn. In modern times, "Shabbat elevators" in tall buildings with many traditional Jews would be set to stop at every floor through Shabbat. It might take a long time to reach the fifteenth floor, but the Jews riding the elevator were not lighting a spark, so they did not violate Shabbat.

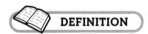 **DEFINITION**

> An **eiruv** is an unbroken barrier or enclosure that allows Jews to carry items while remaining within the borders. In urban areas, an eiruv is often a wire strung along buildings and telephone poles.

There's a wide range of Shabbat observance among the branches of Judaism. Orthodox Jews keep the halachic requirements very strictly. Reform Jews observing Shabbat may focus less on the particular restrictions and more on the intent of the day as a spiritual time away from ordinary work. This might include spending time with family or leisure activities they might otherwise set aside due to job demands, even if this means driving a car or using electricity.

Kabbalat Shabbat—Welcoming Shabbat

Shabbat is a day rich with song and ritual. For many Jews, Shabbat practices constitute the high-light of the week, connecting them to God, their families, and their ancestors. The routine and rhythm of the day can be a great comfort and an incredible spiritual experience.

The *Kabbalat Shabbat* (Welcoming Shabbat) rituals are very special home observances. Shabbat begins with the lighting of candles, usually by a Jewish woman 13 years old or older according to tradition. If no woman is present, a man lights the candles. The lighter uses a match or, in some traditions, a third "helper" candle, covers her eyes, and recites the blessing. This is done because a blessing is usually said before the action, and not the reverse as is done here. The problem with the Shabbat candles is that you can't light the candles until Shabbat arrives, but once Shabbat arrives traditional halachah prohibits lighting a fire. The rabbis solved this problem by allowing the lighter to kindle the lights, covering her eyes and saying the blessing, and then constructively lighting them by viewing the flames when the eyes are uncovered.

Usually, there are two candles lit for Shabbat. One is lit in accordance with the command to "remember" Shabbat found in Exodus 20:8, and the other is lit to "keep" Shabbat as required by Deuteronomy 5:12.

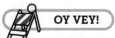 **OY VEY!**

There are different traditions regarding the number of candles lit on Shabbat. Some communities light seven candles, as seven is a mystical number in Jewish tradition and represents the number of days in the week. Some families light the two candles of Shabbat and add an additional candle for each child.

Kiddush, or the blessing over the fruit of the vine, follows the candle lighting. Judaism considers the fruit of the vine to be the symbol of joy because it warms hearts and brings happiness. Jews use sweet wine or juice for this ritual to reflect the sweetness of Shabbat. They fill the cup to its brim, symbolizing that they experience the most joy possible on Shabbat. Then they say the blessing and drink the wine.

Some families then take the opportunity to bless their children. A husband often blesses his wife with the words of Proverbs 31. Traditional Jews then ritually wash their hands as an expression and reinforcement of the holiness of the day.

Finally, before the meal, the blessing is recited over the *challah*. Challah is a sweet egg bread, reflecting the sweetness of Shabbat. It's braided so that it even appears special. Families often use two *challot* (the plural of challah) because God gave the Israelites two portions of the manna that sustained them while they were wandering in the desert. (Exodus 16:22-24) Some families dip the challah in salt before eating it, either as a sign of freedom because wealthy free Romans were the only people who could afford salt in ancient times, or because salt was used with the sacrifices in the Temple.

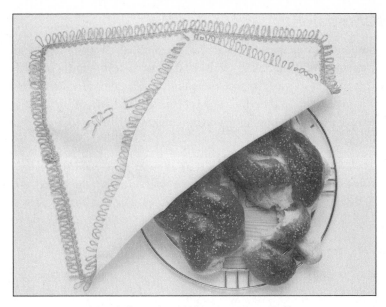

Two challot under a cloth cover eaten on Shabbat.

A festive meal follows these rituals. Traditionally, Jews eat the most special meal they can on Shabbat. The evening doesn't end immediately after the meal is eaten, as they still give thanks to God for their food and celebrate Shabbat with song.

Roasted chicken with vegetables, a traditional Shabbat evening meal.

Shabbat in Community

Shabbat is a time for communities to gather. Synagogues hold worship services on Friday evening and Saturday morning. In Traditional Judaism, Saturday morning is the primary service. Reform Judaism made the Friday evening service the main communal observance in deference to the pressing need of many to keep their businesses open on Saturdays. They deemed this especially necessary when the primary shopping day in America was Saturday due to laws requiring businesses to close on Sunday.

The services include many of the prayers of the daily service as well as special prayers for Shabbat. Jews read a portion from the Torah and a selection from the Prophets called the *Haftarah*. We'll discuss more about these prayers and readings in Chapter 24.

Other Shabbat Customs

Jews traditionally engage in many activities on Shabbat to make the day special. Torah study is especially appropriate on Shabbat. Many Jews give *tzedakah* (righteous acts, charity) and do the mitzvah of *bikur cholim* (visiting the sick). Some Jews eat a special meal called *shalosh se'udah* (third meal) on Saturday afternoon, reflecting the practice of adding joy to Shabbat in Talmudic times when people usually ate only two meals a day.

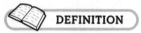

DEFINITION

> **Bikur cholim** is the mitzvah of visiting the sick, a high value in the Jewish tradition. The Talmud says that one who visits the sick takes away one sixtieth of his illness. (Talmud Bavli, Nedarim 39a-b)

Havdalah

As Shabbat nears its end, it would be difficult to simply return to the ordinariness of the rest of the week. Therefore, a special ceremony called *Havdalah* marks the end of Shabbat and prepares Jews to return to everyday life.

Havdalah means "separation." It begins with the lighting of a special braided candle. The candle is braided because the blessing that is later said concerning it refers to lights, not one light. Therefore, multiple wicks are necessary for this ceremony.

The first blessing said at Havdalah is Kiddush, the blessing over the fruit of the vine. Even as Shabbat departs, Jews remind themselves of the specialness and sweetness of this moment.

A second blessing is recited over spices. As Shabbat ends, Jews become sad that this special day is over. Some traditions say they each receive an extra soul on Shabbat, and that they feel unhappy as this extra soul departs. The smell of the spices consoles them, reminding them that Shabbat will return in just a week.

ASK THE RABBI

What kind of spices may be used for Havdalah? Any spice may be used as long as it's fragrant and not man-made. Two should be used together. Common spices used include cloves, cinnamon, and nutmeg.

Next, there's the blessing over the candle that has burned throughout the ceremony. The braids of the candle represent the intertwining of Jewish lives with God, their families, and the community. The braids also may represent the weaving of the sacred with the ordinary that is experienced by performing mitzvot and living honorable lives according to Torah. Because the candle was lit earlier and an action must accompany every blessing, Jews make shadows with the light, holding their hands upward toward it as they say the blessing.

A Havdalah set, with Kiddush cup, spice box, and candle holder that holds the braided candle.

Next they say *HaMavdil,* a blessing marking the actual separation between Shabbat and the ordinary first day of the week about to begin. As this blessing is said, the candle is dipped in the wine or juice, extinguishing it. Songs are sung wishing everyone a good week. Jews also sing a special song called *Eliyahu HaNavi* (Elijah the Prophet). Legend says that Elijah will be the herald of the coming of the *Mashiach* (Messiah). Singing this song at this time expresses the hope that this will be the week when the Mashiach finally comes.

The Least You Need to Know

- The Jewish calendar is primarily based upon the revolution of the moon around Earth. Adjustments are made to keep the seasons in the appropriate months, so the calendar is "luni-solar."
- Traditional Jews add a day to many holidays as Jews did through the centuries to ensure they're observed on the day the holiday occurred in Israel. Reform Jews and Jews in Israel often do not do this.
- Shabbat is the most important holy day in Judaism. It occurs each week.
- Jews traditionally don't work on Shabbat, and observe the day with special meals, songs, and prayers.

Days of Awe:
The High Holy Days

With the exception of Shabbat, the two most important observances of the Jewish year are Rosh HaShanah and Yom Kippur. In English, we usually call these holidays "The High Holy Days."

The High Holy Days mark the beginning of the Jewish year. Many cultures celebrate the beginning of their year with parties and revelry. Judaism views this occasion very differently. The High Holy Days mark a period of renewal, repentance, and devotion to God. They're serious and solemn times, but also refreshing and inspiring, containing some of the most impacting symbolism and contemplations in all of Judaism. They're Days of Awe that inspire our souls and prepare us for the upcoming year.

In This Chapter

- Preparing for the month of Elul
- Rosh HaShanah: a prayerful new year
- The days between the Holy Days
- Yom Kippur, the Day of Atonement

Getting Ready: The Month of Elul

Traditionally, we don't simply jump into the High Holy Days. The tasks set before us during this time require preparation, just like you need to warm up and stretch before doing exercise or playing a sport. We take the entire month, the Hebrew month of Elul, to prepare ourselves for the High Holy Days.

Customs and Prayers Through Elul

During the month of Elul, there are additions made to the traditional prayers in line with the themes of the High Holy Days. We add a series of *Selichot* prayers to the morning service, asking for forgiveness for our sins. We read Psalms, and we hear one blast of the *shofar*, or horn. Many of these are prayers or customs specifically designated for the holidays, and give us a taste for what is to come.

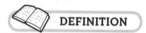 **DEFINITION**

> **Selichot** means forgiveness. The term may refer either to a set of prayers requesting forgiveness from God, or the special night described below.

There are other customs some Jews do prior to the High Holy Days. Some visit the *mikvah*, the ritual bath, as a form of spiritual purifying cleansing. Some visit the graves of the righteous in their families, honoring them through memory and reminding themselves of the realities of life and death. Some synagogues change their Torah covers and ark curtains to white, reflecting the verse in Isaiah that says our sins will be turned from red to "as white as snow." (Isaiah 1:18)

Selichot: A Night of Prayer and Study

Some communities observe a special night, also called Selichot, on the Saturday before Rosh HaShanah, or two Saturdays before if Rosh HaShanah falls on a Monday or Tuesday. There's a special service at midnight in which the Selichot prayers are said, along with psalms and other prayers from the High Holy Day liturgy. The shofar is also blown.

Some communities observe this day with special text or topical study related to the themes of the High Holy Days.

Rosh HaShanah—The New Year

The first of the two High Holy Days is Rosh HaShanah, which literally means "the head of the year." In Jewish tradition, there are actually four New Years. Two are not observed in modern times—the new year for kings, from which the reign of the Israelite kings was counted, and the new year for cattle tithes, from which the amount due to the Temple was calculated. One is still celebrated as *Tu Bishvat*—the new year of trees. The remaining New Year is Rosh HaShanah—the day marking the anniversary of creation. The Jewish year 5775 began in September of 2014 C.E.

Rosh HaShanah is first mentioned in the Tanach in Leviticus 23:24-25: "In the seventh month, on the first day of the month, you shall have a Sabbath, a remembrance with the blowing of the horn, a holy convocation. You shall do no work (on this day)."

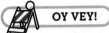

OY VEY!

You might think it strange that the new year is observed at the beginning of the seventh month, and not the first. The number seven has mystical meaning in Judaism, likely accounting for this unusual placement in the calendar.

Traditionally, Rosh HaShanah occurs over two days. This is because in ancient times the authorities declared the exact date of the holiday based on their observations of the moon. Jews living far from the authorities wouldn't know in time what date they selected, so they observed for two days to ensure they had their worship services on the correct day. Orthodox and Conservative Jews maintain this practice, and even Jews in Israel observe two days. Most Reform Jews observe one day, reasoning that they can be certain of the correct day due to advances in astronomy and communication.

Rosh HaShanah is a day when God's review and judgment of the people begins, a process that continues throughout the High Holy Days. Jews view God as having a Book of Life, writing in it the names of those who will live and prosper through the upcoming year, and those who will not. Jews say that, "On Rosh HaShanah it is written, on Yom Kippur it is sealed: who shall live, and who shall die …." Note that this judgment is only for life on earth—it has no connection with anything that might happen after death. Even with this limitation, there's enough at stake to make Rosh HaShanah a quite serious and important day.

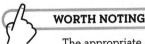

WORTH NOTING

The appropriate greeting for Rosh HaShanah is "L'shanah tovah tikateivu–May you be inscribed for a good year." Jews never say, "Happy New Year."

Special Rosh HaShanah Prayers

The prayer that most fully and dramatically encompasses the idea of judgment and the Book of Life is called the *Unetaneh Tokef.* A legend says that at least part of this prayer was composed by Rabbi Amnon of Mayence at the time of his martyrdom. More than almost any other prayer in

Jewish liturgy, the Unetaneh Tokef emphasizes the fact of human mortality, listing many ways anyone might die during the upcoming year. People are like sheep before the divine Shepherd, ready to be evaluated and judged.

It begins, "Let us declare the power of this day; it is awesome and full of dread." At this most fearful moment, Jews are reminded that God does not desire their deaths, but that they should improve their conduct and live. Jews are told that "repentance, prayer, and charity temper judgment's severe decree." This prayer makes Jews face the reality of life, prepares them for the new year, and uplifts them so that they may confront this reality with hope.

The other distinctive prayer from the Rosh HaShanah liturgy is *Aveenu Malkeinu*—"Our Father, Our King." God's reign over the world as its Creator is a major theme for this holiday. Aveenu Malkeinu praises God for all God does, and pleads with God to hear prayers and show kindness. The melodies associated with this prayer are some of the most comforting and inspiring, including a well-known folk melody and a grand, crescendoing piece by Max Janowski, a composer from Berlin who immigrated to America in 1937.

Readings from Scripture

Different communities read different selections from the Tanach on Rosh HaShanah. Traditional congregations read Genesis 21:1-34, the story of Hagar's banishment from the household of Abraham and Sarah, on the first day of Rosh HaShanah. Hagar was Sarah's handmaiden who Sarah gave to Abraham when Sarah did not conceive. Abraham and Hagar had a son, Ishmael. When Sarah and Abraham had their own son, Isaac, Sarah had Abraham cast Hagar and Ishmael out of the house. It's unclear why this reading was selected for the first day of Rosh HaShanah. Some say it's recognition that we can turn our lives around even at the darkest times, as Hagar eventually lifts herself and Ishmael from their despair. Some say it's recognition that everyone is capable of being unkind, as Abraham and Sarah were to Hagar and Ishmael, but there is still the opportunity for redemption.

Traditional congregations read the *Akeidah,* the binding of Isaac, on the second day of Rosh HaShanah. God tells Abraham to sacrifice his son, Isaac. Abraham agrees, but before he's able to do the act, an angel stops him and tells him he has passed God's test. This story emphasizes God's ruling power, God's mercy, and the Jewish commitment to God, all very appropriate themes for this holiday.

Reform congregations read the Akeidah on the first day and the story of the creation of the world from the beginning of Genesis on the second day. This difference is partially due to many Reform Jews observing only one day of Rosh HaShanah, and the Reform rabbis felt as many people as possible should hear the powerful story of the Akeidah on this day. The creation story is read on the second day because the holiday marks the anniversary of the creation of the world.

The readings from the Prophets also reflect the themes of the holiday. One reading is from the beginning of First Samuel and tells of God hearing Hannah's prayer for a son. This son is Samuel, a prophet who eventually installed the first two kings of Israel. The story brings to mind the stories of Hagar and Ishmael and Sarah and Isaac, as they all include the issue of hope for off-spring. The reading from First Samuel also calls to mind the issue of kingship, which is appropriate, as God's Kingship is an important theme at Rosh HaShanah. The other reading from Prophets is Jeremiah 31:2-20, which speaks of repentance.

The Shofar

The most enduring symbol of Rosh HaShanah is the shofar, an animal horn that's hollowed out and blown like a trumpet. Its deep, mournful sound stirs the soul on Rosh HaShanah, calling us to the important tasks of the High Holy Days. Maimonides said that the purpose of the shofar is to awaken the people, rousing them to alertness.

 ASK THE RABBI

What animals' horns may be used for the shofar? Almost any kosher animal may be used for the shofar. Most of them are rams' horns, but they also may be from goats or sheep. Yemenite Jews make long and distinctive shofarim from the horns of kudus. The horns of cattle usually are not used because of the association with the story of the Golden Calf, when the Israelites at Mount Sinai began to worship a statue of a cow in fear that Moses would not return to them.

The Saadia Gaon listed more specific reasons for the sounding of the shofar:

- Announcing God as King, like a trumpet at a coronation

- Calling for an examination of actions and repentence

- Reminding Jews of the receipt of Torah at Mount Sinai, as the sound of a loud shofar was heard at that moment

- Resembling the voices of the prophets, who shouted for justice like a shofar

- Recalling the destruction of the Temple

- Referencing the Akeidah, because a ram took Isaac's place as the sacrifice

- Asking Jews to be humble, especially in comparison to the greatness of God Jews hear in the shofar's blast

- Sounding the approach of judgment, like the convening of a court

- Foretelling the coming of the Mashiach

- Forecasting the redemption of the entire world, when all peoples will be one

The Talmud also associates the sound of the shofar with the cries of a woman. It names the particular woman as Sisera's mother. Sisera was a ruthless Canaanite general who oppressed the Israelites for 20 years until the prophetess Deborah killed him. It seems strange that the Talmud would compare the shofar blasts to an enemy's mother, but her cries are mentioned in the song Deborah sings in Judges 5:28-30. Some commentators say this teaches Jews to have compassion for all, even our enemies.

Shofarot (the plural of shofar), rams' horns blown to make a mournful sound on Rosh HaShanah.

A total of 100 notes from the shofar are blown on Rosh HaShanah in three sets. Each set represents a different aspect of God's glory: *malchuyot*—God's Kingship; *zichronot*—God's remembrance of the Jewish people; and *shofarot*—God's gift of revealing the Torah. The service leader calls the cadence, and the shofar blower sounds the notes as follows:

- *Tekiah:* a single, unbroken blast

- *Shevarim:* three wails together

- *Teruah:* nine staccato blasts

- *Tekiah Gedolah:* a single, long blast at the end of the third set

Traditionally, Jews don't blow the shofar if Rosh HaShanah falls on Shabbat. This is because the sages were concerned that someone would break the laws of the Sabbath by carrying the shofar to synagogue.

Customs and Practices

One custom of Rosh HaShanah is *Tashlich*. Tashlich is the metaphorical casting away of sins by throwing crumbs of bread or emptying pockets into a flowing body of water. This tradition comes from the words of Micah 7:19, which says, "You shall throw your sins into the depths of the sea." Tashlich is usually done on the afternoon of the first day of Rosh HaShanah unless that day is also Shabbat. Many Jews will do Tashlich on other days in between Rosh HaShanah and Yom Kippur. A similar custom performed after Rosh HaShanah by traditional Jews is *kaperot* which involves the slaughter of a rooster or hen as a means of reminding Jews to seek repentence.

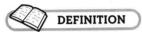 **DEFINITION**

Kaperot is a ceremony in which a rooster or hen is slaughtered to remind us that God's judgment calls for us to die if we do not seek teshuvah. It's not a sacrifice, because sacrifices can only be done at the Temple. The slaughtered animal then is donated to the poor. Sometimes kaperot is done by giving money. Only the ultra-Orthodox and a few others perform this ritual.

There are several foods eaten on Rosh HaShanah, including apples and honey. A special round *challah* is used in place of the usual oval braided loaf. We'll discuss these foods and their symbolism in Chapter 20.

The Intervening Days

The intervening days between Rosh HaShanah and Yom Kippur are called *Yamim Nora'im*—"The Days of Awe." They're also called The Days of Repentance. This is a period of time when Jews examine their souls and conduct over the past year, and resolve to improve themselves. This is also a time when Jews seek *teshuvah* from other people, which we'll examine when we consider Yom Kippur.

The intervening days also contain a commemoration called the Fast of Gedaliah. Gedaliah was the governor of Judea following the destruction of the First Temple. Gedaliah was assassinated, ending any semblance of Jewish rule in Judea for 40 years. The day following the second day of Rosh HaShanah memorializes this event with special prayers and a fast from dawn until dusk.

Yom Kippur

For weeks, Jews have been saying prayers and preparing ourselves. They celebrated the creation of the world and remembered God's sovereignty on Rosh HaShanah. The past 10 days have been a sacred time, the Days of Awe. This climaxes with the most serious of Jewish Holy Days, and the second of the High Holy Days, *Yom Kippur*, which means "Day of Atonement."

I've always found it important to find the right emotional center for Yom Kippur. It's a very solemn day, but for the most part it's not sad. It's a day to cleanse ourselves of our sins, but not a day to punish ourselves. It's serious, but also refreshing and uplifting. Some people dread Yom Kippur because they find it a "downer." But I think it's better understood as an introspective day that leads to renewal of the soul.

Teshuvah and Forgiveness

The main purpose of Yom Kippur is atonement, completing the teshuvah Jews have been working on for weeks, especially the last 10 days. *Teshuvah* means "return." Judaism understands that people are human, and they are imperfect. This means they sometimes fail to follow the mitzvot, or they hurt one another. In other words, they "miss the mark" of being the best they hope to be. This is really what Jews mean when they say they have sinned. In fact, they say in their Yom Kippur prayers, "Who among us is so stiff-necked as to say we have not sinned?" The answer, of course, is no one.

WORTH NOTING

Imagine you're an archer firing at a target. Sometimes you hit a bull's-eye. Sometimes you miss because you weren't thinking, you weren't focused, or you just didn't do the right thing. You're not necessarily bad or evil—you just missed the mark. That's the idea of sin in Judaism.

Teshuvah is a three-step process:

1. Jews need to examine themselves and their souls, which is called *cheshbon nefesh*, and recognize where they've missed the mark and sinned.

2. They need to ask for forgiveness from God and from the people they've hurt by their failures to be the best people possible.

3. They need to resolve honestly not to make these mistakes again, and to try to be better people in the upcoming year.

Seeking teshuvah varies depending on whom Jews need to ask for forgiveness. Jews say in the Yom Kippur prayers, "For sins against God, the Day of Atonement atones, but for sins of one person against another, the Day of Atonement does not atone until you have made peace with one another." So Jews can reach teshuvah for failing to follow mitzvot through their honest reflections, resolve, and prayers to God. However, if Jews have hurt another person through their wrongdoing, they need to approach the other person, admit their offense, and ask for forgiveness.

I think this requirement can be the hardest part of Yom Kippur. It requires honesty and humility. It can be scary to ask someone for forgiveness, because they may not react well. There are two things that ease these concerns. First, the people you ask for forgiveness are asking others for forgiveness, too. The tradition says that no one can expect to be forgiven unless he or she also forgives others when asked. Second, you must restore any harms or losses the other person suffered because of your actions. Between these two considerations, forgiveness is usually given.

But what if the person from whom you are asking forgiveness is really angry or stubborn, and will not forgive you? Does Judaism doom you forever? Not at all. Judaism requires you to go to the other person and ask for forgiveness three times. This is understood from the Biblical story where Miriam spoke against Moses for marrying a Cushite woman, and God punished Miriam. Moses pleads with God to forgive Miriam, beautifully asking God three times for mercy. (Numbers 12:1-13) From this plea, the sages understand that Jews have to ask the person they've wronged for forgiveness only three times. If he or she has not forgiven you after that, you no longer bear the responsibility for your wrongdoing.

Fasting

One of the most striking aspects of Yom Kippur is fasting. Traditionally, Jews don't eat or drink from the beginning of Yom Kippur until it ends. This means absolutely no food, water, or beverage is allowed on this day.

The purpose of fasting on Yom Kippur is not, as many believe, some kind of self-denial that allows a person to get teshuvah. Instead, the fast is intended to remind Jews to think only about matters of the spirit on Yom Kippur, and not on the physical world and personal needs. The hungrier and thirstier they become, the harder and deeper they must focus their souls on the difficult tasks of this solemn day. The fast is intended to help this process, not serve as a punishment.

 ASK THE RABBI

What if I really can't fast? The greatest mitzvah in Judaism is pekuach nefesh—the saving of a life. So if you're unable to fast due to a medical condition like diabetes, or you need to eat and drink with medicine, you are not allowed to fast on Yom Kippur.

Traditionally, every Jew nine years and older is required to fast on Yom Kippur, along with obeying all the other restrictions associated with Shabbat and festivals which apply to this day, too. Not everyone can make it to the end. It's hard to go without food, and especially water, for about 25 hours! Even if one can make it only part of the day, until he or she really, physically can't do any more, it's mitzvah to fast on Yom Kippur.

Day of Prayer

Jews traditionally spend the entire day of Yom Kippur in prayer, stopping only to sleep at night and take a few short breaks. It's not a day for entertainment or luxury, so traditionally, Jews don't wear leather, engage in sexual relations, or even wash, bathe, or use makeup. Some Jews wear white throughout the day, in accordance with the aforementioned verse in Isaiah asking God to make our sins "as white as snow." (Isaiah 1:18) There is a special white garment like a robe, called a *kittel*, that some Jews wear on Yom Kippur.

The evening service is called *Kol Nidrei*, named after a special prayer said only on this night. This prayer asks God to forgive Jews for any vows they made in the past year that they couldn't fulfill, that they didn't even realize they had made, that they made under pressure, or that they made when they weren't completely thinking about what they were saying. The haunting melody of this prayer is one of its most notable features, and some Reform synagogues add a cello or other soulful musical instruments to intensify the emotion of the prayer.

WORTH NOTING

The melody for **Kol Nidrei** is so dramatic it was used as the climatic moment for the first movie with sound, The Jazz Singer.

The prayers throughout Yom Kippur focus on the requirements of teshuvah. These prayers include the *Vidui*, a confession of the sins Jews have committed, and *Selichot*, petitions for forgiveness.

The afternoon service often recounts the entire history of the Jewish people. It's followed by *Yizkor*, the remembrance of those who have died, particularly those who have passed away in the last year.

Finally, the day ends with *Neilah*, which includes one last confession and request for forgiveness. The uplifting prayers end with the proclamation that God has forgiven the people as the Gates of Righteousness, open to receive the prayers of the people on Rosh HaShanah, close. Finally, the prayers of the day end with a loud and long shofar blast.

But the day is not over until Jews have a gathering to "break-the-fast," eating and drinking for the first time in a full day.

The Least You Need to Know

- Rosh HaShanah and Yom Kippur are the most important days in the Jewish calendar, except for Shabbat. They are called "The High Holy Days."
- Rosh HaShanah is the Jewish New Year commemorating the creation of the world more than 5,700 years ago. It's a day of prayer praising God for God's dominion over the world.
- One of the most notable parts of Rosh HaShanah is the blowing of the shofar, the hollowed horn of an animal, usually a ram.
- Yom Kippur is a day of prayer and fasting on which we complete the process of seeking teshuvah ("return, forgiveness") for the times we "missed the mark" of being the best people we can be.

CHAPTER 11

It's a Pilgrimage!

The Jewish calendar preserves the centrality of worship at the Temple in Jerusalem by its inclusion and recasting of three festivals. Tradition says that in ancient times when the Temple stood, Jews would travel to Jerusalem and offer sacrifices on these three holidays. These festivals together are called *shelosh regalim*, the three pilgrimages.

The pilgrimage festivals have their origin in the Torah as they are mentioned in both Exodus and Deuteronomy. The names of the festivals changed slightly from Exodus to Deuteronomy, and those found in the latter book are more commonly used today. As discussed in the Talmud and later rabbinic literature, these festivals are *Pesach*, known in English as "Passover," *Shavuot*, and *Sukkot*.

In This Chapter

- Common elements of the three pilgrimage festivals
- Celebrating the redemption from Egyptian slavery on Pesach
- Commemorating the revelation of the Torah on Shavuot
- Rejoicing in thanksgiving on Sukkot

Common Aspects of the Festivals

Traditionally, all these festivals are times of prayer, special customs, and great symbolism. One of the festivals, Shavuot, occurs over two days according to the traditional calendar and one day according to the Reform and Israeli calendar. The other two festivals occur over a longer period of about a week, with the beginning and ending days deemed the height of the holiday with greater observances than the "ordinary" days of the holiday called *chol hamoeid*. The halachah prohibits work on the heightened days of the festivals, but allows it on chol hamoeid.

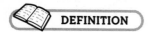 **DEFINITION**

Chol hamoeid, the intermediate days of the festivals of Pesach and Sukkot, is distinguished from the first and last days of the festival, where there are greater observances and requirements and an abstention from work.

Jews customarily give tzedakah during these festivals, reaching out to the poor and less fortunate. Just as the Israelites made offerings to God at the Temple as part of the idea of pilgrimage, Jews give to people in need during these festivals, recognizing that all people are created in God's image.

The Three Themes of Each Festival

Each of these festivals has three distinct themes. Each commemorates or recalls a specific important time in ancient Jewish history. Each accordingly connects a theological meaning to the festival, celebrating one of the three primary roles Jewish thought attributes to God as detailed in Chapter 1. Each festival also incorporates an agricultural meaning, reflecting the ancient roots of these holidays.

Yizkor

One common aspect of the worship of all these festivals is *Yizkor,* a memorial service in which Jews recall and honor those in their families who have died.

The Yizkor service has several distinct prayers, many of which are also used in a Jewish funeral. Psalms are read, particularly Psalm 23, which speaks of God as a Shepherd protecting people from enemies and fear "even as we walk in the valley of the shadow of death." Another distinctive prayer with a similar theme is *Eil Malei Rachamin,* which describes how God, in mercy, takes the departed into the "shelter of God's wings," protecting those who have died. A special prayer of memory also called Yizkor is recited. Finally, the participants recite *Kaddish Yatom,* the prayer said to praise God for the gift of life, which we discuss in Chapter 17.

Pesach (Passover)

The festival of Pesach is named for the sacrifice of a lamb formerly performed at the Temple during this holiday. Pesach literally means "passing over," referring to an important part of the Biblical story of the Israelites in Egypt commemorated by this holiday when the Angel of Death "passed over" the homes of the Israelites during the last plague God sent to the Egyptians who had enslaved them.

Exodus 12:17-18 contains the first mention of the mitzvah to observe this festival, requiring Jews to eat unleavened bread in remembrance of God's liberation of the Israelites from Egyptian bondage. The Torah sets the observance for seven days, and establishes it as a commandment for all generations forever.

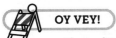 **OY VEY!**

The traditional Jewish calendar extends the festival to eight days to ensure its celebration in the Diaspora on the same days as in Israel. The Israeli and Reform observances last the seven days described in the Torah.

Pesach is one of the most widely maintained observances in Judaism. Even Jews who don't regularly keep Shabbat are likely to participate in at least one of the festive meals of the holiday observance. The traditions and rites of Pesach connect Jews to family and heritage in a greater way than perhaps any other Jewish observance.

The Meaning of Passover

Pesach is a holiday steeped in historical meaning described in the Torah. Following the events in Genesis, the Israelites lived in Egypt. The Book of Exodus begins by telling that a new king, called a Pharaoh, rose to power in Egypt. The Egyptians became afraid that Israelites living with them had grown too strong and too numerous, so they enslaved them.

The Pharaoh feared that slavery wasn't enough to keep the Israelites in line, so he ordered the death of any Israelite baby boys. One Israelite mother put her son in a basket on the river where Pharaoh's daughter found him. She decided to raise him as her own, calling him Moses.

Moses grew up in the Pharaoh's palace. One day he saw an Egyptian beating an Israelite slave to death. Moses intervened, eventually killing the Egyptian. Fearing repercussions, Moses ran away and became a shepherd. However, this occupation did not last, as God called to Moses from a miraculous burning bush that was not consumed. God told Moses to return to Egypt and tell the Pharaoh to let God's people, the Israelites, go free.

Moses went to Pharaoh and told him what God had said. The Pharaoh refused to let the slaves go. God then sent 10 plagues upon the Egyptians to convince Pharaoh to free the Israelites. For the last plague, God sent the Angel of Death to kill all the firstborn male children of the Egyptians. The Israelites placed lamb's blood on their doorposts to indicate to the Angel of Death that the residents were not Egyptian, and the Angel "passed over" these houses. After this final plague, Pharaoh relented and the Israelites finally received their freedom and fled Egypt.

Pesach commemorates this event in Jewish history. The practices and rituals are designed for Jews to symbolically relive and experience the terrible burden of slavery, and to feel that God brought them personally out of Egypt to freedom. The festival embodies the theological meaning of God as Redeemer.

Agriculturally, Pesach also celebrates springtime and the renewal of the earth. Many of the Pesach symbols praise the passing of the cold and storms of winter. The festival marks the first planting of grains and crops.

Matzah and Not Eating Leaven

The most notable way Jews observe the entire festival of Pesach is not eating anything leavened. Anything leavened or otherwise unacceptable for eating during Pesach is called *chameitz*. Jews eat special unleavened bread called *matzah* throughout Pesach instead of ordinary bread. This practice derives from the section of the Exodus story that tells about how the Israelites, when finally allowed to leave Egypt, were worried that the Pharaoh would change his mind and keep them in slavery. They rushed to pack any belongings they had. They couldn't make ordinary bread for the journey because they felt they didn't have time to let the dough sit and rise. They baked the bread without this step, resulting in unleavened bread that looks and tastes like a cracker. The Torah commands Jews to eat only this type of bread during Pesach.

The restriction against eating leaven applies to anything containing wheat, rye, oats, and spelt. If any product containing these grains has been given time to rise and hasn't been supervised and approved by a rabbi, it isn't acceptable for eating during Pesach.

In accordance with Exodus 12:15, many Jews remove all the chameitz from their homes before the festival begins. Some families make this an elaborate ritual called "*bekidat chameitz*—the search for leaven." The family scours and cleans the house, removing all the chameitz. A few crumbs are left conspicuously on a countertop or table, and at the end of the search, the area is examined with a candle, and the remaining crumbs are swept into a spoon with a feather to be burned or scattered to the wind. Many Jews use an entirely different set of dishes during Pesach to avoid the possibility that they eat even a crumb of chameitz.

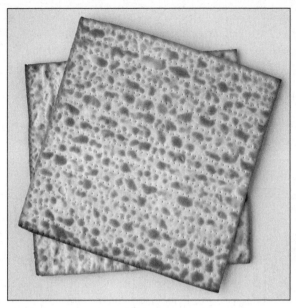

Matzah.

There are differences among Jews as to what matzah is acceptable to eat during Pesach. The strictest level is called *shmurah matzah,* meaning "watched or guarded matzah." The production of shmurah matzah is carefully supervised to ensure that the flour used has no time to rise, and no leavened elements can possibly enter the process. The production of ordinary, non-shmurah matzah is also carefully regulated, but not to the same standard. Jews can find other types of matzah in supermarkets with additions such as egg that some rabbis find acceptable to eat during pesach and others don't unless this is the only type of matzah a person can digest.

ASK THE RABBI

What if a Jew has a large amount of chameitz or doesn't want to throw away lots of good food? Some Jews arrange to constructively sell their chameitz to a non-Jew for the duration of Pesach. They must set aside the chameitz in a defined area, and a special contract is used. The halachah deems such sold chameitz as not owned by the Jew during the festival, and therefore not an issue.

There is a significant difference between Ashkenazic and Sephardic law about chameitz. There's a category of foods called *kitniyot,* which are foods that swell when cooked, such as rice or legumes. Because these foods appear to rise, Ashkenazic halachah considers them chameitz. Sephardic halachah doesn't, so Sephardic Jews may eat some foods that Ashkenazic can't during

Pesach. To avoid difficulties and confusion, the halachah specifically states that a Jew who ordinarily considers himself Ashkenazi can't become Sephardic for Pesach to take advantage of the more lenient requirements.

The Pesach Meal—The Seder

The primary celebration of Pesach is a ritualized festive meal called a *Seder*. Seder means "order," reflecting an established series of prayers, customs, and practices performed as part of the meal. A Seder is usually celebrated at home, and involves a gathering of family and friends. It's a custom to invite guests to the Seder, as the liturgy of the evening says, "Let those who are hungry come and eat." Traditionally, Jews have S*ederim* (the plural of Seder) on the first and second nights of the festival.

> **WORTH NOTING**
>
> The earliest Seder described in the Mishnah resembles an Ancient Greek or Roman symposium meal. The Seder did not appear in the basic form recognizable today until the seventh or eighth century C.E.

The primary purpose of the Seder is to tell the story of the Exodus from Egypt. The book containing the prayers and rituals of the Seder is called a *Haggadah*, which means "the telling (of the story)." According to the Haggdah, every participant should feel as if he or she actually was a slave in Egypt, and that God personally redeemed him or her from bondage. For that reason, participants traditionally recline or sit on a pillow at the Seder, reflecting the idea that a free people have the ability to be comfortable.

Although all *Haggadot* (the plural of Haggadah) contain the same basic prayers and customs, they vary widely. Many contain beautiful artwork, and include creative ways to tell the story and promote the interest and involvement of participants of all ages. A lively Seder will often diverge from the Haggadah to consider modern issues and topics and discuss different interpretations of the Exodus story.

The beginning of the Seder is designed to present the meal in a different and unique way to prompt a child to ask, "Why is this night different than other nights?" This gives the adults the excuse to tell the story of the Exodus. The origin of this custom comes from Exodus 12:26-27, which says, "It will be when your children say to you, 'What does this worship mean to you?' then you will say to them, 'It is the Passover sacrifice to God ....'"

In the earliest known Seder described in the Mishnah, the unusual customs of the meal hopefully caused the child to ask what was happening. If the child didn't ask, the parent would prompt the child to ask a particular set of questions. The Seder eventually evolved to require the youngest child who was able to recite a standard set of questions without expecting the unique customs to pique the child's curiosity. The recitation of these questions by the youngest child or children present at the Seder remains a standard and beloved custom for many Jewish families.

An illuminated Haggadah laid out in an older style.

The Seder furthers the tradition of the inquisitive child by explaining that there are four types of children. The first is the wise child, who knows to ask the questions about the Seder and has deep interest in the answers and all they imply. The second is the wicked child, who asks what all the customs mean to the parents but doesn't see any meaning in them for him or her. The third is simple, and genuinely asks what needs to be done but doesn't have interest in the deep meaning of the Seder. The fourth child doesn't even know if he or she should ask any questions. The inclusion of the four children in the Seder is a metaphor for all participants, for we all act as each of the children at different times in our lives.

Another important observance of the Seder is the drinking of four cups of wine or juice from a "fruit of the vine," usually grapes. These cups, the Jewish symbol of joy, correspond to the four promises of redemption found in Exodus 6:6-7, "I am Adonai, and I will bring you out from the servitude of Egypt, and I will deliver you from their bondage, and I will redeem you with an outstretched arm … and I will take you to Me as a people …."

ASK THE RABBI

The number four has come up often now in the discussion of the Seder. Is that coincidence? No, it's not. The number four is a special number for the Seder. Not only are there four children, four cups of wine, and four promises of redemption, but there are four questions asked by the child, a celebration of the four seasons, and a reference to Jews in the four corners of Earth. The repeated occurrence of sets of four is another signal that this meal is not ordinary.

The actual telling of the Exodus story contains several notable sections. Participants recite each of the plagues God sent upon the Egyptians to convince the Pharaoh to let the Israelite slaves go to freedom. Seder participants take a drop of wine from their glasses as each plague is mentioned, demonstrating the reduction in our joy that God had to impose such pain on the Egyptians to obtain our freedom.

Jews demonstrate their gratitude to God by reading a text and singing a song called *Dayeinu*, which means "it would have been enough for us." This text and song explains that if God had done only one thing for us "it would have been enough," but we are blessed that God did more. Then Jews say that next blessing "would have been enough," but God again did more, and the text and song continues.

OY VEY!

Although Moses has a leading role in the Exodus story, traditionally his name is not mentioned during the Seder. This is to ensure that participants acknowledge it wasn't Moses who brought the Israelites out of slavery, but God.

Another exciting feature of the Seder is the *afikomen*. Afikomen is the Greek word for "dessert." At the beginning of the Seder, the leader breaks a piece of the special bread for Pesach in half and wraps one half, now designated the afikomen, in a cloth. The children watch the leader through the Seder, and the leader tries to sneak away and hide it. After the eating of the main meal, the children go to look for the hidden half, because the Seder can't end without it. Whoever finds the afikomen receives a prize. There are many variations on this tradition, including one where every seeker receives a prize, one where the children cover their eyes as the afikomen is hidden, and one where the children hold the afikomen for ransom for its return.

DEFINITION

Afikomen means dessert, and specifically refers to a piece of matzah that the children present at the Seder must find or redeem to complete the meal.

Every Seder mentions Elijah the Prophet. In Jewish tradition, Elijah is the herald of the Messiah who comes to every Seder to reassure everyone that, eventually, the Messiah or Messianic Age will come. At that time, everyone in bondage or pain will be redeemed. The youngest child opens the door to welcome Elijah, and a special cup of wine, called Elijah's Cup, is set aside and designated for this extraordinary guest. Participants sing a song in Elijah's honor.

Some families have added an additional cup of clear water to the Seder, called a Miriam's Cup. This new custom draws on the midrash saying that whenever the freed Israelites camped, Miriam would be able to show them where to dig for fresh water. The inclusion of the Miriam's Cup is a way to recognize the contribution of women to Jewish history, a fact some find notably absent in the traditional texts.

After additional singing, the Seder ends with everyone saying, *"BaShanah ha'ba-ah b'Yirushalayim—* Next year in Jerusalem,"* representing the traditional Jewish hope for redemption and return to Israel as the Jewish homeland. Many Jews today don't long to leave their home countries and move to Israel, so this line is a reminder that everyone is a slave in one way or another to circumstance or pain, and expresses the hope that next year everyone will be free.

Pesach Symbols

The Seder tells the story of the Exodus not only through words and texts, but through a variety of symbols placed on the table. Many of these symbols are found on a special dish called a Seder plate.

A Seder plate.

One of these symbols is *karpas*, edible green plants such as parsley, which represents the spring-time renewal of Earth. This symbol, eaten at the beginning of the Seder, especially reinforces the agricultural meaning of the festival. Before eating the karpas, the participant dips karpas in saltwater, which represents the tears of the Israelite slaves suffering in their bondage.

Another symbol of the Israelites' slavery is *maror*, bitter herbs eaten to remind the participants of the bitterness of slavery. The Seder plate also contains a roasted egg, which represents both spring and the cycle of life, and the festival offering at the time of the Temple. Similarly, a roast lamb shank bone reminds participants of the special Pesach sacrifice made at the Temple. The shank bone also reminds participants of the lamb's blood placed on the Israelites' doorposts as a sign for the Angel of Death to pass over their homes in the final plague.

WORTH NOTING

The lamb shank reminds the participants of the Pesach sacrifice, but shouldn't be deemed as an actual sacrifice. A sacrifice can only take place in the Temple, which doesn't exist today. Many Seder leaders will not lift the shank bone when speaking about it, but will only point to it, to ensure that everyone understands that this symbol is a representation, not an actual sacrifice.

Throughout the Seder, participants eat *charoset*. Charoset is a combination of fruit, nuts, wine, honey, and seasoning mixed together to resemble the mortar the Israelites used to construct the Egyptians' buildings. In the United States, most charoset is made with apples and walnuts. This symbol has the widest variation in taste and appearance, as there are many recipes for charoset reflecting the different areas of the world in which Jews have lived.

Ashkenazic and Sephardic charoset with matzah.

At the Seder, the leader sets aside three special pieces of matzah for the ceremony. Two represent the bread used in the Temple, and one represents the festival itself. These are broken and eaten at various times at the Seder. Some Jews add a fourth ceremonial matzah to represent people who still are not free.

Scriptural Readings

Congregations read *Shir HaShirim* during Pesach in the synagogue. This poem of love attributed to King Solomon is viewed as an allegory of God's love for the people of Israel. God's redemption of the people from slavery is viewed as a result of that love. Shir HaShirim also prominently features springtime images, reflecting the agricultural meaning of the festival.

Shavuot

The second of the pilgrimage festivals is *Shavuot,* which literally means "weeks." This name reflects that Shavuot occurs seven weeks, or a "week of weeks" following the start of Pesach.

The festival is mentioned several times in the Torah. Exodus 34:22 says, "You shall observe the Feast of Weeks of the first harvest of wheat." Numbers 28:26 and Deuteronomy 16:9-10 contain similar commands to observe this festival.

Unlike Pesach and Sukkot, Shavuot occurs over two days in the traditional Jewish calendar as opposed to the longer observances of the other festivals. The Reform and Israeli calendars shorten the observance of Shavuot to one day.

The Meaning of Shavuot

Shavuot marks the day when Moses received the Torah from God at Mount Sinai. This historical meaning corresponds to the theological meaning of God as Revealer of the Law. This festival also has the agricultural meaning of a celebration of the first harvest of quick-growing crops following the end of winter. This event was especially important in ancient days before refrigeration and modern food transportation and preservation. The communities often needed the fresh food as they had exhausted the stores they had used through the winter, making the first harvest a reason to rejoice.

Counting the Omer

Jews traditionally count the seven weeks leading to Shavuot. This period is called the *omer,* so the practice is commonly called "counting the omer." The counting begins on the second day of Pesach and continues for 49 days, with the fiftieth day being Shavuot.

The omer is a time of semi-mourning, perhaps reflecting the uncertainty of the freed Israelite slaves from the time they left Egypt to the receipt of the Torah at Mount Sinai. No weddings traditionally take place during this period. The one exception to this is the thirty-third day of the omer, called l*ag b'omer.* The word *"lag"* comes from the letters that represent the number 33 in the Hebrew numeric system. According to legend, the students of the Talmudic sage Rabbi Akiva were suffering from a plague that abated on this day. It's possible that this day marked the celebration of a military victory in the final revolt against Rome called the Bar Kochba rebellion in 132 C.E. Children traditionally go to parks and play games with bows and arrows on this day, supporting this theory.

> **WORTH NOTING**
>
> The Hebrew numeric system predates the Arabic numerals. Hebrew uses the letters of its alphabet to represent numbers. The first letter, *aleph*, is 1; the second, *beit*, is 2, and so on. The tenth letter, *yod*, is 10; the eleventh letter, *kaf*, is 20, and so on. The numbers therefore are also words that can be pronounced, as seen by *"lag b'omer—* the 33rd day of the omer."

It's a custom to study the ethical passages of *Pirkei Avot*, the unique section of the Talmud containing ethical sayings of the sages, during the days of the omer.

Scriptural Readings

Congregations read the Ten Commandments and the giving of the Torah as found in Exodus during Shavuot, reflecting the historical and theological celebration of revelation. Traditionally, congregants stand through the reading of these passages, as the Torah says all the people stood at Sinai when Moses brought them the Law.

Congregations also read from the Book of Ruth during Shavuot. The events in the book take place during the barley harvest that the festival also celebrates. Also, Ruth is the story of a woman who accepts the Covenant with God, just as the Israelites accepted the Covenant at Mount Sinai.

Shavuot Customs

Many Jews participate in *Tikkun Leil Shavuot*, which means a night of study of Torah, which takes place during the holiday. Participants study Torah late into the night, with some studying all the way to sunrise.

It's also a tradition to eat dairy foods during Shavuot. The sweetness of dairy reflects the sweetness of Torah study, giving a spiritual meaning to the food eaten during this festival.

Sukkot

The third pilgrimage festival, *Sukkot*, literally means "booths." Like Pesach and Shavuot, the Torah commands its observance in Leviticus 23:34 and Deuteronomy 16:13. Unlike the other two, the Torah specifically calls Sukkot *"zman simchateinu*—the time of our rejoicing." It's especially important for Jews to celebrate this festival with joy.

Like Pesach, Sukkot is eight days in the traditional Orthodox calendar, and seven days in the Israeli and Reform calendars. In the traditional calendar, the eighth day is a celebration called *Shmini Atzeret,* and the next day is *Simchat Torah,* both described in a later section. In the Reform calendar, the eighth day is celebrated as both Shmini Atzeret and Simchat Torah.

The Meaning of Sukkot

Sukkot has the strongest agricultural connection of the three pilgrimage festivals. It celebrates the primary harvest, giving thanks to God for the bounty of the land. The corresponding theological meaning of the festival praises God for creating the earth and giving people sustenance through continual creation.

The distinctive feature of Sukkot is the booths, or temporary structures, that Jews use during this festival. These booths may be traced historically to the temporary dwellings in which the Israelites resided during their 40-year sojourn through the desert after receiving the Torah and before entering the Promised Land. (Leviticus 23:42-43) Later, the Israelites in the Promised Land also lived in booths near their fields during the harvest to maximize the time they had to reap their fields.

Building a Sukkah

The commandments concerning Sukkot require Jews to reside in a *sukkah* (the singular of sukkot) for the duration of the holiday. Some Jews eat, sleep, and fully reside in their sukkah for the entire festival. Others only eat their meals in the structure.

The important feature of a sukkah is that it's a temporary structure. Its fragility reminds Jews of the tenuousness of life, which reminds them to be grateful for all the blessings they enjoy. Generally, the walls of a sukkah aren't solid, but a frame structure perhaps covered with canvas or latticework. The *halachah* allows the building of a sukkah using one permanent wall, such as the wall of a house, but no more. The people in the sukkah must be able to see the sky and stars through its unfinished roof, which is often partially covered with stalks or branches that have been grown from the ground, called *skach*. Children often decorate the walls of the sukkah with fruit, vegetables, grains, gourds, or other colorful adornments.

It's a mitzvah to welcome guests called *ushpizin* into a sukkah for meals and to spend time together. Hospitality and sharing reflect the themes of thanksgiving and gratitude to God central to the festival.

Sukkot Symbols

Sukkot has special symbols called the *arba'ah minim*, or four species, which are used throughout the festival. One is the *etrog*, a bumpy yellow citron grown especially for the festival. Traditional Jews consider the larger, more symmetrical and more elaborate *etrogim* of greater value for *hiddur mitzvah*, the beautification of the mitzvah. The etrog has a stem called a *pitom*, which must remain undamaged and unbroken to keep the etrog usable for the festival.

The remaining of the arba'ah minim are branches from three trees bound together to make a ritual object called a *lulav*. The three branches that comprise a lulav come from the palm, myrtle, and willow trees.

> **WORTH NOTING**
>
> Each of the arba'ah minim represent a part of the body. The etrog is the approximate size and shape of a heart. The palm branch resembles the spine. The willow leaf looks like lips and the myrtle leaf looks like an eye. The items together represent a person's entire body and being, combining everything a person feels, acts, says, and sees in gratitude to God.

It's a mitzvah to hold the etrog and lulav together in the sukkah, say a blessing, and waive them in every direction—in front of the waiver, behind, right, left, above, and below. This represents the presence of God throughout the world, and celebrates that God created all that may be found in every direction.

Scriptural Readings

Congregations traditionally read *Kohelet* during the festival of Sukkot. Like the sukkah itself, Kohelet reminds Jews that life is fragile and impermanent, and it is important to feel gratitude for the blessings they receive from God during life.

Ending Sukkot—Shmini Atzeret/Simchat Torah

In Leviticus 23:36, the Torah calls for a special celebration on the eighth day after Sukkot begins. This is called Shmini Atzeret, literally meaning "the gathering on the eighth (day)." Shmini Atzeret is a day of prayer and refraining from work.

The following day in the traditional calendar is Simchat Torah, literally meaning the "joy of the Torah." During this celebration, the congregation reads the last part of the Torah describing Moses' death, then immediately reads the beginning of the Torah detailing the creation of the world. The important aspect of these readings is the demonstration that the study and reading of the Torah never truly ends, but continues over and over again throughout time.

Simchat Torah is a joyous holiday, as participants carry all the congregation's Torah scrolls throughout the synagogue, and sometimes into the street. Worshippers dance with the Torah in seven circles. Some congregations celebrate Consecration with the students who are beginning their religious studies. Often, children receive special flags to wave as part of the dancing. A modern custom in many congregations has become to unwind the entire Torah scroll so the participants may see all the different sections.

Congregations following the traditional calendar observe Shmini Atzeret on the eighth day following the beginning of Sukkot, and Simchat Torah on the ninth day. Reform congregations combine the observance of Shmini Atzeret and Simchat Torah together on the eighth day.

The Least You Need to Know

- Jews celebrate three pilgrimage festivals when the ancient Israelites would bring sacrifices to the Temple. Each festival has a historical, theological, and agricultural meaning.
- Pesach, or Passover, commemorates God's redemption of the Israelites from Egyptian slavery and the first planting of the season.
- Observance of Pesach is a festive dinner held at home called a Seder. The Seder attempts to make participants feel as if God redeemed them personally from slavery by telling the Exodus story.
- Shavuot commemorates God's revelation of the Torah at Mount Sinai, and gives thanks for the first harvest of the season.
- Sukkot commemorates the Israelites' residence in temporary booths during their 40-year journey through the desert. Sukkot is a harvest festival, giving thanks to God for creating Earth's bounty.

They Tried to Harm Us, They Failed, Let's Eat!

The title of this chapter is taken from a repeated joke said about Jewish holidays. It seems to many that Jewish holidays follow this pattern—someone tries to kill us, we survive, then we celebrate. Actually, this holds true completely for only two holidays: *Chanukkah* and *Purim*. These two holidays are the most joyous and fun in the Jewish calendar, so perhaps this is why some Jews hold this image.

Chanukkah and Purim are considered minor observances. This may be because they developed later in Jewish history. It might be because they commemorate political and military victories, and the Talmudic rabbis wanted us to focus on spiritual concerns. They also might have felt it was dangerous for the powerful secular authorities to see us celebrating such nonreligious triumphs. The two might also be considered minor because ordinary work is not forbidden on these days, or perhaps ordinary work is not forbidden on these days because they are minor!

Whatever the reason, Chanukkah and Purim hold similar positions in Jewish observance—minor days with major, popular celebrations.

Food plays an important part in these holidays, but we'll look at the special treats for Chanukkah and Purim in Chapter 20.

In This Chapter

- The celebration of freedom of Chanukkah
- Purim joy—Esther saves the Persian Jews
- The lighting of the chanukkiah
- Games, fun, and celebration
- Mishloach manot—helping the needy

Chanukkah

The first thing any rabbi will tell you about Chanukkah is that it should not be confused or associated with Christmas. The two holidays have entirely different meanings and standing in their respective religions. Both use lights, which is standard practice for most religious holidays occurring in the middle of winter. Other than that, there's no similarity. It's only their timing that makes many people associate the two in their minds.

The meaning of Chanukkah itself rejects this association. The entire point of the holiday is the assertion that we have the right to exist and practice our religion without being forced to adopt practices from other religions that are contrary to our beliefs. Chanukkah originated at a time when Jews wrestled with questions about this aspect of their identity in the most dramatic ways, in 168 to 165 B.C.E.

The Story of Chanukkah

During these years, the kingdom of Judea was caught between two empires—Egypt and Assyria. Control and influence over Judea went back and forth between these two great powers. At this time, Assyria had control over Judea. The king of Assyria, Antiochus IV, began to try to change the Jews' religion. He banned Torah study, circumcision, and Shabbat observance. He installed idols in the Temple and required pagan sacrifices of pigs, a nonkosher animal, to occur there. It's likely Antiochus wanted to solidify his empire by establishing a uniform Hellenized culture and religion within it.

Some Jews liked the changes and adopted the Hellenistic practices themselves. Antiochus had no trouble finding a Hellenized Jew to become the High Priest in the Temple. Other Jews rejected the efforts, and saw these actions as an attempt to wipe out their religion. One village priest in Modi'in named Mattathias refused to adopt Antiochus' changes, and led a revolt against his forces. He died during the revolt, but his sons continued, becoming known as the *"Maccabees,"* which means "hammer." The strongest of Mattathias' sons was Judah Maccabee, and Judah continued the revolt.

 **DEFINITION**

> **Maccabee** may not only mean "hammer," but also may be an anagram for an important verse in the Tanach the Israelites sang after crossing the Red Sea. The verse states, *"Mi Chamocha Ba'eilim Adonai?*—Who is like You, Adonai, among the gods that are worshipped?"

The revolt of the Maccabees was both a war against Assyria and a civil war, as assimilated, Hellenized Jews challenged them as well. Nevertheless, the Maccabees prevailed and recaptured the Temple. They removed the pagan statues and alters, and purified the Temple. It's from this action that Chanukkah receives its name, as Chanukkah means "rededication." The cleansing of the Temple occurred on the anniversary of the day when the Assyrians began to use it for pagan worship, the 25th day of Kislev, which became the first day of the holiday.

The story of the celebration of Chanukkah extends beyond these historical events. It's clear that the rabbis of the Mishnah and Talmud give a lower priority to this holiday, and it's notable that the Book of Maccabees is not included in the Tanach. Instead, the Talmud contains the midrashic story that became the well-accepted miracle of Chanukkah.

According to the Talmud, while rededicating the Temple, the Maccabees searched for the sanctified, holy oil used to light the *ner tamid*—the eternal light. This light was always kept burning above the ark at the alter, and represented the continuity of God's Presence. The Maccabees found only a small jar of oil that they knew would last only one day. It would take time to produce more of the proper oil. The Maccabees decided to light the ner tamid for the rededication anyway. The little jar of oil miraculously lasted eight days until more oil could be produced! (Talmud Bavli, Shabbat 21b)

ASK THE RABBI

Why is Chanukkah eight days? There are three possible reasons. One is the story of the miracle of the oil. Another is that the Book of Maccabees says the rededication took eight days. (I Maccabees 4:52-59) A third is that Chanukkah was a way to celebrate the eight-day festival of Sukkot (discussed in Chapter 11), which the Maccabees had not been able to do while the Assyrians controlled the Temple.

By emphasizing this story, the rabbis changed Chanukkah's meaning from a celebration of a human victory to a celebration of God's power. They furthered this by requiring a particular part of the Book of Zechariah to be read on the holiday that says everything happens, "'Not by might, not by power, but by My spirit,' says the God of Hosts." (Zechariah 4:6) However, even with these efforts, the human element still remained in the story, providing a possible reason why the rabbis diminished the holiday's importance.

Another possible reason for the diminishing of Chanukkah may be the history that followed the revolt. The Maccabees, also known as the Hasmoneans, ruled Judea for about 80 years following the war with Assyria. The Hasmoneans were brutal to their opponents and also poor leaders, eventually falling to Rome. It's possible the Rabbis did not want to glorify such failed leadership.

Lighting the Chanukkiah

Whatever the reasons for the rabbis' attempt to diminish Chanukkah, the attempt largely failed. Chanukkah is one of the more widely celebrated Jewish holidays. Its observance occurs mostly at home with the lighting of the *chanukkiah*.

A chanukkiah lit for the eighth night of Chanukkah.

A chanukkiah is a nine-branched candelabra. Eight of the branches each represent one of the days of the holiday. The ninth is the *shamas,* or helper candle, which is used to light the others. Jews place a candle in one of the eight daily branches of the chanukkiah for each night of the holiday—one for the first day, two for the second day, and so on. They place the candles in the chanukkiah from right to left, and light them from left to right.

The lighting of the chanukkiah happens each night at sundown. According to the Talmud, it should be lit outside. If it can't be lit outside due to weather, it should be lit so it's visible through a window. It may be lit in an enclosed room if its public display might be dangerous due to threats from the secular government or population, which Jews have encountered throughout their history.

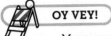 **OY VEY!**

Many people call the chanukkiah a *menorah*. Technically, a menorah is any multi-branched candelabra used for religious worship. A chanukkiah is a specific type of menorah used for Chanukkah. There is another important type of menorah in Judaism, as we will see in Chapter 23, so it's most accurate to call the one we use on Chanukkah a chanukkiah.

Three prayers are said with the lighting of the chanukkiah. The first denotes that the lighting is being done in accordance with the commandment to perform this action. The second asserts God's splendor in performing miracles for the Jewish people. The third is the *Shehechiyanu*, which thanks God for giving Jews life, sustaining them, and enabling them to reach this time. The first two blessings are said every night. The Shehechiyanu is said only on the first night.

The lighting of the chanukkiah also is accompanied by singing. There are many festive songs both in Hebrew and English for Chanukkah. Then Jews eat *latkes, sufganiyot,* or other foods cooked in oil, as we'll discuss in Chapter 20.

Dreidel: The Special Game

Jews keep another Chanukkah tradition by playing a game with the *dreidel*. A dreidel is a four-sided top with a letter on each side that stands for a Hebrew word. In Israel, the letters are *nun, gimmel, hey,* and *pey,* which stand for *"Nes gadol hayah po*—a great miracle happened here." In the Diaspora, the *pey* is replaced by a *shin,* representing the word *"sham,"* which means "there."

Four identical dreidels, each showing a letter on one of its four sides with the letters as they appear on dreidels in the Diaspora.

In the game, each player is given the same number of candies, nuts, or some other small treat. Each player antes one of the treats into a pot, and the first player spins the dreidel. What happens next depends on the spin:

- *Gimmel:* The spinner takes the entire pot, and everyone antes again for the next spinner.

- *Nun:* The spinner gets nothing, and the next player takes a turn.

- *Hey:* The spinner takes half the pot, rounding up in case of an odd number, and the next player takes a turn.

- *Pey or Shin:* The spinner has to put one more treat into the pot.

The game continues until one player has all the treats, or everyone eats what they have.

Gelt and Gift Giving

Many Jews give gifts to family members on Chanukkah, especially to children. At one time, the gift was some coins called *gelt*, given to children on the fifth day. Today, manufacturers make gold and silver foil-covered chocolates in the shape of coins that are accepted as gelt. Some parents give their children a gift every night of Chanukkah, beginning with something small and ending with the largest to build anticipation.

Chocolate Chanukkah gelt.

There's no particular religious significance to the giving of gifts at Chanukkah, and it's likely this practice developed in reaction, and even in competition, to the giving of gifts at Christmas.

Purim

The second popular-but-minor celebration in the Jewish tradition is *Purim*. Unlike Chanukkah, the story of Purim is found in the Tanach, in the Book of Esther.

The Story of Purim

The events of the Book of Esther take place in Persia in a town called Shushan. King Achashveros decides he needs a new queen after Queen Vashti fails to follow his orders. Esther, the heroine of the story, becomes the new queen by winning a contest. Esther doesn't reveal to the king the fact that she's Jewish.

Haman is King Achashveros's prime minister, and is the villain of the story. Haman becomes angry with the Jews after Esther's uncle, Mordechai, refuses to bow down to him. Haman decides that he will kill all the Jews of Persia for this lack of respect. He draws lots, *"purim,"* to determine the date of the mass execution, and sets the date at the 14th of Adar, which eventually will become the day of the celebration.

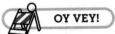 **OY VEY!**

Cities enclosed by walls like Jerusalem celebrate Purim on the 15th of Adar due to an aside in a note in Esther 9:18-19.

In the meantime, Mordechai reports a plot against the king, and the king places a note of this in his records. Later, Mordechai learns of Haman's intention to kill the Jews, and tells Esther she must act to save her people. Esther is afraid, since no one is allowed to go before the king without being summoned, under penalty of death. She knows how this king has dealt with disobedient queens. Mordechai convinces her to act, saying "Who knows? Perhaps you were placed in this position to save us all!"

Esther invites King Achashveros and Haman to a dinner where she reminds the king of Mordechai's loyalty in saving him. She then reveals that she's Jewish, and tells the details of Haman's nefarious plan. The king strips Haman of his power, and the Jews of Persia are saved.

The Schpiel

Unlike Chanukkah, the primary celebration of Purim takes place in the synagogue with the reading of the Book of Esther from a scroll called a *megillah*. This event is unlike any other reading of

Scripture in Jewish tradition. It's quite raucous, with lots of shouting and laughing. Haman's name is shouted down every time it's mentioned, and there are special loud noisemakers called *groggers* used to help in this task. Many congregations also cheer when Mordechai and Esther's names are mentioned.

A Purim grogger to make noise when Haman's name is mentioned during the reading of the megillah.

Some congregations have adopted the practice of telling the story through a skit called a *schpiel*. The schpiel is sometimes a simple retelling of the story. Sometimes the schpiel is adapted with a specific theme, with plenty of parody songs, costumes, and jokes. At non-Orthodox synagogues you might see the Purim story acted out as if it had happened in Hogwarts, with Mordechai and Haman competing over the "kiddush cup," or with songs sung to the melodies of a famous pop star. Purim is a night of fun, where almost anything can happen.

Purim finishes with the eating of a special pastry called *hamentashen*, which we'll discuss in Chapter 20.

Have a Drink? Another?

Purim is a night of outrageous behavior. Both children and adults dress in costume, sometimes as the characters of the story of the Book of Esther, and other times in any costume. Purim is a day when everything is seen to be upside down, and students often take the place of teachers. Some traditions have men dressing as women and vice versa. There's another Purim tradition that states that one should become drunk on the holiday.

 WORDS OF WISDOM

"On Purim it is a man's duty to inebriate himself to the point that he is unable to distinguish between the phrases 'cursed be Haman' and 'blessed be Mordechai.'" —Talmud Bavli, Megillah 7b

Judaism is a religion that usually favors moderation over excesses, so Purim is outstanding for the wild behavior exhibited in some communities. It's clear that the celebration must remain responsible even while being outlandish, and no one is permitted to get so out of control that anyone is harmed. This can be a fine line, and communities need to watch members to make sure the celebration doesn't get out of hand.

Mishloach Manot—Baskets of Love

More seriously, there's a tradition of bringing baskets of food to the elderly and the poor on Purim. These baskets are called *mishloach manot*—"the sending of servings." Traditional practice requires that each mishloach manot contain at least two types of food that require no preparation, but are ready to eat immediately.

There are two reasons for this custom. The first is to ensure that everyone has the opportunity to celebrate joyously and with enough food on the special day of Purim. The requirements of the included food enact this purpose, since the recipient doesn't have to work to eat the gift, and having more than one type of food is considered a luxury. The second reason for this custom is to refute an accusation by Haman that Jews don't get along with each other. The act of caring represented by the mishloach manot strikes another blow against Haman and everything he stands for in the story.

The Least You Need to Know

- Chanukkah and Purim are two similar minor holidays in the Jewish tradition that honor military or political victories in which someone tried to harm the Jewish people, yet they survived.

- Chanukkah is a minor holiday although its practice is widespread, likely due to its proximity to Christmas. It commemorates the victory of the Maccabees over the Assyrians in 165 B.C.E., celebrating the Jews' ability to practice their religion without outside interference.

- Chanukkah is celebrated in the home with the lighting of the chanukkiah, singing, the playing of dreidel, and gift giving.

- Purim commemorates the events in the Book of Esther, in which the Jews of Persia were saved from the genocidal intentions of Haman. It's celebrated with a raucous reading of the book.

More Days of Our Jewish Lives

Everyone in the United States knows the big American holidays. We're all very familiar with Thanksgiving, the Fourth of July, and Presidents' Day. But there are other holidays most American citizens don't think about as much. Is anyone really aware of Flag Day or Arbor Day? How many people born after 1960 notice when it's Pearl Harbor Day? It's not that these holidays are unimportant. They simply don't have the following, awareness, or observance the other, more major American holidays have. A similar thing happens in the Jewish calendar.

There are so many observances in the Jewish calendar beyond the holidays we've already discussed. Some are ancient practices, while others are modern innovations. Jews widely observe some holidays, while others are commemorated by only a few. Some are especially relevant for the State of Israel. This chapter will explore the dates you may see on a Jewish calendar that we have not yet discussed.

In This Chapter

- Starting a month and a holiday for trees
- Remembering the tragedies
- Observances of modern events
- Other celebrations and commemorations

Rosh Chodesh: The Beginning of the Month

As you've learned, the Jewish calendar relies upon the cycle of the months determined by the revolution of the moon around the Earth. In ancient times, observers would view the moon and declare when the new month had arrived. The news was conveyed throughout Israel by the blowing of shofarot that resonated from hill to hill.

The start of a new month became a cause for celebration. The psalms of praise of Hallel are said in synagogue, and a special Torah portion, Numbers 28:1-15, is read. There are also traditionally special additions to the prayers at the daily service.

Rosh Chodesh has evolved to become a women's celebration, likely through the connection of the phases of the moon with the menstrual cycle. Women's groups take this opportunity to gather, study, and pray.

Tu Bishvat—The New Year of Trees

Tu Bishvat is the new year of trees that marked the beginning of the year for the calculation of tithes (the tax of one tenth of a harvest) of fruit in the time of the Temple. It's one of the four new years identified in the Mishnah at Rosh HaShanah 1:1. It occurs on the 15th day of the month of *Shevat.*

> **WORTH NOTING**
>
> Many Jewish holidays are known by their date in the calendar. This takes advantage of the fact that the Jewish counting system predates Arabic numerals. As we've seen, the ancient Hebrews used letters for numerals—the first letter, *aleph*, was 1; the second, *beit*, was 2; and so on. Words therefore received numerical equivalents, and numbers became words. Tu is made from the letters representing 15—*tet* (9) and *vav* (6)—added to make 15, the Tu in Tu Bishvat.

Why Celebrate Trees?

There's a story in the Talmud about a man named Honi. Honi was walking along a path when he approached an old man planting a carob tree sapling. He laughed because he knew the old man would never live to enjoy the fruit from the tree. He continued to walk and felt dizzy. He turned around and saw the tree was now large, and people gathered around it to harvest its fruit. He realized he had slept for 70 years, and appreciated the gift the old man had given to others. Honi dedicated the rest of his life to planting carob trees in Israel. (Talmud Bavli, Ta'anit 23a)

Trees are extremely important to our well-being, and especially important in Israel. In a land that can easily become desert, their fruit, shade, and ability to keep the land together with their roots are essential. This explains why trees merit their own celebration in Jewish tradition. Trees garner so much respect that one midrash even says if you are planting a tree and you hear that the *Mashiach* has come, you must finish planting the tree first and only then go to greet the Mashiach. (Avot deRabbi Natan 31)

This midrash also actually teaches that the trees of Israel reciprocate this appreciation. At creation, other trees wanted to grow in lush valleys or hillsides with lots of sun. The dates, olives, and other trees asked God to plant them in a small, dry land so they could help Israel.

Tu Bishvat Observance

Some Jews observe Tu Bishvat with a Seder similar to the festive meal at Pesach. This custom originated with Kabbalists in the sixteenth century. Participants drink four cups of wine or juice. They start with white wine for the first cup, mix a little red into white for the second, mix a little white with mostly red for the third, and end with all red. This represents the changing seasons. Jews also eat different kinds of fruits, especially those grown in Israel. Each category of fruit—fruits wholly eaten, fruits with pits, fruits with hard shells—receives a different spiritual interpretation. Like a Pesach Seder, this Seder includes singing and fun.

Another custom observed by many Jews is the planting of trees in Israel. The State of Israel has succeeded in large part due to massive efforts to plant trees in the land. Huge forests exist today where none had been for centuries, and Israelis and Jews receive news of a forest fire with particular dismay. Tu Bishvat has grown into a determination in modern times to preserve and protect these forests and the entire ecology of Israel.

 ASK THE RABBI

How do Jews outside Israel plant trees in Israel on Tu Bishvat? Many Jews arrange for the planting of trees in Israel through the Jewish National Fund. They provide a certificate, and many dedicate the planting to someone they love or respect. Religious schools often make this a Tu Bishvat project.

Tisha Be'av—Remembering the Temple

One of the saddest days of the traditional Jewish calendar is *Tisha Be'av*—the 9th day of the month of Av. This date is the anniversary of the destruction of both the First Temple in 586 B.C.E. and the Second Temple in 70 C.E. Amazingly, other tragedies in Jewish history occurred on this date, either by coincidence or intention by non-Jews who knew the meaning of this date to Jews. These other tragic events include the following:

- The breach of the walls of Simeon bar Kochba's last fortress in his revolt against Roman rule in 135 C.E.

- The banishment of Jews from England in 1290 C.E.

- The Edict of Expulsion of Jews from Spain in 1492.

- Many acts of violence by Nazis against Jews in Germany and occupied Europe in the 1930s and 1940s.

Tisha Be'av therefore becomes a day when Jews mourn all the tragedies they have endured. The greatest of these tragedies according to the traditional perspective does remain the loss of the place where Jews could most closely connect with and worship God—the Temple.

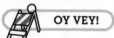 **OY VEY!**

Not all Jews observe Tisha Be'av. The early Reform Movement in particular rejected the commemoration because they felt at home in the Diaspora lands in which they lived and didn't long for a return to Israel and reconstruction of the Temple. They wanted others to see them as loyal to the nation in which they lived, and observance of this day would contradict that impression.

Tisha Be'av is actually the end of a three-week period of mourning and increasing sadness. The process begins three weeks before with *Tzom Tammuz*—the Fast of Tammuz. This day, the 17th of the month of Tammuz, marks the anniversary of the breach of Jerusalem's walls by the Romans. This was the beginning of the siege that ended with the destruction of the Second Temple. Traditional Jews observe this day with what is known as a "minor fast," not because it's less important, but because Jews fast only from dawn to dusk.

No weddings may occur between Tzom Tammuz and Tisha Be'av. The sadnesses and accompanying restrictions increase when the month of Av begins. Traditional law prohibits haircuts, drinking wine, eating meat, and acts solely for pleasure during the first nine days of Av. When Tisha Be'av finally arrives, traditional Jews fast and restrict their behavior exactly as they do on Yom Kippur. Congregations read from the Book of *Eikah* (Lamentations)—words of regret and mourning for the destruction of the First Temple attributed to the prophet Jeremiah. The entire day is gloomy and desolate, reflecting the tragedies that occurred in the past.

Other Religious Observances

There are several other religious observances you might see on a detailed traditional Jewish calendar that have not been discussed. These days are important, but in relative terms, they're observed less widely or don't quite reach the gravity or standing of the other days.

Other Religious Observances in Judaism

Day Observed	Description
Purim Katan	"Little Purim" observed on the 14th of Adar I during a leap year.
Ta'anit Ester	A minor fast the day before Purim reflecting Esther's fast in preparation for confronting Haman and the King.
Shushan Purim	The later day of Purim celebrated in walled cities like Jerusalem.
Pesach Sheini	"Second Passover" in commemoration of the Israelites who could not make the first Passover sacrifice because they were ritually impure at the time. (Numbers 9:6-7) Matzah is eaten on this day.

Modern Observances

Several occasions have been added to the Jewish calendar to reflect events in recent history. Most of them involve the State of Israel where their observance is greater than in the Diaspora.

Yom HaShoah—Remembering the Holocaust

A special day has been added to the calendar to remember the tragedy of the Holocaust—*Yom HaShoah*. After a debate, the Israeli government decided to set this day one week before Israel's Independence Day, on the 27th of the month of Nisan. Some had argued to have this remembrance on the 15th of Nisan because that was the start of the uprising against the Nazis in the Warsaw Ghetto. The government eventually decided the 15th was not a good day to start because it was also the start of Pesach. They chose the 27th because of the defined period of a week prior to the celebration of independence and the fact that the Warsaw Uprising still had been ongoing at that time.

 WORTH NOTING

In Israel, Yom HaShoah is called *Yom HaShoah v'HaGevurah*—The Day of Holocaust and Acts of Courage Remembrance. This embraces the Israeli view of giving particular honor to those who resisted the Nazis.

In Israel, a siren sounds at 11:00 A.M. on Yom HaShoah. People stop wherever they are and stand motionless and in silence. Cars pull to the side of the road and stop as the entire nation remembers.

In the Diaspora as well as Israel, people gather for prayers and to hear stories, often from survivors or the descendants of survivors. Many light six special yellow *yahrzeit* candles, one for each million of the six million Jews killed in the Holocaust. Yellow is used to commemorate the yellow patches the Nazis forced Jews to wear as a badge of identification and shame. The day focuses on one theme: remember, so this will never happen again.

Yom HaZikaron—Memorial Day

Yom HaZikaron is Israel's version of Memorial Day. Occurring the day before their Independence Day, Israelis remember the soldiers who fought and died for Israel's security and existence. Recently, Israelis have also remembered civilians who have died as victims of terrorist attacks. Again, a siren stops all activity in the entire country. Many attend services and public gatherings to mark the day.

Yom HaAtzme'ut—Israel Independence Day

Yom HaAtzme'ut is Israel's Independence Day. It usually occurs on the 5th of the month of *Iyar*, the anniversary of the signing of Israel's Declaration of Independence. Israelis decorate their buildings with colored lights and celebrate with fireworks, parades, and parties. In the Diaspora, Jews often mark the day with cultural events featuring Israeli food, art, and music.

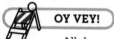

OY VEY!

All these modern holidays are moved a day earlier or later if they coincide with Shabbat.

Yom Yirushalayim—Jerusalem Day

Israelis celebrate the 28th of Iyar, the day of the reunification of Jerusalem in the Six Day War. Many congregations read the Hallel psalms. There are celebrations throughout Israel, particularly in Jerusalem.

The Least You Need to Know

- Jewish women take the lead in celebrating Rosh Chodesh, the beginning of each month.
- Tu Bishvat celebrates the new year of the trees with a Seder and songs.
- Tisha Be'av commemorates the destruction of the First and Second Temples, as well as many other tragedies throughout Jewish history. Reform Jews generally don't observe this memorial.
- There are a variety of additional commemorations and holidays to mark events in modern times.

Jewish Life Events

Celebration and commemoration are such important parts of Jewish life. Almost every people and religion marks milestones with ritual, customs, and practices that give meaning to the stages of life. Judaism is no different. To understand Judaism, it's important to know how life cycle events embody Jewish values and provide a cadence to Jewish lifetimes.

Chapter 14 begins this examination by describing the life cycle events Jewish children experience. Chapter 15 talks about the many laws and customs surrounding marriage. Chapter 16 considers the values and requirements of those who become Jewish not by birth but by choice. Chapter 17 deals with the difficult topic of how Jews mourn and honor someone who has died. Chapter 18 presents Jewish views about what happens after death.

It's a Boy! It's a Girl!

When God calls to Abraham and Abraham accepts God, much of God's promise involves progeny. God promises Abraham his descendants will be a great nation, and they will possess the Promised Land. (Genesis 12:2-7) Later, God elaborates that his descendants will be as numerous as the sands of the sea and the stars in the sky. (Genesis 22:17) Much of Abraham and Sarah's story involves the miracle of Isaac's birth, seen by them as unlikely due to Sarah's advanced age of 99.

Along with all this concern for children and descendants, God instructs Abraham from the beginning to hold a life cycle event for his son. This shows how important Judaism considers marking and celebrating the growth and development of children. This chapter describes the many ways Jews commemorate the lives of their children.

In This Chapter

- Welcoming a baby—brit milah and brit bat
- Beginning religious education with Consecration
- Bar and bat mitzvah: ceremony and celebration
- The innovation of Confirmation

When a Baby Is Born

There is no greater joy for Jews than the birth of a child. Like many religions and cultures, Jews mark this event with a ceremony. Jewish birth ceremonies are a combination of both ancient and modern concerns, and much depends upon whether the child is a boy or a girl.

Brit Milah (Circumcision)

If a child is a boy, the appropriate event is a *brit milah* or circumcision. God commands Abraham from the start that all the males of Abraham's people shall be circumcised at the age of 8 days. God tells Abraham that this will be a sign of the Covenant between God and Abraham's people, and that any male who is not circumcised shall be cut off from the people. (Genesis 17:9-14)

 ASK THE RABBI

What happens to a baby boy who is not circumcised? Is he rejected? Circumcision is extremely important to the Jewish people, but if someone is not circumcised today, he is not thrown out of Judaism. He's still a Jew, but a Jew who has not experienced a very important mitzvah.

Brit milah means the "Covenant of Circumcision." Sometimes you might hear the ceremony referred to as a *bris,* which is simply the Ashkenazic and Yiddish pronunciation of the word *brit.* The Talmud requires the father to fulfill this mitzvah. (Talmud Bavli, Kiddushin 29a) If the father is unable to fulfill this mitzvah, it becomes the responsibility of the mother.

Traditionally, Jews follow the Torah's requirement that the circumcision occur on the eighth day of the boy's life. The requirement means that a brit milah occurs on the eighth day even if that day is Shabbat or a holy day like Yom Kippur. The only reason traditional Judaism allows to not do the circumcision on the eighth day is if the procedure would harm the health of the child.

In counting the eight days, it's important to remember that we count the child's birthday as the first day. So if the child is born on Wednesday during the day, the brit milah occurs the following Wednesday. Remember, though, that Jewish days begin at sundown, so if the child is born on Wednesday after sundown, the brit milah occurs the following Thursday.

Even though the father has the responsibility to circumcise the child, a trained person called a *mohel* performs the actual procedure. One mohel I knew would always hand the scalpel to the father and ask him if he wanted to delegate the responsibility for performing the procedure back to him. Usually, the father, ashen, would quickly hand the scalpel back to the mohel.

A mohel may be a doctor, although this is not required in the Jewish tradition. Orthodox Judaism requires a mohel to be male, but the non-Orthodox movements allow a woman to become a *mohelet* (female for mohel). Usually, the actual procedure occurs quickly as part of the ceremony.

The ceremony includes several honors, blessings, and readings. The child is brought into the ceremony by the *kvatter* or *kvatterin,* the closest honor to godparents in Judaism. In some traditions, these people accept responsibility for the Jewish education of the child should something happen to the parents. They place the baby on a special chair designated as the *Kisei Eliyahu* (the "chair of Elijah"), as the prophet Elijah is considered to be the protector of children. The *sandak,* an honored male or family member, often a grandfather, then takes the child and holds him through the ceremony. The sandak also has the important role of giving the baby a little wine during the ceremony and procedure.

The rabbi or mohel recites the passages from Genesis about God's command to Abraham for this act as a sign of the Covenant. There are several blessings denoting the procedure is being done in fulfillment of the mitzvah. There's a blessing for the health of the child, and the child receives a name. Some communities read a verse from the Tanach for every letter of the child's name, each verse beginning with the letters within the name. The child and family receive a blessing, and then everyone celebrates and eats.

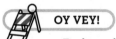

OY VEY!

Traditionally, there are no invitations to a brit milah because it's a mitzvah to attend and witness the event. Jewish parents will tell people, "The bris is on Thursday at 2:00," and people know they may attend.

Some parents today have the circumcision performed in a hospital while the mother recovers from childbirth. Often this is done for safety concerns or for insurance coverage. Due to the length of stays in hospitals, this often means the procedure occurs before the eighth day. This doesn't comply with the traditional requirements. The appropriate blessings must be said prior to the circumcision to denote it as a religious act in accordance with the mitzvah.

Not every circumcision is a brit milah according to traditional Judaism. The Orthodox remedy for this is to do *hatafat dam brit* at a later time, as discussed in Chapter 16. Some non-Orthodox authorities will still accept the circumcision as a valid brit milah, or will consider it sufficient retroactively following a naming ceremony.

Pidyon HaBen—Redemption of the Firstborn

Numbers 18:15-16 pledges the firstborn male of any woman or animal to God's service. However, the text quickly states that a woman's son may be redeemed by a payment in lieu of dedicating the child to God.

Many traditional Jews still follow this procedure today, holding a ceremony including a payment to a *Kohein*, a descendant of the priestly tribe of the Israelites. The ceremony occurs after the baby is 1 month old. The Torah sets the amount at 5 *shekels* or 20 *gerahs*. Today, many parents use silver coins to effectuate the payment. A minyon is required to witness the ceremony, which takes place after a meal.

A Ceremony for Girls: Brit Bat

While baby boys have the brit milah ceremony welcoming them to the community and fulfilling the mitzvah set forth in Genesis, girls don't have a similar ceremony in traditional Judaism. Some communities have addressed this by creating a ceremony for girls called a *brit bat* ("Covenant for a Daughter") or *brit chayyim* ("Covenant of Life"). This ceremony celebrates the birth of a girl, and does everything you would see at a brit milah except the circumcision procedure and references to it. The baby girl receives a name and a blessing, and everyone eats and celebrates.

Consecration

Many synagogues hold a ceremony for students beginning religious school, called Consecration. They invite the children to the *bimah* and give them a gift, often a small reproduction of a *Sefer Torah*. Some congregations give the children honey, following the tradition demonstrating the sweetness of learning.

Bar/Bat Mitzvah

Many religions and cultures have "coming of age" ceremonies marking when children become adults. The "coming of age" ceremony in Judaism is called a *bar/bat mitzvah*, meaning a son or daughter of the commandments. This ceremony marks the time when a Jewish young man or woman becomes responsible for his or her own adherence to the mitzvot.

Becoming a Jewish Adult

The traditional age of a bar mitzvah is 13. The texts differ as to whether a girl becomes a bat mitzvah at the age of 12 or $12\frac{1}{2}$. Many non-Orthodox congregations make the age of both bar and bat mitzvah 13 to reinforce the value of gender equality.

WORDS OF WISDOM

"Blessed is God, who has freed me from responsibility for this boy."—Genesis Rabbah 63:10, citing the words Rabbi Eleazar ben Rabbi Simeon attributes to a father when his son reaches the age of 13.

It's difficult to find a religious reason for setting the age of adulthood at 13. The only mention of this age in the Torah is that Ishmael was circumcised when he was 13. The midrashim describe other events as happening when a Biblical figure reached the age of 13, including Avram's destruction of the idols in his uncle's shop, Jacob and his brother Esau's parting, Simeon and Levi's revenge against Shechem for assaulting their sister Dinah, and Bezalel's building of the Tabernacle in the desert.

The sages may have been at least partly influenced to set the ages for bar and bat mitzvah based upon the physical maturity of boys and girls. People had much shorter life spans, and soon after children reached these ages, they were married. Once ready to establish an independent household, the community needed to declare that the children to have become adults. Today, Jews tell their children they have become Jewish adults, but they still have a lot to learn and experience before they're ready to leave their parents' house and make all their decisions about their lives.

The Purpose of the Service

The young adult participates as a leader in a worship service in most *b'nei mitzvah* (the plural of bar mitzvah) today. The amount the child does in the service varies among communities and sometimes depends on the needs and desires of the young adult and his or her family. Some b'nei mitzvah lead all or most of the service, read from the Torah and the Haftarah, and deliver a teaching lesson on the Scripture called a *d'var Torah* ("words of Torah"). Others may merely receive an aliyah and say only the blessings before and after someone else reads a portion from the Torah, or read some or all of the Haftarah. Some congregations have only one student become a bar or bat mitzvah at a service, while larger synagogues may have several students sharing the roles and honors.

OY VEY!

Many people say a young man "gets bar mitzvah-ed." This is not only incorrect Hebrew, but it misrepresents the ceremony. Bar or bat mitzvah is not something that happens to a young adult. A young adult "becomes" a bar or bat mitzvah by reaching the appropriate age and hopefully experiencing an inner transformation. No one gets bar mitzvah-ed.

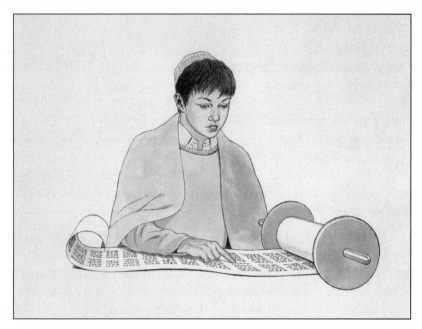

A boy reading from the Torah at his bar mitzvah.

Technically, a worship service is not required for a young adult to become a bar or bat mitzvah. A Jew attains this status simply by reaching the appropriate age. If the young adult hasn't studied, he or she simply is a bar or bat mitzvah who does not know how to fulfill the mitzvot, including leading a service. From a religious standpoint, he or she is a Jewish adult who doesn't know what the Covenant means or how to meet the ritual expectations of a Jewish adult. Nevertheless, in recent decades the bar or bat mitzvah has become the seminal life cycle event for many Jews.

Many congregations have the b'nei mitzvah students perform other mitzvot as part of the learning process in becoming a bar or bat mitzvah in addition to those involving worship services. Many require *gemilut chasadim* projects, acts of loving kindness that help someone in the community in need. Some ask the student to contribute some tzedakah. These requirements attempt to reinforce the idea that being a Jewish adult means more than performing rituals, but also acting as a *mentsch* who helps others and improves the world.

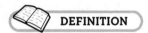 **DEFINITION**

> **Mentsch** is a Yiddish word meaning a good, honorable, modest person. One of the greatest compliments a Jew may receive is to be called a mentsch.

Celebrations

Celebrating a *simcha* ("joyous occasion") is an important tradition in Judaism. Many Jews have a celebration following the worship service of a bar or bat mitzvah, which may range from a light lunch to a large party. It's important to remember that the celebration is not the bar or bat mitzvah itself, but the rejoicing occasioned by the young adult reaching the age of maturity in Jewish tradition.

A Ceremony for Girls—Bat Mitzvah

Reflecting the exemption from many ritual requirements, Jews traditionally did not celebrate a *bat mitzvah* with a service or subsequent celebration. This began to change in the twentieth century.

The first recorded bat mitzvah occurred in 1922. Judith Kaplan, the daughter of Rabbi Mordechai Kaplan, read the blessings and a portion from the Torah in Hebrew and English. She read from her own book and not from the Sefer Torah, even though the covered Torah rested on a reading table. She stood below the bimah. At the time, this event was shocking to many.

As the non-Orthodox movements accepted gender egalitarianism, girls became able to celebrate a bat mitzvah in the synagogue. Some congregations treat boys and girls exactly the same. Others have maintained some differences, such as having a bat mitzvah at a different service than Shabbat morning or having the girl perform a different part of the service than boys. Nevertheless, the bat mitzvah has become normative for many Jews.

 WORTH NOTING

Some adults who didn't have a bar or bat mitzvah ceremony as a child have had them as adults. These include adults who chose Judaism later in life and women whose congregations didn't have any b'not mitzvah (the plural of bat mitzvah) when they were children. There's also a tradition of having a second bar or bat mitzvah at the age of 83.

Confirmation

Many non-Orthodox congregations have added an additional life cycle event for children called Confirmation. Modeled after the ceremony they saw occurring in churches, these congregations saw reasons to institute a similar ceremony in Judaism.

The Origin of Confirmation

Confirmation began in the Reform Movement. The early American Reformers saw limitations to the bar mitzvah ceremony. They noted that many adult Jews couldn't read Hebrew, so they believed asking a child to learn the language and chant from Scripture at a worship service had become antiquated. There was also a concern that calling a child of 13 years an adult was premature, and that the bar mitzvah unfairly ignored girls in the congregation.

WORDS OF WISDOM

"The original significance (of bar mitzvah), which was to indicate ... the admission of the lad into membership of the congregation, has been forgotten and consequently ... meaningless ... [A] form of consecration for the young of both sexes was instituted in its place and the beautiful rite of confirmation was adopted."—Rabbi Kaufmann Kohler, 1907

Connection with Shavuot and Customs

Many rabbis saw a natural connection between Confirmation and the Jewish holy day of Shavuot. They reasoned that there was no better time for young men and women who truly were entering adulthood to appreciate their connection to Judaism than the holy day celebrating the receipt of the Torah at Mount Sinai.

Confirmation occurs in one service for an entire class a few years after they celebrate becoming b'nei mitzvah. This gives each young man and woman the ability to confirm what they pledged at their b'nei mitzvah about being a Jew and observing the mitzvot. The class usually leads the worship service, including the reading of the Ten Commandments from the Torah as traditionally done on that holiday. In many congregations, some or all of the students read a personal statement about their connection to Judaism or their interpretation of the Tanach. Additionally, the clergy often give each of the students their own blessing.

The Least You Need to Know

- Jews celebrate the birth of a male child with a welcoming ceremony called a brit milah at which the boy is circumcised and named. Some girls have a similar ceremony without the circumcision called a brit bat or brit chayyim.

- The Jewish "coming of age" ceremony is a bar or bat mitzvah, meaning son or daughter of the commandments. The young man or woman becomes responsible for performing the mitzvot. They generally lead all or part of a worship service.

- Many b'nei mitzvah have a party celebrating the event after the service. The party isn't the bar or bat mitzvah, but an affair to rejoice that the young man or woman has reached this religious milestone.

- Some communities celebrate Confirmation, a ceremony held a few years after the bar or bat mitzvah confirming what the young man or woman said about being a Jew following the *mitzvot* at the earlier life cycle event.

Breaking the Glass: Jewish Weddings

Judaism highly values marriage as the ideal way for a person to live life and achieve happiness. The beginning of the *Torah* describes how God saw that it wasn't good for the first man, Adam, to be alone, and so God created a "helpmate" for him in Eve. (Genesis 2:18) The Torah further teaches from this the lesson that "a man will leave his father and his mother and join to his wife, so they become one flesh." (Genesis 2:24) The Talmud teaches that "when a man lives without his wife, he lives without joy, without blessing, without good." (Talmud Bavli, Yevamot 62b)

The union of man and woman in marriage has cosmic significance in Judaism, as according to some Jewish sources, a man's connection to God depends upon his being married. The Midrash explains that "no man [should be without a] woman, no woman [should be without a] man, and neither without the Divine Presence. (Genesis Rabbah 22:2) The Talmud extends this even further, stating that "when there is no union of man and woman, men are not worthy of beholding the Divine Presence." (Talmud Bavli, Aharei Mot 59a)

In This Chapter

- Jewish preference for marriage
- Making the match
- Preparing for the wedding
- The wedding ceremony
- Divorce in Judaism

None of this means that Judaism rejects unmarried people or views those without a spouse with scorn. Instead, Judaism emphasizes the importance of marriage, and the hope that everyone will find a suitable spouse. Marriage is the highest joy in Judaism, and a wedding traditionally is viewed as the seminal Jewish experience in one's life. The laws, traditions, and customs surrounding the wedding gain importance in enhancing that joy and beginning the ideal relationship of marriage that Judaism values so highly.

Finding a Spouse

The Midrash tells a story about a Roman matron who asks the Rabbi what God does all day.

The Rabbi replied, "God spends all day matching the right man with the right woman."

The matron scoffed at this answer, thinking that she could do the same with ease. She returned home, and began matching her servants, pairing each male servant with a female servant she thought would make the best pair.

The next morning, the matron awoke to find great unhappiness in her home. The servants were bruised and had broken limbs, and each complained that he or she couldn't live with the spouse the matron had chosen. The matron returned to the Rabbi and admitted she was wrong. (Genesis Rabbah 68:4)

 WORDS OF WISDOM

> "When love is strong, a man and woman can make their bed on a sword's blade. When love grows weak, a bed of sixty cubits (about 90 feet) is not large enough."
> —Talmud Bavli, Sanhedrin 7a

Throughout much of Jewish history, there has been great concern to ensure that spousal pairings were appropriate, beneficial to the couple and the families, and lasting. Despite the previous Midrash, without a clear message from God as to who should pair with whom, many Jewish communities did the next best thing—they created a process to arrange the marriages.

Matchmaking

Matchmaking and arranging marriage became an important part of Jewish life in communities through the ages. The communities created a special position for the matchmaker, who was called a *shadchan*. The shadchan would learn about the prospective brides and grooms and their families, and work with the parents to create suitable matches. The shadchan considers the prospective bride and groom's character, interests, modesty, adherence to halachah, scholarship, family reputation, and any other relevant factors to create a good match. Originally an honorary role within the community, the shadchan eventually became a full profession with payment for his or her services.

Even though the parents of the bride and groom selected their children's prospective spouses, Jewish law required that both children consent to the match. According to the halachah, the bride couldn't be forced to marry someone she didn't want. This law may be traced to Genesis 24:58, where Rebecca's mother and brother ask her if she will agree to marry Isaac. The match is set only after Rebecca says, "I will go."

 WORTH NOTING

The most popular image of the matchmaker comes from the play and movie *Fiddler on the Roof*, in which the character Yenta takes the role of arranging marriages. Usually played for comic relief, the character of Yenta is endearing but doesn't fully convey the respect the shadchan received from the community. The story does demonstrate the tensions the practice of matchmaking began to face with the onset of modernity.

Today, the role of the shadchan and the practice of matchmaking have fallen out of favor in many Jewish communities. Most non-Orthodox communities no longer use a shadchan, and brides and grooms find each other through the same process of dating and falling in love as done in most communities in America. In recent years, many matches have been made through online dating sites catering specifically to Jews. Nevertheless, some Orthodox communities today still arrange marriages and use a shadchan to attempt to create the best, lasting match.

Prohibited Spouses

Jewish law prohibits marriage between certain people. For example, Leviticus 18 contains a list of relatives who can't marry as prohibited by the law against incest. The rabbis expand these prohibited relationships in the Oral Law. Essentially, a person may not marry his or her parent, grandparent, aunt, uncle, children, in-laws, half-relations, or someone who is connected through a prior marriage, such as a spouse's child from a previous marriage.

The halachah also prohibits polygamy. The Talmud asserts that a woman may not simultaneously be the wife of two men. (Talmud Bavli, Kiddushin 7a) It took longer for the law to prohibit a man from having multiple wives, especially since there are examples of this in the Torah, most notably by the patriarch Jacob. Rabbi Gershom wrote a document called the *Cherem d'Rebbeinu Gershom* in the Middle Ages that barred men from having multiple wives for the purpose of keeping peace in the home. The document applied only to Ashkenazic Jews, but the Sephardic Jews in Israel have also adopted its reasoning. Today, polygamy remains in practice in Judaism only among a few Yemenite Jews.

Even though the Temple was destroyed almost two thousand years ago, the status of the families who composed the priesthood has been maintained within traditional Judaism. These people, called the *Kohenim*, enjoy certain honors in some congregations such as the privilege of the first *aliyah*, or blessing, for the first reading of the Torah at a worship service. It's important for the Kohenim to maintain a level of holiness and purity, so the halachah imposes certain restrictions upon them to retain their status. Consequently, a male *kohen* may not marry a divorcee or a convert to Judaism, categories of women the sages deem would create a situation inconsistent with the honor of being a kohen.

 ASK THE RABBI

What about same-sex marriage? As traditional Judaism holds homosexually to be an inappropriate sexual act, the halachah doesn't allow same-sex marriage. The halachah views marriage as appropriate only between a man and a woman. However, many rabbis and cantors in the nonhalachic Reform and Reconstructionist movements disagree with this interpretation and understanding of homosexuality in the Written and Oral Law, and will perform a same-sex marriage.

The halachah prohibits some other marriages as well. The Torah explicitly forbids adultery in Exodus 20:13, Leviticus 20:10, and Deuteronomy 5:18. It would be illogical to forbid adultery but then allow the marriage of the two people who committed the sin. The Law prohibits sanctifying the marriage of a couple who have participated in an adulterous act. The children of two people who were not married or married in a way not condoned by the halachah are called *mamzerim*, and there are restrictions in traditional Jewish Law about whom they may marry. A person also may temporarily be unable to marry under traditional law, as a mourner may not marry until 30 days have elapsed after the funeral of the deceased.

Intermarriage

Traditional Jewish law prohibits marriage between a Jew and a non-Jew. Deuteronomy 7:3 commanded the Israelites not to marry someone from the Canaanite people. The Prophets contain several exhortations to the people urging them not to marry non-Jews, such as Malachai 12:11-12 and Ezra 10:11.

Throughout history, Jews have been wary of intermarriage because they worry the practice will lead to assimilation and, eventually, the abandonment of Jewish practice and status. As a minority, Jews have held great concern that intermarriage is the first step toward the disappearance of the Jewish people. For this reason, the halachah strictly forbids intermarriage, and it's the position of Orthodox Jews and the Conservative movement that a rabbi or cantor may not perform a marriage ceremony for an interfaith couple. As we shall see later in this chapter, an essential part of the wedding ceremony has the groom taking the bride "in accordance with the laws of Moses and Israel." Many Jewish authorities have the concern that if these words are said by or to someone one who doesn't follow these laws, the wedding ceremony will lose an essential meaning.

In contrast, many Jews in the nonhalachic movements have a different view. They believe that an intermarried couple who raise their children as Jews enhances the Jewish people, and keeps Jews within Judaism. They argue that rejecting the couple at the moment of their marriage means that they, their family, and their descendants will be lost to the Jewish people forever, which will actually increase assimilation and the evaporation of the Jewish people. For this reason, many in the Reform and Reconstructionist movements will perform intermarriage, albeit under certain conditions and possibly with some changes or restrictions in what is done at the ceremony.

The issue of intermarriage is perhaps the most hotly debated controversy in Judaism today, especially in the United States. There are rabbis, scholars, and lay leaders who feel passionately about both sides of the issue, resulting in a wide range of practices among rabbis and congregations.

Making the Plans

Once a couple decides to marry or has a match arranged, attention quickly turns to the wedding arrangements. People want to know when and where the wedding will take place, and eventually they begin to wonder what the bride (and to a lesser extent, the groom) will wear. Jewish custom and tradition provides some guidance to answering these questions.

Prohibited Days

The halachah teaches that a Jew should experience each joyful occasion separately. This maxim ensures that everyone gets full enjoyment out of every joyful occasion, and people fully focus upon the cause for celebration. This rule also increases joy in people's lives, since it's usually more joyful to be happy on two days than one. Jewish law therefore prohibits holding weddings on any day in the Jewish calendar for which there is already a commandment for joy, such as Shabbat and the pilgrimage festivals.

Jewish law also prohibits marriages on days when Jews focus on other spiritual tasks and observances, such as Rosh HaShanah and Yom Kippur. A Jew may not have a wedding during a day of mourning, including the three weeks from the 17th of Tammuz through the 9th of Av when Jews mourn the loss of the Second Temple, during the days of the Omer except for *Lag B'omer*, and during the 30 days following the funeral of a relative or someone for whom a Jew has the obligation to mourn. Weddings also may not take place during fast days, including the tenth of Tevet and the Fasts of Gedaliah and Esther.

Place

Jewish law and tradition don't require couples to have their wedding in a designated place. Anywhere that's tasteful and respectful is appropriate. Some couples choose to have their weddings outside, hoping they will have as many children "as the stars in the heavens" as God promised Abraham about his descendants. (Genesis 15:5) Many communities encourage couples to hold their weddings in the synagogue as a place suitably modest to create a sense of holiness for the ceremony. However, it isn't uncommon to hold a Jewish wedding ceremony in a hotel, function hall, or other venue.

Dress

Throughout history, Jewish brides and grooms have adopted much of the wedding attire characteristic for the cultures in which they lived. Ashkenazic brides often wear white dresses as the color of purity. In contrast, Sephardic brides often wear colorful gowns. Grooms typically wear suits reflecting the community's style for important occasions. Some grooms wear a *kittel* (white robe symbolizing purity) or *tallit* (prayer shawl) as well.

Approaching the Wedding Day

Judaism includes many rituals in the months, weeks, and hours leading to the actual wedding ceremony. There are a wide range of practices among Jews. Some elaborately perform every ritual step, while others engage with very few. The choices depend upon the desires of the bride and groom and their families, the customs and religiosity of their communities, and the practice of the *mesader kiddushin*, the person performing the ceremony.

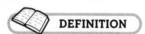 **DEFINITION**

> **Mesader kiddushin**—the wedding officiant—is traditionally a rabbi, as the person knowledgeable of the laws and rules for the ceremony. However, any learned Jew, particularly *hazzanim* (cantors) may serve as a mesader kiddushin in Jewish practice, although civil law may impose other requirements.

Tenaim

Tenaim means "conditions." This word refers to an Ashkenazic ceremony held by some families at which the family reads a document setting the terms of the betrothal and the plans for the wedding ceremony. After the reading of the document, the families break a plate, recalling the destruction of the Second Temple, and emphasizing that if either side breaks the terms of the document the relationship can't be repaired. The breaking of the plate also foretells the breaking of the glass performed at the end of the wedding ceremony.

Aufruf

An *aufruf* is an opportunity for the bride and groom to receive a blessing in the synagogue, allowing everyone in the entire community to share in the joy of the wedding even if they aren't attending the ceremony. An aufruf usually occurs on the Shabbat before the wedding, although many couples and communities agree to an earlier date. In some communities, it's traditional for the groom to read from the Torah or deliver a *d'var Torah*, an interpretation of the Torah reading. After the blessing, many communities toss candy or nuts toward the couple, wishing them sweetness in their lives.

Other Customs

Some couples go to the *mikvah* in the days before the wedding. As we'll see in Chapter 25, the mikvah is a ritual bath Jews use as a means of spiritual purification. Brides more commonly use the mikvah than grooms, although it's not unusual for a groom to go to this special and holy place for his own spiritual preparation for his wedding as well.

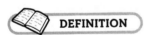 **DEFINITION**

A **mikvah** is a ritual bath used for spiritual renewal and purification. A mikvah must have a certain percentage of its waters flowing naturally into the pool from rain or flowing bodies of water such as a river or stream. Jews may use a natural body of water as a mikvah.

Some couples don't see each other for as long as a week leading up to their wedding day. The absence from each other heightens the anticipation for their wedding, and increases the joy of the day and its celebration once they reunite.

The Wedding Day

The wedding day can become quite exciting and chaotic, with friends and relatives to greet, photographs to be taken, and unanticipated needs and crises to satisfy or resolve. Jewish law and custom provide several practices for the wedding day leading to the ceremony, which instill a sense of holiness into the events and prepare the couple and their guests to both appreciate the blessing of the moment and begin the celebration.

Fasting

There are several connections between a wedding and Yom Kippur. The wedding is a time of renewal and beginnings, just as Yom Kippur is a day of spiritual return and revitalization for a new year. As we've seen, the bride in Ashkenazic tradition wears white, the color of spiritual renewal and purity also associated with Yom Kippur, and the groom often wears a kittel, the robe men traditionally wear during Yom Kippur prayer. The couple sometimes visits the mikvah, another custom also performed just prior to Yom Kippur.

Another shared practice of a wedding and Yom Kippur is that a bride and groom sometimes fast during the day leading to the ceremony. Like Yom Kippur, a fast provides the bride and groom an opportunity to focus on the spiritual elements of the day instead of their physical needs, and may be seen as a means of purification in preparation for the sacred moment of their union. A fast also has the benefit of increasing the bride and groom's joy at their celebration, and there is nothing that makes a person happier when he or she is hungry than good food.

Ketubah

The *ketubah* is the document outlining the terms to which the bride and groom agree as the foundation of the marriage. Often, Jews refer to the ketubah as the wedding contract. A traditional ketubah is written in Aramaic, although some are written in Hebrew, and many contain a translation into the language normally spoken by the couple in everyday life. *Ketubot* (the plural of ketubah) may be illustrated with exquisite and beautiful artwork, sometimes individually commissioned from an artist with personal meanings applicable to the wedding couple.

In Jewish tradition, a marriage was an act of *kinyan* or "acquisition." The groom "acquires" the bride as part of his family, and pledges to care for her and provide her with the benefits and protections of marriage under Jewish law. Kinyan is not an act of ownership or slavery, but a change of personal status and an understanding of property rights. In this sense, the ketubah historically was a revolutionary step protecting women and providing for them at a time when women had no rights in many cultures. The traditionally worded ketubah retains this character, providing details of the bride's rights and the dowry. A groom must give property of at least nominal value—*shaveh perutah*—to the bride as part of kinyan, and the ketubah also describes this.

 OY VEY!

Many Jewish couples today aren't comfortable with the wording of the traditional ketubah and its emphasis on kinyan and technicalities of exchanges of property. Many couples and rabbis from non-Orthodox movements use ketubot that speak of agreements to love each other and pledges of their commitment to each other. Some nontraditional ketubot are specially written for same-sex or interfaith couples. A wedding couple needs to consult with their mesader kiddushin to be certain the ketubah they choose is appropriate for them.

As a Jewish legal document, two witnesses must sign the ketubah attesting that they saw the bride and groom assent to the wedding and the agreement. The halachah requires the witnesses to be Jewish men over the age of 13. Most sources also prohibit relatives by blood or marriage to witness the ketubah. Some rabbis in the non-Orthodox movements ease these restrictions, especially allowing women to witness the ketubah.

Tish and Bedeken

As the time set for the beginning of the wedding ceremony approaches, Jewish custom provides a series of steps and ceremonies for the attendees. As much as any time in Jewish practice, it's important to remember that couples may or may not choose to have some or all of these traditions as part of their special day. A wedding is one of the most personal and meaningful experiences in a person's life, and the choices people make depend upon their personal practices, traditions, desires, and opinions. If you go to a Jewish wedding, you might see some of these ceremonies, or you might not.

Many couples decide to have traditional *Tish* and *Bedeken* ceremonies. The men and women separate, with the men in one room and the women in another. The men hold the Tish, which means "the groom's table." Sometimes the groom invites all the male guests to the Tish, but it isn't uncommon for the groom to limit the Tish to his closest friends and relatives. At the Tish, the groom and witnesses sign the tenaim and the ketubah, and the mesader kiddushin or other representative of the bride accepts the ketubah on the bride's behalf. Often, friends and relatives toast the groom, tell stories, and sing. Sometimes the groom or a guest teaches about a text from the Torah.

While the men attend the Tish, the women gather in another room for *hachnasat kallah*— "gathering with the bride." The women also sing, share stories, and do everything possible to entertain and care for the bride.

Eventually, the groom comes to the bride for the *Bedeken*, or "veiling." The tradition of the bride wearing a veil comes from the story of Jacob, Leah, and Rachel. Jacob wants to marry Rachel, daughter of Laban, and younger sister of Leah. Jacob agrees to work for Laban for seven years to earn permission to marry Rachel. At the wedding, Laban gives his eldest daughter, Leah, to Jacob instead of Rachel, hiding her identity according to tradition by a veil. Laban explains it's customary that the eldest sister marries first, and Jacob has to work another seven years to marry Rachel. (Genesis 28:15-28) Jewish tradition calls for the groom to veil his bride to avoid such a misunderstanding.

The veil also serves as a crown, as the community treats every bride as a queen at her wedding. Additionally, the white veil represents purity.

Some couples forego the traditional Tish and Bedeken, and hold a simple ceremony for signing the ketubah with the mesader kiddushin, close family, and witnesses with both the bride and groom present prior to the ceremony.

The Wedding Ceremony

Following all the preparations, the tenaim, the Tish, and the Bedeken, the bride and groom are ready for the actual wedding ceremony. A Jewish wedding ceremony is filled with sacred prayers and moments, times of joy and times of commemoration, and profound symbolism, all bound together to create a special celebration for the couple, their families, and the entire community.

Two Ceremonies in One

A Jewish wedding technically is two separate ceremonies. The first has been called *erusin* or *kiddushin,* meaning "engagement" or "betrothal." This ceremony announces the intention of the bride and groom to marry. The second ceremony is *nissuin,* meaning "to carry." This ceremony celebrates the actual union of the couple, and may have gained its name for a custom of carrying the bride to her new home.

Centuries ago, the two ceremonies occurred at separate times, with many months between the two. After a while, problems with this practice emerged. The gap in time created an uncertainty of the bride and groom's status, which could become particularly troubling if something happened to one of them or if one of them met someone else before they were actually married. It was also expensive and cumbersome for the family to hold two feasts. Eventually, the practice arose to merge the two ceremonies into one event.

One remnant that remains from the double ceremonies is the inclusion of two *kiddushim,* or blessings over the fruit of the vine. Jews use the fruit of the vine, usually grape juice or wine, as a symbol of joy, and they say a blessing before drinking to designate a time as holy or joyous. In a modern Jewish wedding ceremony, *kiddush* is said twice, which is extremely unusual, but one marks erusin and the other marks nissuin.

WORTH NOTING

Some couples use separate kiddush cups for the two blessings. The bride and groom each drink from the first cup for one blessing, and then use the second cup for the other. This particularly designates the blessings as separate acts for different reasons. It also allows the bride and groom to each have a cup from the wedding ceremony for his and her own use at home.

Coming to the Chuppah

Jewish weddings occur under a canopy called a *chuppah*. The chuppah may be any cloth or fabric, although often the couple uses a large tallit, which we'll talk about in Chapter 25. The chuppah is mounted on four poles at its corners that either stand on their own on bases or are held by four honored guests.

There are several explanations for the use of the chuppah. Some say it represents the formation of a new home, one of the beautiful tents of Jacob as blessed by Bilaam in Numbers 24:5. Other traditions hold that the chuppah represents the Presence of God in the home. The openness of the chuppah on all sides reflects the hope that the couple's home will be open and welcoming to all, as Abraham's tent was known as a place of hospitality. Still others say the chuppah represents the marital bedroom.

OY VEY!

A few synagogues don't allow wedding ceremonies to take place on their *bimah,* the stage on which a worship service is held, because they don't feel it's appropriate to have a symbol of the marital bedroom close to the Torah.

There are different traditions of who proceeds with the wedding couple to the chuppah. Reflecting general American custom, many couples choose to have a wedding party with a best man, maid or matron of honor, ringbearers, and flower girls. Traditionally, the bride and groom select two friends each to serve as *shushvinim,* or attendants. Often, the parents of the groom escort him to the chuppah, and the parents of the bride escort her. In some traditions, there is a separation by gender, where both fathers escort the groom and both mothers escort the bride. In either case, the parents escort the bride and groom to the chuppah, but do not bring them underneath it. The couple meets before the chuppah and enter it together without their parents, representing their leaving their parents' homes and forming a new home together.

ASK THE RABBI

Why don't I hear some of the same music I'm used to hearing at Jewish weddings? Non-Jewish weddings often use music from Wagner, particularly *Lohengrin,* or Mendelsohn's *Midsummer Night's Dream* at weddings for the processional and recessional. However, Wagner was notoriously anti-Semitic, and Mendelssohn was born Jewish but converted to Christianity, so Jews deem their works inappropriate for a Jewish wedding.

There are also different traditions concerning who stands beneath the chuppah. Some communities expect only the bride, groom, and mesader kiddushin to stand under the chuppah. Others include the parents and shushvinim as well.

The Wedding Rings

The wedding ring is a symbol of kinyan, the groom's "acquisition" of the bride. The groom must give the bride something of at least nominal value, and the ring has become this item. Of course, most wedding rings today have significantly more value than this minimum requirement.

To ensure that the ring has the requisite value, the halachah requires it to be a solid unbroken metal band. Any holes in the ring may make it less than the worth, and any jewels could be fake, so neither is found in a traditional wedding band. The single simple band also represents the unbroken connection of the bride and groom.

The groom gives the ring to the bride during the wedding ceremony, saying the important words that bind the couple together, "*Harei at m'kudeshet li b'taba'at zo k'dat Moshe v'Yisrael*—Behold, you are consecrated to me as my wife in accordance with the Laws of Moses and Israel." Some Jewish grooms place the ring on the bride's right index finger, which some sages thought had a direct connection to the heart. The bride says nothing, but demonstrates her assent by moving the ring from the right index finger to the left ring finger where she will wear it.

 WORTH NOTING

The words said by the groom to the bride have 32 letters when written in Hebrew. The word in Hebrew representing the number 32 is *lev,* which means "heart."

Some couples today perform a dual-ring ceremony at the wedding, in which both the bride and groom give a ring to each other. They each say the words that bind the couple to each other, with the bride adjusting the traditional wording to the appropriate gender for her groom.

The Sheva Brachot

An important part of the ceremony is the *sheva brachot,* or "seven blessings." These blessings include the themes of happiness, joy, redemption, and praise to God for creating man and woman. They also include the second Kiddush of the ceremony.

Traditionally, the bride circles the groom either three or seven times during the recitation of these blessings. The origin of this custom may arise from Jeremiah 31:21, which states "A woman shall go around (or protect) a man." The circling demonstrates the union of the couple, and the commitment of the bride to guard her husband. The choice of the number of circles depends upon the source used as the basis for the circling. Three circles comes from Hosea 2:19, which states the word "betroth" three times. Three also may represent the three obligations of a husband for his wife: food, clothing, and physical intimacy. Seven is a mystical number in Jewish tradition representing completeness, and corresponds to the number of blessings.

Some couples find the circling of the bride around the groom anachronistic, and possibly giving a message of inequality as they interpret the act to mean the groom is the central figure of the relationship. In some non-Orthodox weddings, the circling is not done, or the bride and groom circle each other.

Breaking the Glass

Perhaps the most well-known part of the wedding ceremony comes at the very end, as the groom breaks a glass with his foot. The origin of this custom comes from a story in the Talmud where Mar ben Rabina viewed everyone celebrating at a wedding and broke a glass to pause the revelry. The reason he did this is a matter for debate, but it may have been that he felt the party was getting out of hand or that the sages present were behaving in an unseemly manner. (Talmud Bavli, Berachot 30b)

The breaking of the glass has several possible interpretations today. Some believe it represents the destruction of the Temple, and that even at our happiest moments like a wedding, Jews must remember the loss of this important institution. Some believe it's a message to the bride and groom to care for their marriage or else it will shatter, or that their spiritual connection shouldn't break like mere items from the physical world like the glass. Still others find its meaning in Jewish superstition, believing that demons look for the opportunity to spoil the couple's happiness when they least expect it at the wedding, but the breaking of the glass frightens them away.

Whatever meaning the bride, groom, and guests give the breaking of the glass, it's a moment of happiness and release, ending the ceremony with cries of *"Mazel tov—Congratulations,"* signaling the start of the celebration.

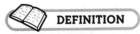 **DEFINITION**

Mazel tov is an expression used to say "Congratulations." It literally means "good luck" or "good fortune," but it's never said to someone before he or she performs the act in the way we would say "good luck" to someone in English.

Yichud—First Moments Alone

It's a Jewish custom for the bride and groom to spend the first moments of their marriage alone. They leave the chuppah and go to a private room, taking the opportunity to enjoy each other's company, eat some food if they have been fasting, and catch their breath prior to the celebration.

Celebrating with the Bride and Groom

Judaism holds celebrating with the bride and groom to be an important mitzvah. The Talmud teaches that someone who attends a wedding and doesn't increase the joy of the bride and groom transgresses five voices: the voice of joy, the voice of gladness, the voice of the groom, the voice of the bride, and the voice of praise to God. (Talmud Bavli, Berachot 6b)

Wedding celebrations typically include a *seudah mitzvah*—a special meal, toasts, stories, and dancing. Typically, guests participate in a Jewish cultural dance called a *hora,* in which dancers join hands and move in a circle. Often, strong guests lift the bride and groom on chairs with each holding one end of a kerchief or napkin, especially in an Orthodox wedding where the men's and women's celebrations are separated by a partition called a *mechitzah* for purposes of modesty. An old custom is to have a *badchan,* a person whose role is to spread joy at the celebration.

 **DEFINITION**

> A **badchan** is a jester who has the task of telling jokes, increasing merriment and joy, and entertaining the bride and groom at a wedding celebration. The badchan often is the master of ceremonies who guides toasts as well.

Some families participate in special dances, including the *mezinke,* a dance for the bride's mother if the bride is the mother's last unmarried daughter. A similar dance is a *krenzel* for parents when either the bride or groom is their last child to marry.

Some traditional communities maintain the tradition of celebrating with the bride and groom for seven days. They host the couple for a week of meals and gatherings, extending the couple's joy.

Divorce

For some couples, the joy and expectations felt at the wedding do not last. In Judaism, divorce isn't sinful or prohibited. It's almost always sad, as Rabbi Elezar says in the Talmud, "When a man divorces his wife, even the Temple alter sheds tears." (Talmud Bavli, Gittin 90b) However, Jewish law considers divorce preferable or even necessary at times.

When Divorce Is Allowed in Judaism

Traditionally, divorce isn't something done lightly. The husband and wife should make every effort to resolve their differences and rediscover the love they felt at their wedding. The sages knew this wasn't always possible, so they allowed divorce if the couple causes each other unhappiness that can't be resolved, what today we would call "irreconcilable differences." The husband may initiate a divorce if his wife consistently and without reason denies him sex. The Talmud even allows the husband to divorce his wife if she spoils his meals (Talmud Bavli, Gittin 90a) or fails to provide him a child after 10 years of marriage. (Mishnah, Yevamot 6:6)

Basically, if the husband decides the marriage isn't working, he may divorce his wife under Jewish law. Indeed, if his wife commits adultery, the halachah requires the husband to divorce his wife.

Giving the Get

The divorce procedure is entirely the husband's prerogative in Jewish law. The wife can't institute or force a divorce proceeding. A divorce occurs only when the husband gives his wife a special document called a *get*.

The get shares several similarities with the ketubah. The get is a formal legal document, specially written by a scribe, with language that describes the monetary settlement and declares the marriage ended "according to the laws of Moses and Israel." Like the ketubah, the get requires two witnesses. The husband gives the document to his wife, and it's ritually torn to finalize the divorce. He must then fulfill the financial obligations outlined in the ketubah.

The Problem of Abandoned Women

The requirement that the husband give his wife the document to effectuate a divorce, and the wife's inability to initiate divorce proceedings under traditional Jewish law, creates serious problems in some circumstances. Some husbands have refused to give their wives a get, causing them to become *agunot,* or "chained women." Agunot may not remarry because they remain their husbands' wives.

Jewish communities have taken several steps to alleviate this problem. Some Jewish courts have ordered husbands to give their wives a get, or have organized communal pressure to compel the husband to participate in the divorce. Some grooms sign a prenuptial agreement promising to give their wives a get if she requests one. Some ketubot include special words called the Lieberman clause, named after its author Rabbi Saul Lieberman, requiring the husband and wife to submit their case to a rabbinic court and abide by the decision.

The Reform movement has rejected the need for a get for a woman to remarry, especially if the husband unreasonably withholds his participation in the required procedure. The Reform Movement instead has a ceremony of separation that doesn't involve a traditional get, or recognizes a divorce granted by a civil court. Nevertheless, some women find themselves in very difficult circumstances due to their beliefs, the beliefs of the community, and their husbands' refusal to provide the get.

The Least You Need to Know

- Marriage is one of the most joyous occasions in a Jew's life, and Judaism traditionally views marriage as an ideal for everyone.
- There are several rituals for a Jewish couple leading up to the wedding ceremony. These include the veiling of the bride (Bedeken) and the signing of the wedding agreement (ketubah).
- The wedding ceremony takes place under a chuppah. There are several meaningful rituals in the ceremony, including the giving of a ring to the bride, the recitation of seven special blessings (sheva brachot), and the breaking of a glass.
- It's a great mitzvah to rejoice with the bride and groom, making them happy and treating them like royalty.
- Judaism allows divorce, finding it to be a cause for sadness but desirable in some circumstances. Traditionally, a divorce occurs only when a husband gives his wife a special document called a get.

Choosing to Become Chosen: Conversion to Judaism

There are two ways for a person to become Jewish. One is to be born Jewish. The other is to convert to Judaism.

The model for conversion to Judaism comes from the beginning of the Book of Ruth. A Jewish woman named Naomi had two sons who each married a Moabite woman, one named Orpah and the other named Ruth. Naomi's husband and sons died, leaving the women alone. Naomi urged her daughters-in-law to return to their people. Orpah did, but Ruth refused. She told Naomi, "Don't ask me to leave you, or stop me from following you. Wherever you go, I will go. Where you stay, I will stay. Your people shall be my people, and your God shall be my God. (Ruth 1:16)

The rules and procedures for conversion to Judaism have become much more complicated since Ruth's time. Jewish sages and authorities over time adopted a particular perspective and rituals for conversion. Today, conversion to Judaism is not uncommon, but it's also not something that happens all the time due to the sages' viewpoints on the matter.

In This Chapter

- Jewish reluctance to seek converts
- Reasons why some people become Jewish
- A year of exploration
- Rituals performed in the conversion process

Jewish Perspectives on Conversion

Judaism takes a somewhat split perspective on conversion. On the one hand, Judaism does not seek converts; but on the other, Jews venerate and honor those who do choose to join them.

Rejection of Proselytization

Some religions view part of their mission as bringing the teachings of their religion to others. They seek to convince others to adopt their beliefs.

Judaism takes the opposite view. While conversion to Judaism is possible, Jews don't try to convince people to adopt Judaism or become part of their people. A person may become a *ger*, the Hebrew word for proselyte, but the desire to become Jewish must spring entirely from the person choosing to join the Jewish people. This rejection of seeking converts may arise from the perspective that Jews have never believed their religion is the only way to become close to God and be a moral person. Another reason might be that others have targeted Jews for conversion and they haven't liked it. As Hillel taught, "What is hateful to you, do not do to another."

WORTH NOTING

The Jacob Rader Marcus Center of the American Jewish Archives in Cincinnati, Ohio, keeps records of anyone in the United States who chooses Judaism and sends them a copy of their *te'udat ger* (conversion certificate).

There have been exceptions to this rule throughout history. Abraham and Sarah sought people to join them when they first accepted monotheism. Some scholars believe there's some evidence of Jewish efforts to proselytize in early Rome. Today, the Reform Movement has shown a greater openness to *gerim* (the plural of ger), and several Jews from different movements have questioned whether Jews should be more encouraging of conversion to bolster their numbers. The weight of history and tradition still curbs these opinions, and Jews don't seek converts in any way in comparison to those of other faiths who make such efforts a central focus of their religion.

Once, Twice, Three Times Discouraged

The reluctance to proselytize gave rise to the practice of discouraging prospective gerim three times. Rabbis would tell the ger about all the challenges of being Jewish, including the burden of ritual requirements and the hostility Jews have encountered throughout history. If the prospective ger returns after the third attempt to dissuade him or her from becoming Jewish, the rabbi accepts his or her desire as true, and the conversion process may continue.

Many in the non-Orthodox movements don't try as hard to discourage people from choosing Judaism as rabbis did in the past. These rabbis want to be more welcoming and present a more compassionate appearance. I have told prospective gerim that I will not try to discourage them from becoming Jewish three times, but if they're like most gerim, they'll encounter at least three challenges or obstacles in the process. These may be family issues, things they have to give up, or the burden of learning Judaism and living a Jewish life. It may be the difficulty of truly feeling Jewish, or feeling that they don't know as much as those who are born Jewish. Whether stated explicitly or received through experience, a ger is certain to confront discouragement. However, if they truly want to join the Jewish faith, they will.

Acceptance and Blessing of Gerim

Once someone has converted to Judaism, it is a mitzvah for other Jews to respect and accept that person completely. They've persevered through the discouragement, and successfully completed a long process to fulfill their wish. If someone is known as a ger, it's not mentioned nor do Jews treat him or her any differently. As Jewish tradition teaches, all Jews were at Sinai and accepted the Torah, including those who choose to become Jewish. (Talmud Bavli, Shavuot 39a)

WORDS OF WISDOM

"The Holy One of Blessing said, 'The names of proselytes are beloved to Me like the wine of libation brought to the alter.'"—Leviticus Rabbah 1:2

One of the reasons the texts may emphasize this acceptance is that some Jews find it difficult to extend a full welcoming to gerim. Jews often have insular communities, viewing outsiders with suspicion. A person seeking to join this community from the outside might raise even more concerns. Nevertheless, Jewish teachings tell Jews to overcome any negative thoughts they might have about gerim and to accept them completely.

Why Do Some People Choose Judaism?

Many different paths lead prospective gerim to choose Judaism. There's no single pattern or set of circumstances that defines a Jew-by-Choice except the honest desire to become Jewish on his or her own.

Some choose Judaism based on the appeal of the culture or the religious philosophy. They might disagree with some aspects of the religion in which they were raised, or find after consideration and study that Judaism is a better fit for what they believe.

Some find the customs and traditions of Judaism very appealing. The closeness of the community attracts them to join. In some ways, these gerim desire an attachment more to the people of Israel than the religion of Judaism, which suffices for many rabbis and communities to justify conversion.

Some people encounter Judaism for the first time through the person with whom they fall in love. Someone who is not Jewish may fall in love with a Jew, and they may want to marry. The question of religion for the couple and any children may arise. What kind of wedding ceremony will they have? Who will perform the ceremony? What holidays will be observed in the home? What will they teach the children about their religious identity? Answering these questions can be difficult, and the decision might be made that the non-Jewish partner will convert to Judaism.

WORTH NOTING

A number of gerim discover they had Jewish relatives in their ancestries. Sometimes they know this before they convert, and other times they only learn of this afterward. Some people in this situation have described to me their desire to become Jewish as "a draw I felt in my bones" or "a feeling of returning home."

This can be somewhat tricky for the rabbi. A person must want to become Jewish for himself or herself, and not for someone else or to make their family life easier. Conversion to Judaism is not something one should do to make someone else happy. It's one thing if the prospective ger has been exposed to Judaism by his or her love and has decided to accept Judaism as part of who he or she is. It's something very different if the person wants to convert "for my spouse," "for the children," or "for my in-laws' acceptance." A rabbi and a prospective ger need to have deep conversations about the person's motivations to become Jewish and decide whether this truly is the right thing to do.

The Conversion Process

A conversion must be done with the guidance and supervision of a rabbi. You can't simply declare yourself Jewish, or say you accept Jewish beliefs, and immediately become Jewish. Instead, conversion to Judaism requires a great deal of personal exploration and experience as a student of a rabbi.

Rabbis will have varied expectations for a prospective ger. An Orthodox rabbi will expect the ger to adopt an Orthodox perspective and lifestyle. Non-Orthodox rabbis might expect the ger to adopt practices more in line with their respective movements. A prospective ger needs to consider the philosophy and perspectives of the rabbi as much as the rabbi needs to consider the views and practices of the ger.

ASK THE RABBI

Will every rabbi accept every conversion guided by other rabbis? The acceptance of a ger depends on the beliefs of the rabbi. Some more traditional rabbis will not accept conversions directed by rabbis of the more liberal movements because they can't be sure the proper rituals were performed to their standards. It might be that a rabbi didn't require a ger to adopt the viewpoints and requirements of traditional Judaism.

A Year of Study and Experience

Most rabbis require their prospective gerim to study Judaism and experience Jewish life for at least a year. This allows gerim time to understand Judaism and appreciate everything about the religion and the people they seek to join. They have a year of observing Shabbat and experiencing each of the holy days at least once. This year gives gerim ample time to reflect upon their choice to convert and the changes it will bring to their lives. The extended time period gives the gerim the opportunity to change their minds, and to prove to themselves, the rabbi, and the community their commitment to becoming Jewish.

The year is not a fixed period. Much depends on the individual circumstances of each ger. Some gerim have lived as part of a Jewish family and have studied for years before finally deciding to convert to Judaism. In such a case, a rabbi might decide that the time the ger must be actively in the conversion process can be shorter. Others may need more time to study, consider their choices, and become ready for a Jewish life. In such a case, it may take much more than a year for someone to become Jewish.

WORTH NOTING

If parents have a child converted, the child may renounce the conversion at the time of bar or bat mitzvah. This is the only opportunity the child has to reject the conversion.

Very few rabbis will perform a conversion in a short timespan, such as a few weeks or a few months. No matter the stated needs or time pressures that may be caused by a pregnancy or a scheduled wedding, rabbis generally will not allow the conversion unless they're certain the candidate is ready and has met the requirements.

Circumcision or Hatafat Dam Brit

Traditionally, a Jewish male must be circumcised as the sign of the Covenant required by Genesis. Adult males who desire to convert almost always must be circumcised as part of the conversion process. Unlike a bris for a baby, modesty and the extent of the procedure means the circumcision usually occurs in private and not as part of a community celebration. Like a bris for a baby, the appropriate blessings must be recited to designate the act as done for religious purpose.

If the prospective ger already has been circumcised, the rabbi usually requires *hatafat dam brit*. This is a tiny elicitation of blood from the area of the circumcision performed after reciting the proper prayers and blessings. In effect, this gives the prior circumcision the intent of being the sign of the Covenant as required of all Jews.

Some Reform rabbis don't require an adult male to undergo circumcision to convert, although the trend is that more are requiring or encouraging the procedure.

The Beit Din (Rabbinic Court)

After the prospective ger has studied and experienced Judaism, and the rabbi believes he or she is ready, the ger must appear before a *Beit Din*.

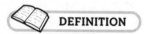 **DEFINITION**

> **Beit Din**, meaning "house of law," is a court of three learned Jews, most often rabbis, entitled to hear and decide legal matters. A common use of a Beit Din is to determine whether a prospective ger is ready to become Jewish.

The Beit Din is an opportunity for the ger to tell his or her story and answer questions about the Jewish life he or she wishes to lead. The Beit Din then decides whether the ger has the true desire and commitment to be a Jew. If so, the ger may continue to the next stage of the process.

The Mikvah (Ritual Bath)

The next step for the ger is to go to the *mikvah*. The mikvah is a ritual bath covered in more detail in Chapter 25. For the purpose of conversion, the ger immerses himself or herself in the water three times with the intention of doing so to become Jewish. The spiritually transformative power of the water in this case completes the process, and the ger emerges from the water as a Jew.

Ceremony and Celebration

Many rabbis have their gerim perform an additional step in the conversion process with a ceremony. Some perform the ceremony before the entire congregation. Others do it privately, perhaps witnessed only by family and friends. Ceremonies vary among the movements and different rabbis, but often the ger is invited to hold the sefer Torah and recite the words of the Sh'mah.

Many gerim also have a celebratory meal to rejoice in the completion of the process and the beginning of their lives as Jews.

The Least You Need to Know

- Jews traditionally don't proselytize; however, it is possible to convert to Judaism.
- Once a person converts to Judaism, halachah requires that person to be treated exactly the same as anyone born as a Jew.
- Conversion to Judaism is usually a long process involving at least a year of study and experience.
- A ger generally must perform several rituals, including circumcision or hatafat dam brit if male, appearing before a Beit Din, and immersion in a mikvah.

When a Jew Dies

A midrash explores the meaning of Ecclesiastes 7:1, which states, "The day of death is better than the day of birth." The midrash compares a person's life to two ships in a port, as one leaves on a voyage and the other arrives after its journey. It remarks that people gather at the water's edge to rejoice as the first ship leaves, but no one rejoices for the returning ship. The midrash questions the people's actions, noting that no one knows if the departing ship's journey will be a success, but everyone knows the returning ship has completed its voyage safely. Shouldn't people rejoice for the returning ship instead of the departing vessel?

Judaism views death as a part of life. Just as Jews celebrate and praise God when a new life begins, they also give thanks, praise God, and even celebrate a life well lived when it ends. Judaism commemorates death with a complex set of rituals, prayers, and practices that encourage memory and respect for the person who has died, and aids those who survive to grieve and return to their lives.

In This Chapter

- The goals of Jewish mourning
- Respect for the body
- Giving honor at the funeral
- Continuing support and remembrance

Guiding Values When a Jew Dies

The customs and practices surrounding death developed from important guiding principles. Everything that happens to the deceased's body and through Jewish ritual reflects one or more of these concerns.

Kavod HaMeit—Honoring the Departed

Judaism requires that each person receive honor upon his or her death. God created everyone *b'tzelem Elohim*—in God's image. Judaism teaches that each life has infinite value. A death requires the deceased's family, friends, and community to demonstrate respect and appreciation for the deceased's contributions, achievements, and everything that made that person's life special. Jewish tradition teaches that no matter a person's wealth, social standing, or behavior, there are always aspects of that person's life to honor.

Importantly, *Kavod HaMeit* doesn't require the living to lie about the deceased, or exaggerate his or her admirable qualities. It also doesn't allow the mourners to ignore the deceased's faults or struggles. Kavod HaMeit instead requires an honest memorial of the deceased. The deceased receives honor by others remembering him or her as he or she truly lived, for the good and for the bad, as long as people speak about the person with respect, care, honesty, and love.

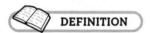 **DEFINITION**

> **Kavod HaMeit** is the honoring of the dead, one of the primary requirements during the mourning and remembrance process for someone who has died.

Nichum Aveilim—Comforting the Mourners

The second value guiding the Jewish practices and customs concerning death is *Nichum Aveilim*—comforting the mourners. The tradition recognizes that some people were closer to the deceased than others, and these people need greater care and solace. Jewish tradition also acknowledges that it's difficult for a person to stand alone when buffeted by the winds of sadness and grief. However, when people lean upon each other and give each other support, it's far easier to remain standing, weather the storms of sorrow, and endure to return to life and joy. Comforting the mourners therefore becomes an essential part of Jewish practice after someone has died.

Dust to Dust

The sages interpret several verses in the Tanach to describe appropriate treatment of the body after someone has died. In Genesis 3:19, God tells Adam, "By the sweat of your brow shall you get bread to eat until you return to the ground, for from [the ground] were you taken. For you are dust, and to dust you shall return." Ecclesiastes 3:20 reiterates this idea, saying, "Everyone goes to the same place, all come from dust, and all return to dust."

The sages understand these verses to mean that nothing should interfere with the natural process of the body returning to the earth and its natural decomposition. As we shall see, this has a significant influence on the timing, rituals, and care of the deceased's body following death.

When Someone Is Dying

One of the hardest experiences anyone can endure is watching someone they love in their final moments. Judaism provides a theology and several rituals that aid and bring comfort to both the person dying and his or her loved ones.

God as the True Judge

Judaism acknowledges that God is the True Judge of when we are born and when we die. We know a great amount about the process of birth and dying, and we can do much to affect the timing of these events. Science has given us a great amount of understanding. Nevertheless, Jews understand that humanity's power over these events is limited. Ultimately, when we are born and when we die lie in a power beyond humanity that Judaism calls God.

WORDS OF WISDOM

"God has given; God has taken away. Blessed be the Name of God."–Job 1:21

In this respect, Jews call God *Dayan HaEmet*—"The True Judge." God determines the timing of birth and death, and there's an aspect of these processes that remains a mystery to us. Many Jews find this idea comforting, for even though they may not understand why someone dies at a particular time, they may accept that the event isn't within their control. They can trust that the process of dying remains within God's governance, and they know that this event, as sad as it may be, can be trusted to God.

Vidu'i and Sh'mah

Jews may recite two prayers as someone's death approaches, for themselves and on behalf of the person who is dying. The first is the *Vidu'i,* a confessional prayer similar to a prayer said on Yom Kippur. The purpose of the Vidu'i at someone's deathbed isn't to ensure a cleansed soul leading to a better afterlife. Instead, it's part of the obligation everyone has to do teshuvah, returning to the state they were in before they sinned. Normally, Jews do this on Yom Kippur, but the dying person won't have that opportunity. Reciting Vidu'i as the moment of death approaches allows the dying person to fulfill this obligation to atone for everything they've done since Yom Kippur prior to their passing.

> **ASK THE RABBI**
>
> Is euthanasia permitted in Judaism? There are differences of opinion between the movements of Judaism on some of the details on this topic. In general, euthanasia isn't permitted in Judaism, and no one may take an affirmative action to cause or hasten someone's death. However, in some circumstances where death is imminent and inevitable, some authorities allow the family to let the natural process of death occur, forgoing efforts to extend life further.

The other prayer Jews may recite as death approaches is the Sh'mah. This assertion of belief in God and affirmation of God's Oneness reinforces Jewish faith. Death is the time when Jews most need to hear that there is something meaningful, eternal, and good, even when a life ends. The Sh'mah gives that message at the most difficult time people experience.

Preparing the Body

The intense mourning period from the moment of someone's death until burial is called *aninut*. During this time, Jewish law designates each person in seven categories of relatives of the deceased to be an *onen*. Leviticus 21:1-3 sets these relatives as the deceased's father, mother, sisters, brothers, sons, daughters, and spouse. An onen is exempt from many of the mitzvot so that he or she may cope with the shock and feelings of their relative's passing, and make sure proper actions occur to care for the deceased's body.

Chevre Kadisha

The *chevre kadisha*, or "holy society," is the group of people entrusted to care for the body of the deceased. Participation in the chevre kadisha is a great honor, and it's one of the most important institutions in a Jewish community.

The members of the chevre kadisha must be learned Jews, knowledgeable of the laws concerning care of the body and the prayers to be recited when someone dies. They also need to be able to perform their duties with respect and care, avoiding joking or disrespect while doing so. They also must be able to handle the body while maintaining their poise, health, and equilibrium, a difficult task for some while viewing or touching a dead body.

Men comprise the chevre kadisha for men, and women do the same for women. Even in death, the importance of *tzni'ut* (modesty) applies.

Care for the Body

It's crucial in Judaism for the deceased's body to receive the highest level of care, because God created each person b'tzelem Elohim—in God's image. Consequently, Judaism requires the chevre kadisha to treat a person's body with the same kind of care and respect they would give to anything else to do with God. The practices of caring for the body also enact the idea of Kavod HaMeit—honoring the deceased.

The chevre kadisha approaches the body with honor, handling it gently. They perform a ritual washing for spiritual purification called *taharah,* and ensure that the body reaches its destination safely. Traditionally, the body is never left alone from the moment of death until burial, and many Jews have a person stay with the body through the night reading psalms.

Prior to burial, the body is wrapped in a plain white shroud of simple cloth. The white represents purity, and the simplicity of the garment demonstrates that everyone leaves life with no property or worldly possessions. The garment's simplicity also demonstrates the equality of people in death, as everyone, rich or poor, enters and leaves life the same way. Instead of or in addition to the shroud, some people are buried wearing a kittel or tallit.

The value of allowing the body to naturally return to dust according to the natural process affects the procedures for care of the body. Jewish law prohibits the use of embalming or any preservative that delays the natural process. It requires burial of the body whole and in its natural state, precluding the practice of cremation and the adornment of the body with jewelry or cosmetics. The halachah prohibits donating the body for medical study or experimentation. Similarly, Jewish law prohibits autopsies unless required by the civil authorities or necessary to gain knowledge to imminently save the life of someone else.

WORTH NOTING

Organ donation is permissible and encouraged by most Jewish authorities, because the value of *pekuach nefesh*—saving a life—exceeds even the important value of allowing the body to return to dust.

The Funeral and Interment

The funeral and interment of the body is the primary commemoration for the dead in the Jewish tradition. Unlike many faiths, there isn't a formal gathering or remembrance prior to the funeral. There also isn't any public viewing of the body. Jewish tradition observes that people tend to gawk or react with shock to the viewing of a dead body, especially for Jews because the halachah prohibits the use of cosmetics or preservatives that would make the body appear more as he or she did in life. Jewish tradition considers this gawking or shock to contradict the value of Kavod HaMeit, so there aren't open caskets at Jewish funerals.

Timing and Location

Jewish funerals take place very quickly. They usually occur during daylight within 24 to 48 hours after the person has died. As Deuteronomy 21:23 describes, leaving a body unattended or unburied is considered disrespectful, even for a sinner put to death. A delay may occur to allow a family member an extra day or two to travel to attend the funeral, or because the civil authorities require the delay. Jews also don't hold funerals on Shabbat or the first or final days of festivals, although they may occur on *Chol Hamoeid.*

A Jewish funeral may take place in a home, synagogue, chapel, or at the cemetery itself at grave-side. The idea of setting aside a sacred place for the burial of a loved one comes from Abraham's purchase of the cave of Machpelah for his wife Sarah when she died. (Genesis 23) Traditionally, Jewish cemeteries consist of consecrated land set apart from other parcels by a fence or wall. Most traditional Jewish cemeteries allow the burial of only Jews within these walls, although a growing number of Jewish cemeteries have at least a section where non-Jewish family members may be buried alongside Jews.

The Casket

The common phrase for a Jewish casket is a "plain pine box." Reflecting the idea of modesty and equality among rich and poor in death, Jewish caskets usually are unadorned and simple. They're commonly made of pine, although any wood will suffice.

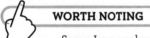 **WORTH NOTING**

Some Jews are buried with earth from Israel, symbolically expressing hope for the return of the Mashiach as described in Chapter 18.

The other factor affecting Jewish caskets is the need to allow the body to naturally return to dust. This need prohibits the use of metal in the casket's construction, or the inclusion of fabrics that don't decompose. Some Jewish caskets have holes in their bottoms, further connecting the body to the earth and allowing its easier return to dust.

Keriah

The Tanach describes several occasions when someone tears his or her clothing upon hearing of the death of a loved one. Jacob tears his clothes when he sees Joseph's bloody coat of many colors, believing the tale of his other sons that Joseph has died. (Genesis 37:34) David tears his clothes upon hearing of Saul and Jonathan's deaths. (II Samuel 1:11) Job tears his clothing after hearing of the death of his children. (Job 1:20)

Jews maintain the tradition of tearing their clothing when someone has died, a tradition called *keriah*. Some Jews tear their clothes as soon as they hear of the death. Others make the tear immediately before the funeral. Some Jews tear the clothing they're wearing, while others tear a black ribbon specially worn and designated for the ritual.

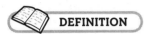 **DEFINITION**

Keriah is a ritual tearing of clothing or a special black ribbon upon hearing of the death of a close relative.

Traditionally, the same relatives designated as onen perform keriah: the deceased's mother, father, sister, brother, son, daughter, and spouse. A child tears over his or her heart on the left side upon the passing of a parent, and other relatives tear on the right. Although the tradition limits keriah to these relatives, some rabbis and families feel the purpose of keriah is to connect the closest relatives to the deceased and begin the formal mourning process. Knowing that the traditional definition of the seven relatives doesn't necessarily include the closest relatives in modern families, some rabbis allow other relatives to participate in keriah, such as grandchildren or in-laws.

The Funeral Service

The funeral service begins with comforting words from the Tanach. Several psalms and passages bring solace, reassuring the mourners of the presence of God even when a death occurs. Psalm 23 is especially notable among these selections. Its heartening and familiar message that God stands with people "even as [they] walk through the valley of the shadow of death" provides Jews comfort at the most difficult time of a funeral.

Other psalms and readings at the beginning of the funeral include:

Reading	Message
Psalm 15	God cares for the righteous
Psalm 16	God doesn't abandon people
Psalm 90	Though we return to dust, and our lives are short, God allows the work of our hands to endure
Psalm 121	We look to the mountain, and help comes from God
Proverbs 31	Special praise for a woman of valor

The funeral service continues with at least one *hesped,* a telling about the deceased's life designed to honor the deceased's character, achievements, and joys. Importantly, a hesped doesn't ignore the deceased's faults or failures. Jews recognize that no one is perfect, acknowledging this truth even after a person dies. A hesped needs to be a true recounting of the entirety of the deceased's life, finding ways to tell the deceased's story in a way that both gives honor and is truthful. If someone goes to a funeral, listens to the hesped, and remarks that the hesped didn't describe the deceased at all, the hesped hasn't served its purpose.

Sometimes, only the rabbi delivers the hesped. It has become more common for some relatives and friends also to deliver *hespedim* (the plural of hesped) although it's not necessary for anyone besides the rabbi to speak.

Following the hesped or hespedim, the funeral continues with an important prayer called *Eil Malei Rachamin,* which means "God full of mercy." This prayer specifically names the deceased, and expresses faith that he or she will be taken "into the shelter of God's wings." This prayer is both an assertion of belief and an offering of comfort for the mourners that the deceased's soul continues with God beyond life.

The mourners then accompany the deceased to his or her final resting place in the cemetery if the service until now has occurred in a home, synagogue, or chapel. Relatives and friends often serve as pallbearers, carrying the casket to the grave. Some communities have the tradition of pausing the procession at various times to show the sadness and reluctance to say goodbye, even though this is something that must occur.

 WORDS OF WISDOM

"Caring for the deceased is one of the highest mitzvot because it is a favor the deceased can never repay."

—Traditional Jewish teaching

The mourners then recite *Kaddish Yatom,* a special prayer said in memory of someone who has died. A *Kaddish* is a prayer that praises God for life that Jews recite whenever they finish a section of a service, a course of study, or the end of a life.

It's noteworthy that a form of the Kaddish came to be associated with death because it never mentions death. Instead, it praises God for the joy and sweetness of life. A story explains that the Kaddish first became the prayer recited upon completion of a Torah lesson or study of a tractate of Talmud. The sages then decided that every teacher's life was a lesson, so they should recite the prayer after a teacher died.

The story continues to say that a young boy told the sages he wanted to recite the Kaddish for his father who had died. The sages scoffed at the boy, explaining that this prayer was reserved only for teachers. The boy replied, "My father was my greatest teacher." From that moment, the Kaddish became the prayer recited for everyone, because everyone's life is a lesson with value worthy of praise to God.

At this point in the funeral service, the casket is lowered to its resting place. Jews then take part in an important custom of placing earth within the grave. The purpose of this ritual is to honor the deceased and care for him or her until the final moment. Some Jews use their hands to place earth into the grave. Others use a shovel, placing three portions of earth upon the casket. Traditionally, the mourner uses the back side of the blade for the first portion of earth and the normal side for the other two portions, and then replaces the shovel in the mound of dirt instead of handing it to the next mourner. These actions demonstrate that even though it's a mitzvah to perform this act, it's something we do reluctantly, without appearing eager to say farewell. Some communities fill the entire grave with earth, and others feel the obligation is completed if the casket is covered, allowing the cemetery's staff to fill the remainder of the grave.

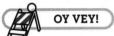 **OY VEY!**

Losing a loved one is one of the hardest experiences anyone experiences. Different communities and people vary in their customs and preferences, especially at this difficult time. Don't be surprised if you go to a Jewish funeral and the practices diverge from those described here.

Friends then form two lines of condolence so that the onen may walk away from the grave hearing words of comfort. It's traditional to tell the mourners, "May God comfort you among all the mourners of Zion and Jerusalem."

Sitting Shiva

Following the interment, the mourners return to the home of the deceased or a relative for *shiva*. Shiva is a period of mourning, reflection, and remembering the deceased. Traditionally, Jews "sit shiva" for seven days, although some Jews may shorten the time to anywhere from one to three days.

The Purpose of Shiva

Shiva provides the mourners an opportunity to reflect upon the loss they've just suffered. The idea of shiva is to stop the ordinary course of life because a significant change has happened with the death of their loved one. Shiva is a time to tell stories, give honor to the deceased, and care for those who feel the loss most keenly. By the end of shiva, the mourner hopefully has accepted the change and is prepared to return to most of the ordinary activities of life.

Shiva Practices and Restrictions

Upon returning from the cemetery, many Jews wash their hands before entering the house where shiva takes place. This is a ritual purification that reflects the transition from caring for the deceased to the beginning of shiva. Immediately upon returning from the ceremony, the mourners eat a *seudah haberiah*—a meal of condolence. Traditional foods for this meal include hard-boiled eggs and bread, as these foods represent life, reminding the mourners that life continues even in the face of loss.

The relatives traditionally required to sit shiva are those who were onen. These relatives of the deceased reside in the home, not going out to work, doing errands, or anything usually done in ordinary life. Others come to the house to offer comfort, allow the mourners an opportunity to talk about their memories and their feelings, and make sure the mourners are taking care of themselves during this difficult time.

The mourners required to sit shiva have several restrictions upon them, including refraining from cutting hair or shaving, no grooming or bathing for pleasure, no cosmetics, no sex, no wearing new clothing, and no wearing leather. This is a time to refrain from any luxuries or pleasures. Many people sit on low stools during shiva. They cover mirrors in the home because shiva is a time to avoid any sign of vanity. People sitting shiva also refrain from studying Torah, as this act is seen by the Jewish tradition to add joy, which is to be avoided at this time.

A *shiva minyon* occurs in the home. Members of the community have conflicting requirements. They must comfort the mourners and they must go to worship. Because shiva occurs in the home and the minyon occurs in the synagogue, performing both requirements presents a challenge. The tradition resolves this problem by moving the service to the shiva home.

What to Do, Say, and Bring

It's always appropriate to make a shiva call, even if you don't know the person who has died. It's a mitzvah to comfort the mourner, and the presence of friends and community members helps the mourners cope with their grief.

Many families set a specific time when the house will be open for people to visit. Often, you may check the obituary, or call the synagogue or funeral home to learn these times.

The appropriate greeting for the mourner is "May you be comforted with the mourners of Zion and Jerusalem." Jews generally don't say "shalom" or any of the usual greetings at this time. It's then important to allow the mourner the opportunity to speak about his or her feelings or memories. The presence of friends and community members provides this opportunity, allowing the mourner to receive comfort and emotionally process the loss. A shiva visitor shouldn't try to explain the death or offer platitudes, but should listen and share the mourners' sorrow. There are many emotions experienced during shiva as the mourners both feel their sadness and remember joyous times with the deceased—but it never should become a party or festive atmosphere.

It's appropriate to bring food to the home, remembering the dietary restrictions of *kashrut* many Jews observe. Sometimes, friends organize who will bring food on different days, so the family isn't inundated with food one day and have nothing on the next.

ASK THE RABBI

Should I bring or send flowers? Generally, the answer to this is no. Jews don't use flowers to symbolize death; in Judaism, flowers are a symbol of life. As a practice different from other religions, most Jews don't have flowers at funerals or shiva. Instead, it's appropriate to give tzedakah, making a charitable donation to a cause designated by the family or connected with something the deceased valued.

After Shiva

The mourning process continues after the days of Shiva. Jewish practice gradually brings the mourner back into ordinary life, helping him or her cope with the loss in the months after the death.

Sheloshim

Sheloshim means "thirty," and refers to the first thirty days after the death. As during shiva, the seven relatives have limitations on their actions, although they're less severe than those imposed during shiva. The mourners may leave the home, return to work, and conduct most ordinary activities. However, they still may not shave, cut their hair, get married, or attend parties. Sheloshim is an intermediate step between the intense days following the loss and the return to ordinary life.

After Sheloshim

During the year following the death, the mourner may say the Kaddish prayer for the deceased at synagogue. Some Jews make a special effort to attend the minyon every day to remember their loved one.

On Yom Kippur and the festivals, a special service called *Yizkor* occurs that remembers those who have died. Jews remember their relatives at these services for the rest of their lives.

Additionally, the relatives commemorate the *yahrzeit*, the anniversary of the death, every year by lighting a special yahrzeit candle and going to the synagogue to say Kaddish in the minyon.

Unveiling

Genesis 35:19-20 says Jacob set a pillar on Rachel's grave. Jews today follow this practice by erecting a headstone or monument at the graves of their loved ones.

These markers may be ornate or simple, and often contain the person's name in Hebrew and the language of the country, the date of birth and death, the family he or she left behind, and an expression of prayer that God care for his or her soul.

> **WORTH NOTING**
>
> When Jews visit a cemetery, they often mark their visit by placing a small stone on the marker or monument. Perhaps borrowed from the ancient practice of marking the location of a grave to allow the living to avoid ritual impurity, the placement of a stone is a sign of caring and respect for the deceased.

The marker is consecrated through a special ceremony called an Unveiling. Many of the same psalms and prayers said at the funeral are recited at the Unveiling, including the Eil Malei Rachamim and the Kaddish. Some Jews believe the Unveiling must take place one year after the death, but it actually may occur at any time after a few months following Sheloshim.

The Least You Need to Know

- Jews grieve and commemorate a death according to the values of Kavod HaMeit (honoring the dead), Nichum Aveilim (comforting the mourner), and returning the body to the earth.
- The chevre kadisha cares for the body, ritually washing it and making sure it's treated with respect. No preservatives may be used and no changes to the body may occur.
- Jewish funerals usually take place within 24 to 48 hours after death. It's an important mitzvah to mourn and care for someone who has died.
- The seven relatives—mother, father, sister, brother, son, daughter, and spouse—are required to sit shiva after the death, and refrain from ordinary activities and pleasures. The tradition then gradually eases the restrictions, aiding the mourners to return to ordinary life after suffering the loss.

CHAPTER 18

The Next Frontier: After Death

The midrash often expresses itself creatively, using parables, making comparisons, or giving life to the letters of the Torah. In one such midrash, the letter *aleph* comes before God with a complaint. The aleph said, "God, I am the first letter of the alphabet. Why don't I get the honor of being the first letter of the Torah?"

God said to the aleph, "First, you do get an honor. You are the first letter of the Ten Commandments: *Ani Adonai Elochecha*—I am Adonai your God. But, second, I wanted the beit to be the first letter of the Torah to give a message to the Israelites. (The beit is closed on three sides—the top, the bottom, and the right. It is open only on the left, in the direction Hebrew reads—right to left). The message is that the Israelites can't know what is above, what is below, or what is before. They can know only what is in the Torah." (Genesis Rabbah 1:10)

Jews have understood this midrash to acknowledge that human understanding is limited, particularly when it comes to the question of what happens after death. Generally, Jews don't believe they can know exactly what happens after people die. They may adopt some general ideas and concepts, and there has been some speculation about what might

In This Chapter

- A lack of definitive answers
- The everlasting soul
- The biblical idea of Sheol
- The world to come and resurrection
- A note on reincarnation

happen. However, in general, Judaism is devoid of the clear detailed descriptions of life after death some other religions provide.

Judaism's views of what happens after death are undeveloped, with few precise details and many questions deliberately left unanswered. Judaism views the purpose of life to be fulfilling the Covenant with God, doing mitzvot, and focusing attention on the world of the living. Whatever comes after death will inevitably come to everyone soon enough, and everyone will discover what happens after death eventually. However, some significant concepts and ideas about what awaits us after death have evolved that are important to understanding Judaism.

The Immortality of the Soul

Judaism says each person has a soul given to him or her by God. The Torah describes God as creating the body of the first person, Adam, from the dust of the Earth. However, Adam receives life only when God breathes into him the breath of life, giving Adam a "living soul." (Genesis 2:7) This differentiation between the body and the soul persists throughout most of Jewish thought. The two are related, but though the body will die, the soul is immortal. This actually becomes a problem between God and Adam and Eve. After Adam and Eve eat from the Tree of Knowledge against God's will, God expresses concern that they will also eat from the Tree of Life and gain physical immortality. God expels Adam and Eve from the Garden of Eden because of this. (Genesis 3:22-23) This guaranteed that humans would have limited physical lives.

However, the soul God breathes into every human remains immortal. Traditional Jews express this belief in the morning prayer called the *Elohai Nishamah*, which reads in part, "My God the soul that You implanted within me is pure. You created it, You formed it, You breathed it into me. You keep body and soul together. One day You will take my soul from me, to restore it to me in life eternal." This is a concept implicit in the prophet Ezekiel's famous vision of a valley of bones returned to life. The bodies have died, but the souls remain alive and available to return to physical life if God wills. (Ezekiel 37)

 **OY VEY!**

Some Jews reject the idea that there is *anything* after death. They believe death is a complete and final end, and we live on only in the memories of those we affected in life and in the good deeds we did in our lives. However, most Jews throughout history have taken the view that there is *something* waiting for us after death.

Some Jewish sages have expressed the idea of the immortal essence of a human being not as a soul, but as an immortal intellect. They define *nefesh* not as soul, but as rationality that joins with the Absolute Intellect, God, after death.

The difference between viewing the nefesh of a human being as a soul or an intellect has important philosophical and theological implications well beyond the scope of this book. For our purposes, the important point is that Judaism maintains the idea that God gives each person something that exceeds the physical body and that is immortal.

WORTH NOTING

Maimonides, the great sage of the Middle Ages, infers the belief in an immortal intellect, but doesn't state it explicitly. (Mishneh Torah, Teshuvah 8:3) Even so, Jews of the time considered even the implication to be heresy, and Maimonides had to write a treatise reaffirming his belief in the traditional view of the soul. A later Jewish scholar, Baruch Spinoza, clearly supported the immortal intellect idea in the seventeenth century, and was excommunicated from the Jewish community for it.

Biblical Ideas

The Tanach expresses the first Jewish ideas of what happens to us after death. Like the ideas that will come later, the biblical conceptions of what happens after a person dies are vague and contain only a few definitive elements.

Sheol

The Tanach describes a place called *Sheol* where people go after they die. The term is used many times in the Tanach, from Genesis through the Writings. For example, Jacob expresses his sorrow that his son, Joseph, has gone to Sheol after Joseph's brothers bring him Joseph's bloody coat of many colors. (Genesis 37:35) Similarly, Proverbs warns people not to stray from God's words through the heart's desires because that way leads to Sheol. (Proverbs 7:27)

Sheol is a shadowy place, usually described as located under the earth or in some other low place. It's a place of silence and darkness (Psalms 88:13, 115:17), from which God doesn't hear prayers or pleas. (Psalms 6:6, Isaiah 38:18) According to the Book of Job, there is no return from Sheol. (Job 7:9)

Everyone goes to Sheol when he or she dies. It isn't a place of either punishment or reward. Jacob believed his son, who he thought was a good and honorable person and who Jewish Scripture portrays as one of its heroes, had gone to Sheol when Joseph's brothers brought him the bloody coat. Equally, the rebellious band following Korach, the epitome of misbehaving Israelites in the Tanach, also went to Sheol as their punishment. (Numbers 16:32-33)

Connection with the World of the Living

Sheol has no connection with the living world in terms of communication or interaction. Not only is there no return to the living world from Sheol, but the living may not attempt to communicate with the dead there. Moses forbade the Israelites from consulting with a necromancer, grouping those who claimed to speak to the dead with witches, enchanters, and soothsayers. (Deuteronomy 18:11) The Tanach contains numerous examples of people ignoring this injunction and attempting to communicate with the dead, including King Menasheh of Judah. This is one of the reasons the Tanach says he did "evil in the sight of God." (II Chronicles 33:1-6) The Tanach also prohibits sacrificing to the dead. (Psalms 106:28-30)

Post-Biblical Ideas

Judaism didn't hold to the idea of Sheol following the destruction of the Second Temple. Rabbinic Judaism formed a new idea of what happens to us after death that remains the primary belief in the religion today: *olam haba*.

Olam Haba—The World to Come

The sages formulated an idea called *olam haba*, meaning "the world to come." They explained that at some point in the future, people who had died would live again in a happier, perfect world. Like the Tanach's treatment of Sheol, the sages don't explicitly describe olam haba. However, they clearly view olam haba favorably as a desirable place to go.

Initially, the sages wrote that almost everyone would go to olam haba. The Mishnah said "all Israelites will have a share in olam haba except deniers of resurrection, anyone who says the Torah didn't come from heaven, and Epicurians (a hedonistic philosophy that denies Divine Providence)." (Mishnah, Sanhedrin 10:1) The Mishnah also states that certain groups such as the generation of the Flood also would be excluded from olam haba. (Mishnah, Sanhedrin 10:4)

Eventually, the sages developed the idea that whether someone would go to olam haba depended on their general behavior in life. Those with good admirable characters and deeds would go to olam haba, while those who led a sinful life wouldn't. The poor and Jews who studied Torah would receive a share in olam haba, as would people who were meek, humble, and didn't claim greatness due to their knowledge of Torah. (Talmud Bavli, Sanhedrin 88b) In contrast, those who didn't do mitzvot or generally weren't kind to others wouldn't have a place in olam haba.

People who misbehaved during their lives would go to *Gehonnim*, an undesirable place that shared a name with the valley near the Old City of Jerusalem where a Canaanite sect sacrificed children as part of their worship. (Jeremiah 7:31; II Kings 23:10) The rabbis disagreed as to whether a person's time in Gehonnim was temporary or permanent, and if the former, what happened to a person afterward. The Mishnah says Rabbi Akiva believed people would stay in Gehonnim for only 12 months. (Mishnah, Eduyyot 2:10)

Rabbi Shammai said people who die fall into three categories: one category goes to olam haba, one goes to Gehonnim, and the third goes to Gehonnim *only* for a limited time and then may go to olam haba. (Talmud Bavli, Rosh HaShanah 16b-17a) Some sages say everyone who goes to Gehonnim stays for a limited time, and then the soul is destroyed. (Talmud Bavli, Rosh HaShanah 17a) Like almost everything concerning this issue, the rabbis' opinions vary and don't provide many explicit details or a clear picture of what comes after death.

WORTH NOTING

There are a few complete Jewish descriptions of what happens after death composed by some leaders and rabbis, notable as exceptions to the general practice. One of the most remarkable is a Jewish version of Dante's *Divine Comedy* written by Immanuel ben Solomon of Rome composed in 1321 C.E. following Dante's death.

The sages do provide a few details about life in olam haba. It will be a good life, with peace and contentment for all. It will be a spiritual life. There will be no need for physical pleasure or activity such as eating or sexual intercourse. Everyone will live together without hatred, and all will unite in praise to the one true God. (Talmud Bavli, Berachot 17a)

The Idea of Mashiach (Messiah)

The idea of the Messiah is closely related to olam haba. Messiah comes from the Hebrew word *mashiach*, which literally means "anointed one." In today's world, kings and queens gain their status with a coronation, the placing of a crown upon their heads. In ancient Israelite society, kings gained their status by a priest or other authority pouring or rubbing scented olive oil on the new monarch's head or body.

The idea of the Mashiach is a worldly and political concept. He is the King of Israel, a descendant of King David. Jews throughout history have generally believed the Israelite Kingdom in the Promised Land would be reestablished, led by the Mashiach. This new Mashiach wouldn't have any personal mystical powers, but would be an instrument of God's power in bringing olam haba. In this sense, the Mashiach would be similar to Moses—a leader who God uses to express the Divine Will, but not a miracle worker himself.

In Jewish thought, the coming of the Mashiach will be heralded by the great Jewish prophet Elijah, and will mark God's gift of full redemption to the world. Everything on Earth will be good, similar to life in the Garden of Eden. Maimonides describes this time as, "In that era there will be neither famine nor war, neither jealousy nor conflict. Blessings will be everywhere, within the reach of all." (Mishneh Torah, Hilchot Melachim 12:5)

WORDS OF WISDOM

"I believe with perfect faith in the coming of the Mashiach. Although he may tarry, I will wait for him."

—Traditional Jewish song, "Ani Ma'amim," sung during services, and notably sung by victims of the Holocaust.

Some Jews have adapted the idea of the Mashiach to the political philosophies of the Enlightenment and post-Enlightenment, particularly in the Reform Movement. Instead of a single king, these Jews speak of a Messianic Age, when the world envisioned to come at the time of the Messiah will happen without a king. Instead, the world will reflect democratic ideas of governance held by most in the Western world today.

Resurrection

The mystical aspect of olam haba comes with the idea of resurrection. Maimonides named resurrection as one of his 13 Principles of Faith every Jew must believe, although questions arose as to how strongly he personally held this belief. Nevertheless, the daily liturgy contains the idea of resurrection, as the prayer speaking of God's mightiness, the *Givurot*, calls God *m'chayei meitim*—"the maker of the death." Generally, this is understood to refer to God's power and intent of resurrection of the dead.

The sages don't describe the details of resurrection, and many questions about it remain unanswered. However, the basic idea is that God will resurrect almost everyone who has died, allowing them to live another wonderful life in olam haba. There will be enough room for everyone, although the sages don't explain how that will happen. They don't fully explain whether someone born with an infirmity or enduring an illness or injury during his or her life will suffer the same condition in the resurrected life.

The sages also don't fully explain what happens after a person has lived his or her resurrected life. However, they do express the belief that, however it works, God will ensure the resurrected person's life is blissful and happy. As Rabbi Joshua ben Chanina said in the Talmud about whether the resurrected would require a purification ritual, "When they come to live again, we will discuss the matter." (Talmud Bavli, Niddah 70b)

ASK THE RABBI

Can God resurrect someone with missing body parts? Is this why Judaism requires the burial of complete bodies as much as possible? Judaism says God's power is infinite, and therefore God can resurrect someone completely regardless of the condition of the body. However, keeping the body whole and complete demonstrates Jewish faith in resurrection and represents our partnership with God in making sure everything happens as God wills.

The Reform Movement rejected the idea of resurrection from its beginnings. Article 6 of the first platform adopted by American Reform Rabbis in Philadelphia in 1869 reads, "The belief in bodily resurrection has no religious foundation, and the teaching of immortality is to be expressed exclusively in relation to continued spiritual existence." Some Reform Jews have become more open to the possibility of resurrection in recent years, but they mostly still reject this traditional idea.

Reincarnation

While not a major stream of thought or belief in Judaism, some Kabbalistic Jews have adopted the idea of reincarnation. Called *gilgul nishmamot*—"the turning of souls," resurrection found its way into Kabbalistic thought in the twelfth century. The ideas of resurrection answered the question of why bad things happened to good people: they were suffering as a result of sinful ways they had adopted in an earlier life.

Belief in reincarnation didn't affect belief in olam haba and resurrection. A person would continue to live lives through reincarnation, purifying and perfecting the soul, until the arrival of olam haba.

Some Chassidic sects and Jews studying Kabbalah today still believe in resurrection. But most Jews haven't adopted these beliefs.

The Least You Need to Know

- Judaism doesn't provide clearly developed ideas of what happens to a person after death beyond the belief in the immortality of the soul.
- The Tanach describes a shadowy place called Sheol where everyone goes when they die.
- The idea of Sheol evolved to a belief in olam haba, the World to Come, where God would resurrect righteous people in a world of peace and prosperity led by a king called the Mashiach.
- Some Jews have adopted a belief in reincarnation, although that remains a minority view held by those adhering to the Kabbalah.

A Jewish Home

The inner world of the Jewish home is the place where Jews' unique beliefs and culture are most apparent. Jewish homes truly are the castles most Jews throughout history could only dream about—a place of safety where Jewish views and practices dominate.

Part 5 considers the many aspects of the Jewish home. Chapter 19 describes the importance of the home and some of the features you may see within it. Chapter 20 shares the enjoyment of delicious Jewish food. Chapter 21 takes you into the Jewish bedroom to consider Jewish views of gender roles and sex. Chapter 22 deals with issues of parenting and children.

Unique Treasures in a Jewish Home

There are many institutions in Jewish life. Jews build synagogues, Jewish community centers, schools, and museums. They have more organizations and foundations than can possibly be counted, often using confusing acronyms. But there's no place or institution more important to Jewish life than the home.

The Jewish home is the place where the Jewish past is celebrated, the Jewish present is lived, and the Jewish future is ensured. It's where the Jewish past is celebrated because it's where family members are remembered and traditions are maintained. It's where the Jewish present is lived because it's where Jews experience their Judaism on a consistent basis without undesired or unsought influence by other ideas or cultures. It's where the Jewish future is ensured because it's where children learn to appreciate their religion and culture. Without distinctive and active Jewish homes, there is no Judaism.

In This Chapter

- A home for the Jewish heart
- Inscribing Jewish doorways
- Jewish art and Jewish books
- Ritual objects that beautify the home

The Importance of Home in Judaism

From the beginning, Jews have recognized the Jewish home as their most important space. This recognition comes from an unusual source—a non-Jewish prophet in the Torah who sought to curse the Israelites. The Book of Numbers tells how King Balak of Moev feared the Israelites, and engaged Bilaam to curse them. Bilaam goes to the Israelites and tries to do as Balak had asked, but instead, Bilaam blesses the people. He says, "How good are your tents, O Jacob; your dwelling places, O Israel!" (Numbers 24:5) Jews include this blessing in their morning prayers because it describes how they view their home—a place of beauty, love, learning, and connection to God.

Judaism has a special name for the home: *mikdash me'at*—"the small sanctuary." After the Temple was destroyed, public worship and gathering centered in the synagogue. Much of the emotional connection to God came to rest in the home.

The Jewish home also has served as a place of confidence and safety. Times could be bad and secular society could be hostile, but when Jews entered their home, they had a place of security. They could act according to their desires and according to the tenets of Judaism. As the sage Rava said, "In his home, even a weaver is a ruler." (Talmud Bavli, Megilla *12b*)

 WORDS OF WISDOM

"It is a joy to live in one's home."–Talmud Yirushalmi, Moed Katan 2:4

"On food, spend as much as you can afford; on clothing, spend less than you can afford; on your home, spend more than you can afford."–Genesis Rabbah 20:12

In light of the importance of the home, Judaism believes it's crucial to maintain *shalom bayit*—"peace in the home." This doesn't mean that family members can never argue, or that children must be seen and not heard. It means the Jewish home needs to be a place of love and respect. It means everyone in the family must cooperate with each other, help in supporting and maintaining the home to the extent each is able, and try to make the home the special, sacred place it can be. The midrash teaches that this creates a blessing that extends far beyond the individual home, for "peace in the home helps to create peace for all of Israel." (Avot de-Rabbi Natan 28)

Essentials of the Jewish Home

Jewish homes have great variety, and each family possesses different Jewish treasures. However, there are a few items, or categories of items, that truly characterize a home with a vibrant and visible Jewish presence.

Mezuzah

Anyone approaching a Jewish home will likely notice something different as soon as they reach the front door. Looking to the right, the visitor will see a small box or tube attached to the doorpost. This is called a *mezuzah*.

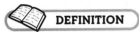 **DEFINITION**

A **mezuzah** *is* a small box or tube containing a scroll with passages from the Torah affixed to the doorpost or doorframe of a Jewish home.

Most people pay particular attention to the casing of a mezuzah. Casings may be metal, glass, pottery, or virtually any type of waterproof material. They may be simple, or they may be ornate and beautiful works of art. The only commonality among mezuzah casings is that they have the Hebrew letter *shin* on it, standing for one of the names of God—*Shaddai*.

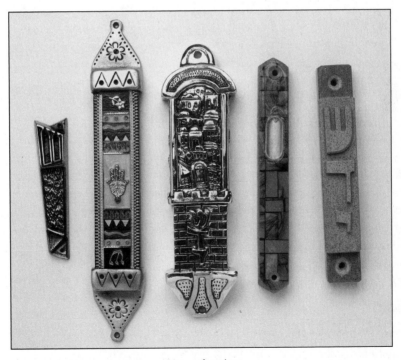

Mezuzah casings.

The important part of each mezuzah isn't the casing; it's what's inside. Every mezuzah contains a *klaf*—a scroll of parchment upon which is written the words of Deuteronomy 6:4-9 and 11:13-21. These passages contain the Sh'mah—the statement affirming God's existence and Oneness. They speak of the mitzvah of learning and passing knowledge and the Jewish heritage to children. They also contain the mitzvah to affix the mezuzah in its location.

A kosher scroll is made of parchment and is handwritten by a *sofer*, a special scribe who produces Jewish sacred documents. It's possible to find mezuzah scrolls that have been photocopied onto ordinary paper, but almost no rabbi from any branch of Judaism would approve of them. There's something mystical and meaningful about having these words written in the traditional manner with reverence in a mezuzah that a photocopy simply can't provide.

Jews traditionally place a mezuzah upon almost every doorway in the home. The only exemptions are bathrooms and most closets and storerooms. There are complicated rules that govern whether a mezuzah is required in archways or other unusually shaped or sized doorways.

Many Jews kiss their hand and touch the mezuzah as they enter a doorway as a sign of respect and blessing. It's also a mitzvah to leave the mezuzah for the next occupant of the home when a Jew moves, if that new occupant is Jewish.

Jewish Art

Jewish art also adds to the spiritual atmosphere of the home. It's comforting to see pictures and items that remind Jews of their heritage and values.

The natural question that arises is what exactly is Jewish art. There are probably as many opinions about this as there are Jews. Certainly, Jewish ritual objects often are examples of Jewish art. Pictures, paintings, sculptures, or crafts of scenes from Tanach, Jewish life, or Jewish people may be Jewish art. But a picture of someone who happens to be Jewish is not necessarily Jewish art unless the subject somehow exemplifies a Jewish action or value. Similarly, a piece of art from a Jewish artist isn't necessarily Jewish art, and it's certainly possible that a non-Jewish artist can produce a beautiful work of Jewish art, depending on the subject. Like all art, the answer to this question is very subjective.

Jewish Books

Reflecting the high value Judaism places upon learning, an active and vibrant Jewish home will usually contain Jewish books. It's unlikely for the home to have all the books of Jewish law, for there are so many. However, it is common to see many Jewish books in the home, including the following:

- The Tanach

- A Siddur

- Books on Jewish history, including the Holocaust

- Books on Jewish practice

- Jewish cookbooks

- Books of Jewish fiction or poetry

Tzedakah Box

The final item that characterizes an active Jewish home is a *tzedakah* box. As described in Chapter 7, tzedakah has a high value in Judaism. The presence of a container for tzedakah contributions reminds everyone of the mitzvah to care for others who are less fortunate. The presence of the tzedakah box in the home especially reinforces this value with children.

A tzedakah box.

 **WORDS OF WISDOM**

"The charitable will have children wealthy and wise."—Talmud Bavli, Bava Batra 9b

Tzedakah boxes may be any size or shape. Some are elaborate and works of art themselves. Others are simple containers of tin or cardboard. The most common characteristic of these boxes is that they are marked for tzedakah. This prevents people from seeing them as just another piggy bank. The funds deposited within them are reserved for those in need.

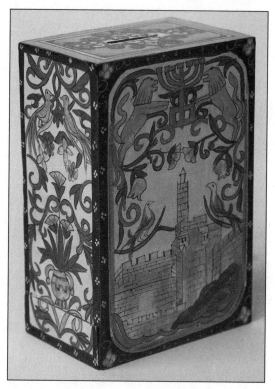

A tzedakah box illustrated with pictures and symbols of Israel.

Other Items You May See

There's almost no end to the amount of *judaica* you might see in a Jewish home. You also might see almost none at all. Some of this depends on the strength of the homeowner's Jewish identity. Some depends upon the home's religiosity, as some of the items or features have a religious connection. For some, it's just a matter of taste and preference. There's no formula to say exactly how much obvious Jewish content you'll find when you enter a Jewish home, just as you never know how much Christian content you'll see when entering a Christian's home. However, the following are some other items and features you might see in a Jewish home.

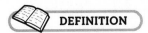 **DEFINITION**

Judaica refers to any item that reflects Jewish ideas or thought, such as Jewish art, Jewish books, or Jewish ritual objects.

An Unfinished Corner

If you glance at a corner of a ceiling or wall in a Jewish home, you might see that the paint or covering is incomplete. This isn't because the workers were sloppy or neglected to finish their work. This is a religious observance connected to the destruction of the Temple.

The custom of an unfinished corner comes from the Talmud. A story is told of Rabbi Joshua right after the Temple's destruction. He came across a group of despondent men who had decided they would no longer use anything connected to Temple worship, like bread, water, or wine, as part of their mourning. Rabbi Joshua convinced them that this was impossible, because they would starve and die of thirst. Rabbi Joshua reasoned with them that they should mourn, but the mourning should not become more than they could bear. He counseled them that they should enjoy life, but always leave everything a little incomplete, because their lives were incomplete without the Temple. (Talmud Bavli, Bava Batra 60b)

A home's unfinished corner is another way traditional Jews mark and mourn the loss of the Temple. The amount unfinished might be small, or it might be quite noticeable. Less traditional Jews who do not mourn the Temple's loss, particularly Reform Jews, likely will not follow this custom.

Mizrach

The Talmud teaches that Jews should always say their morning prayers while facing the Temple Mount. For Jews outside of Israel, this means facing Israel. For those in Israel, this means facing Jerusalem. For those in Jerusalem, this means facing the Temple. (Talmud Bavli, Berachot 30a)

For most Jews outside of Israel, facing the Temple means facing east. In Hebrew, "east" is *mizrach*. It became customary to place a marker on the eastern wall of the home to designate the proper direction to face for prayer, and the marker became known as a mizrach.

Some *mizrachim* (the plural of mizrach) became elaborate and beautiful works of art as part of the practice of *hiddur mitzvah*. They appear in many mediums, including stained glass, paper cuts, and whatever else artists may conceive to use. Most of them do contain the word mizrach to be clear of the work's religious purpose and to note that it's not just another work of art.

Items for Shabbat

A Jewish home may have several special objects for celebrating Shabbat.

Most homes have two special candlesticks designated for lighting the Shabbat candles. Some traditions use three-branched candelabra, two holders for the Shabbat candles and one for a *shamas* to light the other two. If the family's tradition is to light more than two candles, they will have more than two candlesticks.

A special cup, often made of silver, is used to hold the fruit of the vine for kiddush. The kiddush cup sometimes rests in a small tray or holder to catch any wine or juice that might spill because the cup traditionally is filled to the brim or overflowed to represent our unbridled joy on Shabbat. Some special devices allow the head of the family to pour wine into a central container that then flows into smaller glasses for all the members of the family and guests.

The *challah*, a braided bread, has several items devoted to it. The challah is often placed on a special ornate tray or plate. It's draped in a special cover that is removed only immediately before the blessing is said. Some don't use knives to cut the challah with the reasoning that an instrument of war should not be used on an item representing the peace of Shabbat. Some don't follow this custom and have a special knife they use for the challah.

The Havdalah Set

Jews use a special group of three items for *Havdalah*, the ceremony to separate Shabbat from the ordinary days of the week at sundown on Saturday. Artists often sell these items together as matching sets with a tray to hold them. You may also obtain them separately.

Havdalah sets contain a kiddush cup similar to that used to welcome Shabbat. The second item is a spice box that contains the spices for the second blessing of the ceremony. Spice boxes may be any shape or size. Some of the more notable spice boxes are shaped like windmills, possibly after the famous Montefiore site in Jerusalem. The third item in a Havdalah set is a candleholder specially made for the braided candle of the ceremony.

ASK THE RABBI

Do I need to buy a whole set to do Havdalah? No, you don't. A lot of people do buy a set for hiddur mitzvah, but this is not absolutely necessary. For a quick and easy Havdalah, you even can use any cup for the fruit of the vine, place cloves and pieces of cinnamon bark into an orange for the spice box, and use any two candles held with their wicks together for the braided candle.

Items for Pesach (Passover)

Pesach is another holiday requiring ritual items you may see displayed in a Jewish home. Seder plates are a common item. They contain spaces for the ritual items needed for the Seder meal we discussed in Chapter 11, including the saltwater, charoset, maror, karpas, egg, and shank bone. Some families have a special matzah cover to hold the three ceremonial pieces of unleavened bread needed for the ceremony. Many of these covers have a matching afikomen bag to hold the piece of matzah the children will seek after the meal. Some families have a special cup for Elijah and, reflecting a more recent tradition, a Miriam's Cup.

Items for Chanukkah

There are two main items used in Chanukkah you may see in a Jewish home. The first is a chanukkiah, the nine-branched menorah with a holder for each of the eight days of the holiday and a shamas. The second is a dreidel, the top used for a holiday game. It's not uncommon for each member of the family to have his or her own chanukkiah and dreidel, so you may see a collection of these items.

The Least You Need to Know

- Home is extremely important in Judaism. Jews call the home the mikdash me'at—"the small sanctuary."
- Most Jews affix a mezuzah, a container enclosing a small scroll with verses from Deuteronomy, upon their doorposts.
- Some Jewish homes leave a corner of the ceiling unfinished to represent the incompleteness of Jewish life without the Temple. Some Jewish homes also include an artwork called a mizrach indicating the proper direction of prayer toward Israel.
- Most Jewish homes contain Jewish books and art, some with cultural or historical meanings.
- Many Jewish homes contain ritual objects that add artistic beauty to the home as well as providing the means for religious celebration. Common objects include kiddush cups, candle sticks, Havdalah sets, dreidels, chanukkiot, and Seder plates.

Jewish Food for Jewish Thought

In the early 1980s, a prominent cream cheese company aired a television commercial. A customer sits in a fancy restaurant eating an omelet and croissant. The customer asks the waiter to leave the company's cream cheese on the table.

The waiter returns to the table with a plate, saying, "A bagel for your cream cheese, sir?"

The customer looks at the plate and then directly into the camera and says, "A bagel? What's a bagel?"

There aren't many places in the United States where that commercial would work today. There's a much greater familiarity and appreciation of Jewish food than there has been in years past. Food plays a significant role in Judaism, both religiously and culturally, and knowing about Jewish food is helpful in understanding Judaism.

In This Chapter

- Religious eating: kashrut rules
- Challah—a distinctive bread
- What to eat on the holy days
- A taste of ethnic dining

Keeping Kosher

The most notable feature of Jewish food is the restriction that Jews eat only foods that are kosher. The word *kosher* means "fit," or "suitable." Food that isn't kosher is called *treif.* A recent study by the Pew Foundation found that 22 percent of American Jews keep kosher in their homes. The laws of *kashrut* (the Hebrew form of kosher) are complex and varied, and different rabbis and sages have disagreed about the details of what's kosher and what's treif. However, the general rules of kashrut described in this chapter are universal.

DEFINITION

Kosher food is any food Jews are permitted to eat according to traditional Jewish ritual law. A rabbinic authority must certify food as permitted for it to be kosher. Any food that isn't kosher is called **treif.**

The General Rules of Kashrut

The first set of rules about kashrut concerns which animals Jews may eat and which they may not. The Torah says kosher animals must have cloven or split hoofs and chew their cud. Jews who keep kosher may eat cows, goats, sheep, and like animals. The laws of kashrut prohibit Jews from eating animals that chew their cud but don't have split hoofs, like camels. Similarly, the laws of kashrut prohibit Jews from eating animals that don't chew their cud but have split hoofs, including the most notable prohibited animal, swine. (Leviticus 11:2-8; Deuteronomy 14:3-8)

Other restrictions apply to fowl. A Jew who keeps kosher may eat chicken, turkey, and similar birds. They may not eat any other birds, including eagles, vultures, falcons, ravens, owls, hawks, and others. (Leviticus 11:13-19; Deuteronomy 14:11-18) The Talmud identifies these unclean, prohibited birds as those that hunt or eat carrion. (Talmud Bavli, Chullin 59a)

Fish and every animal that lives in water also must meet a particular set of criteria to be kosher. A fish is kosher only if it has scales and fins. The Torah thereby prohibits eating any animal that dwells on an ocean or lake floor and scavenges for food. This notably designates shellfish such as lobster, scallops, and shrimp as treif. (Leviticus 11:9-12; Deuteronomy 14:9-10)

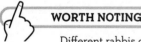

WORTH NOTING

Different rabbis disagree about how the standards apply to different species of fish, especially sturgeon and swordfish. Some rabbis say they're treif, while others adjudge them to have fins and scales, and find them to be kosher.

The Torah and Oral Law are a bit less definitive about whether there are any kosher insects permissible for eating. Leviticus 11:20-23 prohibits eating insects and other creatures that have wings, swarm, and walk on four legs. This text designates four-legged winged creatures with jointed legs as kosher, including locusts, crickets, and grasshoppers. In contrast, Deuteronomy 14:19-20 prohibits eating any winged swarming creature. The halachah resolves this conflict by allowing communities that have a tradition of eating a particular type of insect meeting the description in Leviticus to continue to do so. No one else may eat any insect, and if a Jew is not a regular member of a community allowing this consumption, he or she still may not eat the insect while he or she is visiting a community where it is permitted.

The Torah specifically prohibits eating other animals, including anything with paws, and moles, mice, lizards, geckos, crocodiles, and chameleons. (Leviticus 11:29-30) Animals, insects, or other life forms that crawl on the earth on their bellies or have many legs are also prohibited. (Leviticus 14:41-43)

The laws of kashrut even have requirements for otherwise permissible foods to meet, such as fruits or vegetables, or anything processed and made with permitted foods, such as wine. These items are kosher only if someone called a *mashgiach* supervises their harvest or production to ensure nothing unkosher touches or mixes with them at any point during the process. A mashgiach must be a Jew with knowledge of the halachah who lives according to the practices required by the authority certifying that an item is kosher.

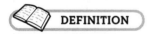 **DEFINITION**

> A **mashgiach** is a knowledgeable Jew who observes the laws of kashrut who reviews, inspects, and certifies that food or a restaurant is kosher.

The second set of rules of kashrut concerns how animals are slaughtered. The halachah requires kosher animals to be slaughtered in a manner it considers to be the most painless and humane possible. A special, respected person called a *shochet* slaughters the animals. The shochet must know all the laws of kashrut and receive special training to ensure an animal is slaughtered in the appropriate manner.

A shochet uses a finely sharpened knife to slay an animal, saying a prayer before the act and killing the animal with a single quick motion. The shochet also drains all the blood from the animal because Judaism sees blood as a symbol of life, and deems it wrong to consume or enjoy the life essence of the animal. (Leviticus 17:10-14; Deuteronomy 12:23-25)

The third set of rules of kashrut involves the eating of meat with dairy. The Torah says three times that a Jew may not seethe a calf in its mother's milk. (Exodus 23:19, 34:26; Deuteronomy 14:21) The sages of the Talmud understand this to prohibit the consumption of dairy and meat together. Judaism divides food from animals into three categories: *fleishig,* meaning "meat" or "flesh"; *milchig,* meaning "dairy"; and *pareve,* meaning "something that may be eaten with either fleishig or milchig."

For many Jews, the prohibition against eating meat and dairy together is more than forbidding the inclusion of fleishig and milchig in the same dish. These Jews maintain separate sets of dishes, pots, pans, and even sinks—one for meat and another for dairy—to prevent any possibility that a morsel of one will mix into the other. The sages even consider the time required to elapse between eating meat and milk based upon prohibition to ensure that the two types of food don't mix during digestion. Rabbis require anywhere from an hour to six hours before a person eats dairy after eating meat. They generally require a much shorter time to elapse before eating meat after eating dairy, usually about a half hour.

 ASK THE RABBI

Is fowl milkig, fleishig, or pareve? What about fish? Why? The sages answer these questions by seeking to avoid confusion. They judge that people might consider fowl to be meat, but they never would consider fish to be meat. So fowl is *fleishig* and fish is *pareve.* (Shulchan Aruch, Yoreh De'ah 87:3) However, the Talmud prohibits eating fish with meat because it considers this unhealthy. (Talmud Bavli, Pesachim 76a)

Why Keep Kosher?

Jews have questioned the reasoning for some or all of the complicated laws of kashrut throughout history. The laws pervade Jewish life on a moment-to-moment basis, and it's natural for Jews to wonder about their purpose and meaning. Jewish sages and scholars have offered several possible explanations.

Some argue that the laws of kashrut are an early health code. They note that many nonkosher foods have a higher probability of carrying disease or causing illness if prepared improperly. An often-cited proof for this opinion is the prohibition against eating swine, which could cause trichinosis, especially without modern cooking guidelines and safeguards. Other scholars and sages vigorously dispute this claim, asserting that it's unreasonable or even sacrilegious to reduce the laws of kashrut to a mere health code, and that the claim doesn't explain many of the laws and prohibitions.

Others argue for a cultural and tribal purpose for the laws of kashrut. The laws require Jews to remain together and build social structures and institutions to produce edible food. They also separate Jews from other people. It's hard to fully join and relate to other people if you can't eat in their homes and restaurants. The supporters of this argument note that pagans featured some of the prohibited foods such as swine in their worship and festivals, so the prohibition against these foodstuffs kept Jews away from participating in these prohibited religious practices.

> **WORTH NOTING**
>
> Some Jews today have used moral or ethical reasoning to construct new forms of kashrut. Some keep an "Ethical Kashrut," eating only items and meats produced without cruelty to animals and by industries that treat their workers fairly. Others have adopted an "Eco-Kashrut," paying attention to the effect of their food choices upon the environment, world sustainability, and fair distribution of food.

Most Jews who keep kosher adopt a more spiritual view of the rules. Some simply see keeping kosher as part of the mitzvot they're obligated to follow as part of the Covenant. God says to eat this way, so they eat this way. Others note that the Torah relates keeping kosher with the idea of living a holy life. (Leviticus 14:44-45) They reason that if Jews pay attention to everything they eat and drink, they'll constantly focus themselves on making even their smallest acts holy. Keeping kosher becomes a reminder to be a holy people and always give thanks to God.

Different Ways of Keeping Kosher

Just as there are different rationales for the laws of kashrut, there are a myriad of ways Jews keep kosher.

Some Jews keep kosher very strictly. They follow the laws for everything they eat and drink, no matter where they might go. One person who keeps kosher very strictly once told me he believed that nonkosher food was poison to him. Some Jews keep an even higher standard of kashrut called *glatt kosher*. Glatt kosher involves whether an animal's lungs are found free of blemish, making an animal with even the slightest imperfection unsuitable for eating.

This level of scrutiny has been extended by some who keep glatt kosher to increased requirements of supervision by the mashgiach. The different levels of kashrut and the differences among standards of authorities certifying a food is kosher leads to different *hekshers*. A heksher is a mark or symbol on a food or food packaging designating that an authority has certified the food kosher. Some Jews will eat foods marked with one of many different hekshers, while others will eat only those marked with a heksher they know represents the application of a stricter standard and has been approved by their rabbi.

A **heksher** is the mark of a governing authority on a food or food packaging certifying a food is kosher to that authority's standard. The most common heksher in the United States is a "U" in a circle, representing the authority of the Orthodox Union, although there are dozens of different national and local hekshers.

Other Jews keep kosher in a more limited fashion. They may keep kosher in the home, but eat anything when they're outside the home. They may keep "Biblical kosher," refraining from eating nonkosher animals and mixing milk and meat, but setting aside requirements instituted in the Oral Law such as strict supervision of foods and the particular method of slaughter. Some don't formally keep kosher at all, except that they won't eat pork or shellfish. The halachah doesn't distinguish between the laws of kashrut, requiring Jews to keep all the Written and Oral laws equally. However, this doesn't prevent some Jews from finding their own way and creating their own practices that suit them.

The Reform Movement initially rejected all the laws of kashrut quite vigorously. The Pittsburgh Platform of 1885 expressed the thinking of Reform Jews of the time, saying, "all such Mosaic and ritual laws concerning diet … originated in ages and under the influence of ideas altogether foreign to our present mental and spiritual state …. Their observance in our days is apt rather to obstruct than further modern spiritual elevation." In more recent years, the Reform Movement has expressed a greater openness to kashrut practices, finding value in the dietary laws and encouraging Reform Jews to keep kosher if they find it meaningful.

A Distinctive Bread: Challah

The word *challah* comes from a practice described in Numbers 15:20-21 where a baker takes a piece of dough and throws it into the fire as an offering of thanks to God. Many Jews still do this practice today, and some Orthodox Jews believe women are specifically obligated to perform this mitzvah.

Challah today also refers to the special bread Jews use for Shabbat and holidays. Challah is made with eggs that often give it a golden crust and a yellow inside. Some bakers use raisins or honey to make the challah especially sweet.

In some ways, challah is a symbol of our partnership with God in improving the world and helping to complete the work of creation. In one Midrash, a cynic asks a rabbi why Jews circumcise their sons, claiming that if God was perfect, anything created by God should also be perfect. The rabbi explains that just as grain needs to be made first into flour and then into bread, so too do Jews need to give their sons the sign of the Covenant. (Genesis Rabbah 11:6) In the Jewish tradition, Jews see themselves as united with God in making the world, and the fact that both God and people have a part in producing the challah reflects and celebrates that cooperation.

Braided Bread

The dough used for a challah is braided before it's baked, creating a distinctive appearance. There are many different traditions for braiding challah, with some very elaborate techniques producing beautiful loaves. Some people braid three strands of dough to represent the creation of the world, the redemption from Egypt, and the Messianic times to come. Others who use three strands say two strands represent the commandments to "keep" and "remember" the Sabbath, and the third binds the two commandments together as one. Some fashion their loaves to have twelve sections to represent the twelve loaves used in worship at the Tabernacle, and also the twelve tribes of Israel. (Leviticus 24:5)

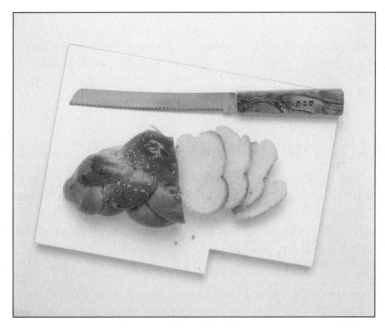

Challah with knife.

This also may be the reasoning behind the common practice of braiding a challah with six strands. On Shabbat, Jews traditionally have two loaves of bread on the table, representing the double portion of manna God gave the Israelites on Friday in the wilderness so they didn't have to gather food on Shabbat. (Exodus 16:29) Two challot (the plural of *challah*) with six strands each equals a total of twelve strands, reflecting the twelve tribes of Israel. Others believe the six strands represent the six ordinary days of the week that Jews reflect upon and spiritually prepare for during Shabbat.

Challah Rituals

Eating challah on Shabbat is an important ritual. Many families use a special plate and covering for the challah, which combines with the unique braided appearance and sweet taste of the bread to fulfill the requirement of *hiddur mitzvah* ("beautifying the commandment"). The people at the table don't eat any challah until they say a special blessing to thank God for bringing the bread from the earth. Many Jews dip the bread in salt before eating it, recalling that sacrifices at the Temple were eaten with salt. (Leviticus 2:13) Since salt never spoils, it represents the eternality of the Covenant between God and the people of Israel. The salt also reflects the verse in Genesis saying "You will eat bread with the (salty) sweat of your face." (Genesis 3:19)

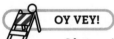 **OY VEY!**

Often you'll see a special knife designated for the challah. However, many Jews don't use a knife for the challah because it represents to them an offering performed at the Temple, and an instrument of war should never be used on such an offering. Instead, these Jews divide the bread with their hands.

Food for the Holy Days

Jewish tradition and ritual law frequently combine food with observance. Nearly every major holy day in the Jewish calendar has at least one traditional food that's part of its obligations or customs. It's also customary to celebrate many holy days and life cycle events with a *seudah*, a joyous, plentiful meal, or a solemn meal of commemoration. A person who understands Judaism often doesn't need a calendar to know what holy day it is—he or she just needs to smell the wonderful aromas from the kitchen or taste the delicious food at the table.

Pesach meals may have the greatest association with their holiday. They represent aspects of the Israelites' experience with slavery in Egypt and also springtime, and are inseparable from the festive Pesach Seder, so you'll find them described in Chapter 11.

Cholent for Shabbat

The halachah concerning work on Shabbat greatly affects the way a Jewish home prepares meals for this special day. The traditional law considers lighting a fire as work prohibited on the day of rest. However, a fire lit before Shabbat may remain lit, and may be used to prepare food. This has caused Jews to create the innovation of *cholent*, a stew that can remain on a low flame or oven for an entire day. Cholent allows a Jewish family to have a hot meal on Shabbat and still follow the law.

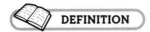 **DEFINITION**

> **Cholent** is a stew specially made for Shabbat that cooks slowly, allowing Jews to use a flame or oven lit before Shabbat to have a hot meal during the day. Cholent is also called *chamin* in Hebrew.

Cholent usually contains a hearty grain like barley and beans, meat, and potatoes. Ashkenazkic recipes sometimes include *kishke,* a beef sausage casing stuffed with flour and onions. Sephardic recipes often feature chicken and rice as primary ingredients instead of the red meat and beans favored by the Ashkenazi.

Rosh HaShanah Specialties

There are two special foods that are distinctive for Rosh HaShanah, the Jewish New Year: a round challah, and apples and honey.

The challah used for Rosh HaShanah and the meal prior to Yom Kippur usually have a distinctive round shape. The round challah represents the cyclical passing of the years, celebrating God's continuous creation of the world. Some say the round challah looks like a crown, marking God's sovereignty over the world, which is one of the primary themes of Rosh HaShanah.

The second food Jews traditionally eat on Rosh HaShanah is apples and honey. This treat symbolizes the hope for a sweet year to come. The apple has several meanings. It recalls the Garden of Eden, and also represents God's love for the Israelites as recorded in the Song of Songs, which says, "Beneath the apple tree I called you forth." (Song of Songs 8:5) Similarly, this text says, "As the apple is rare and unique among the trees of the forest, so is My beloved amongst the maidens of the world." (Song of Songs 2:3) The Kabbalists believed the apple represents the *Shechinah,* the comforting Presence of God, who acts in mercy at this time of judgment.

Lots of Oil on Chanukkah

Many traditional Chanukkah foods reflect the spiritual story of the holiday. After the Maccabees won their revolt, they found that the Eternal Light representing the Presence of God in the Temple had been extinguished. They wanted to relight it, but found only enough kosher oil to last one day. They lit the oil, and it lasted the eight days it took to produce more oil.

In honor of this miracle, Jews eat items fried in oil on Chanukkah. The most well-known food is *latkes,* a fried potato pancake usually eaten with either sour cream or applesauce. Some Jews also eat a fried pastry like a donut called *sufganiyot.*

Latkes.

Hamentashen on Purim

The traditional food of Purim is *Hamentashen,* or "Haman's pockets," which are triangular filled cookies. Some classic favorite flavors include poppy, apricot, and prune, though many bakers use chocolate or a variety of jam fillings.

There are different interpretations of the meaning of the cookies and how they relate to Purim. Some believe they resemble the villain Haman's pockets, ears, or three-cornered hat. There's also a theory that the cookies resemble the lots Haman used to determine the day on which he intended to kill the Persian Jews.

Jewish Ethnic Foods

Jewish ethnic foods largely derive from the surrounding cultures in which Jews lived. Jews and non-Jews who lived in a particular area largely used the meats, vegetables, and seasonings in similar ways. As long as the foods met the criteria of the kosher dietary laws, Jews would prepare and eat them in the same ways others did. Like many, the Jews in some areas were poor, so their diet reflected the same concerns for heartiness and low cost as other people.

Ashkenazic Foods

When most people in the United States think of Jewish food, they think of Ashkenazic recipes. This is because most Jews in the United States today are Ashkenazic.

These foods include such Jewish delicacies as chopped chicken liver and *schmaltz*, which is chicken fat used as a spread. *Kugel* is a potato or noodle casserole or pudding. Potato kugel is a side dish with potatoes, onions, and eggs. Noodle kugel is a sweet dessert with eggs, sugar, cream, cottage cheese, and sour cream. Another well-known food is the *k'nish*, which is either a tough crust or flakey dough filled with mashed potatoes or spinach. *Gefilte* fish, a fish meatball made with ground and molded whitefish, pike, or carp, is also renowned in Jewish circles.

Common meat dishes include roast chicken and brisket, a tough cut of beef cooked long and slow to make it tender and delicious. *Matzo* ball soup, which is chicken soup with dumplings made of *matzah* meal, egg, and oil, is also popular.

A Jewish woman making matzo balls.

 WORTH NOTING

Jews debate whether matzo balls should be large, soft, and fluffy or small and firm. While this may not seem like a significant issue, many families have great debates as to which style is the best.

Also favored are bagels and *bialys,* the former being a crusty type of bread with a hole in the middle, and the latter a similar bread without a hole. They're often eaten with cream cheese and lox, the Jewish name for smoked salmon. "Jewish deli" is also very popular, and includes kosher cuts of meats such as pastrami, corned beef, and turkey.

Bagels.

Sephardic Foods

Sephardic foods reflect the Spanish and Middle Eastern cultural foods eaten by the peoples among whom Sephardic Jews lived. These dishes include *hummus* (a smashed chickpea paste), *couscous* (a steamed wheat dish), *kebabs* (skewers of meat), and *mujadrah,* a dish with lentils and rice. Another favorite dish is *borekitas,* a turnover or dumpling filled with cheese or vegetables such as eggplant.

Unlike Ashkenazic food, Sephardic food includes a greater variety of fresh vegetables, fish, rice, and spices. Both cuisines are delicious and a key part of Jewish culture.

The World of Jewish Food

Jewish communities from around the world have their own unique cultural foods. For example, Roman/Italian Jews, to keep the laws of kashrut, use eggplant instead of meat to create eggplant Parmesan. They also traditionally bake biscotti, also called *Mandelbrot*, for dessert. Similarly, Greek, Turkish, Yemenite, Moroccan, and Persian Jews all have rich food traditions worth exploring.

The Least You Need to Know

- Many Jews "keep kosher," following dietary laws that prohibit eating foods such as pork and shellfish, and eating milk and meat together.
- Challah is a sweet, braided egg bread eaten by Jews on Shabbat and many Jewish holy days.
- Many of the Jewish holy days are associated with particular foods with historical, Biblical, or spiritual meanings.
- The two ethnic divisions in Judaism, Sephardic and Ashkenazic, have different traditional foods reflecting the areas in which they live or lived.

The Jewish Bedroom

The Talmud tells a story about one of the great scholar Rav's students, Rabbi Kahanah. Rabbi Kahanah wanted to learn everything he could from his sage and teacher. One day, Rabbi Kahanah hid under Rav and his wife's bed, and waited for them to arrive. He soon heard the couple laughing, joking, and having conjugal relations.

Rav eventually discovered his student, and told him to leave. Rabbi Kahanah replied, "It (sex) is a matter of Torah, and I must learn."

Judaism has never been afraid to talk about sex. Jewish texts contain discussions of everything important in life, and it's undeniable that sex is an important aspect of human relationships. Judaism establishes guidelines about gender roles, relationships, and sexual behavior that seek to make this part of life holy and spiritual. However, like most aspects of Judaism, there is both significant agreement and disagreement among Jews about what is appropriate and what is not.

In This Chapter

* Judaism's view of gender roles
* Sex for procreation and pleasure
* Forbidden sexual relationships
* The importance of being modest

Roles of Men and Women

The variation in Jewish thought about the roles of men and women reflects many of the same debates found in general society today. Some Jews view men and women to have separate and distinct roles, while others have adopted a more egalitarian view.

Tradition and Change

Traditional Judaism maintains separate, definitive roles for men and women. Women are obligated to maintain the home and bear and raise the children. As noted in Chapter 2, this means women are not obligated to perform positive, time-bound mitzvot, simply because they have other priorities that may require their attention at any time. Men do have the obligation to perform these positive time-bound mitzvot, including prayer at the set times. Men also have the obligation to study Torah, while women are free from that requirement.

This doesn't mean traditional Jewish women work only in the home, cooking, keeping house, and raising children. Many traditional Jewish women work outside the home, and represent the primary or significant breadwinner for the family. This is because their husbands spend their time learning Torah, an endeavor that takes an incredible amount of time.

Traditional Judaism doesn't view these separate roles for men and women as discriminatory or unfair. They view these roles as at least equally important, and often give a higher value to the woman's role, especially if she enables the man to study Torah. The women also largely cherish their role in the traditional Jewish family structure.

Non-Orthodox Jews tend to reject these fixed roles for men and women, and vary from the traditional Jewish family structure. In the United States, these Jewish families resemble much of American society. The woman may work outside the home or not, depending upon what she wants to do and the family's economic needs. The man may become the primary homemaker and caretaker of the children. Gender egalitarianism has become a strong value in many Jewish families.

Gender and Prayer

Traditional Jews see gender having a great effect upon prayer. Men have the obligation to pray; women don't. Women still may come to worship if they're able. The halachah views the beauty of a woman as a distraction to men due to her sexuality. Even a woman's voice, called in Hebrew *"kol isha,"* likely will distract men from prayer. This means traditional congregations must take steps to ensure that the men are able to focus their hearts and souls upon God during prayer without distraction. Traditional Jewish practice therefore requires separation between men and women during prayer, often having a barrier called a *mechitzah* dividing the men and women in the sanctuary.

DEFINITION

Kol isha, means "voice of a woman," and refers to the idea that a woman's voice will distract a man from his obligatory devotions to God if it's heard during prayer. A **mechitzah** is a barrier that separates the men and women in a sanctuary or prayer space.

Traditional congregations vary in how they set up their mechitzah. Some place the women in the back of the sanctuary, while others run the mechitzah down the middle of the sanctuary. One congregation may have a mechitzah that's tall and solid, making it impossible for people on one side to see the people on the other. Other congregations may use a lower mechitzah only a few feet high, a curtain, or latticework that a person can see through. These congregations believe a less drastic separation suffices to ensure men will focus on their prayers without distraction. On the other end of the spectrum, some congregations don't use a mechitzah at all, but have the women and their children sit in a balcony or a separate room.

The non-Orthodox movements generally have moved in a different direction. Some Conservative congregations maintain a mechitzah, while others allow mixed seating. Gender egalitarianism in all respects is a high value in the Reform Movement, and even its *siddur* ("prayer book") uses gender-neutral language for God. The non-Orthodox movements also have abandoned or modified the idea of kol isha, allowing women to become rabbis and cantors for their congregations.

WORTH NOTING

One of the more heated current controversies in Jewish life involves gender roles, gender separation, and the Western Wall in Jerusalem—the holiest site in Judaism. Some women would like to pray together and read Torah at the Wall; the Orthodox authorities that control the site disagree that this would be appropriate. The Israeli government and representatives from the movements and groups with interest in allowing women at the wall are attempting to find an acceptable solution.

Jewish Perspectives on Sex

As we'll consider more completely in Chapter 22, Judaism views procreation to be the primary purpose of sex. The first commandment God gave to human beings was "Be fruitful and multiply." (Genesis 1:28) However, Judaism delves much deeper into the questions involving human sexuality than merely the idea of producing progeny, on both philosophical and practical levels.

Yetzer Tov and Yetzer Ra

Judaism envisions human beings to have two types of inclinations: the *yetzer tov*, which is the good inclination, and the *yetzer ra*, the evil inclination. The yetzer tov includes the noble and spiritual aspects of a human being, including the desire to live a holy life, study Torah, and perform unselfish and caring acts. The yetzer ra includes appetites, ambition, and the drive for sex.

It's clear that yetzer tov and yetzer ra are misnomers in some respects. The acts that fall into the category of yetzer ra aren't necessarily bad acts or sins. There's no achievement without ambition, and there's no procreation without sex. It may be better to view yetzer tov as the impulses we have to act as we envision God in heaven would act, and yetzer ra as the impulses we have to act like creatures of the Earth. This may help to understand why sex, performed in its proper context, isn't a sin. Rather, it's an important part of being a human being, usually leading to positive and desirable outcomes when conducted as a holy act.

The Holiness of Sex

Traditional Judaism views sex as holy when it's part of the loving and caring relationship of marriage. The Torah explains that a man will leave his parents and cleave to his wife, and they will become one flesh. (Genesis 2:24) Sex within marriage is treasured and valued, especially because it leads to the blessing of children and family.

While Judaism sees procreation as the primary purpose of sex, it also views sex as an important aspect of a married couple's healthy and happy relationship. Judaism values sex for the joy and pleasure it brings to the married couple and their lives. There's a story in Genesis where Isaac tells a king that Rebecca is his sister so the king will not kill him to free her to become his queen. The king sees Rebecca and Isaac "laughing" together, understood as a euphemism for sex, and the king realizes the two actually are married. (Genesis 26:8) This proves to the sages that an important part of sex within marital relationships is pleasure and fun.

Jewish texts encourage husbands and wives to engage in sexual activity. It's an axiom of Jewish law that sex is a woman's right and a man's duty. Exodus 21:10 says "a man may not withhold from his wife food, clothing, or conjugal rights." The text calls the latter *onah*, meaning the intercourse a husband is required to provide his wife as part of the marriage agreement. The Talmud goes further, saying husbands should provide sex to their wives when she desires it beyond the obligations of *onah*. (Talmud Bavli, Pesachim 72b) Sex is an aspect of *simchat ishto, the* "rejoicing in one's wife" derived from the Biblical commandment that a man may not enter the army for battle in the first year of his marriage. (Deuteronomy 24:5)

May rabbis marry? Not only may rabbis marry, but Judaism says that, ideally, they should marry and have children. Family has such a high priority in Jewish life that the halachah says rabbis should perform this mitzvah like any Jew.

Similarly, the *halachah* says a wife should modestly encourage her husband to participate in sex. There's an element of responsibility placed on both parties for a healthy and fulfilling sex life. The Talmud explains that a woman who solicits her husband to engage in intercourse with her will have children the like of whom didn't exist even in the generation of Moses. (Talmud Bavli, Eruvin 100b)

It's especially meritorious in Jewish thought to include sex as part of the ways to make Shabbat a joyous and special day.

When It's Not Okay

The value of sex within the marital relationship naturally leads to traditional Judaism's disapproval of sex outside of marriage. This may be one of the reasons that the Mishnah named intercourse as one of the means by which a man acquires a wife. Non-traditional views of Judaism still express a preference for sex solely within the sanctity of marriage, but have a greater tolerance for sex between consenting adults if treated seriously and respectfully.

Judaism describes several relationships in which sex is forbidden. The same incestuous relationships created by blood or linkage through a spouse or former spouse that prohibit marriage also prohibit sexual relations. (Leviticus 18:7-18) Minors don't qualify as appropriate partners for marriage, and therefore sex with minors is also prohibited. (Talmud Bavli, Sanhedrin 76b) Sex with animals is a sin. (Leviticus 18:23, 20:15-16)

The holy aspect of sex requires that it must be consensual. It's sinful for a husband to force himself upon his wife. (Talmud Bavli, Eruvin 100b) This demonstrates one of the ways Jewish law was revolutionary for the time in which it was formulated, giving women some rights and protections not provided by other peoples and cultures.

The laws of *niddah* also create a time when sex is forbidden. Niddah refers to the time of a woman's menstrual period, a time when the halachah forbids any sexual contact to occur. To ensure that the woman has passed the time of niddah, the halachah requires a minimum of 11 or 12 days to pass from the time menstruation begins before sexual contact may resume. Even then, the woman must go to the mikvah—the ritual bath—for a spiritual cleansing and renewal before she resumes normal sexual activity. Orthodox Jews follow these laws, while many non-Orthodox Jews shorten the time after the period of menstruation has ended, don't require a mikvah visit, or don't follow these laws at all.

Another sexual prohibition arises from the story of Er and Onan, the sons of Yehuda. God killed Er because he was evil, and Yehuda told Onan to have a child with Tamar, Er's wife, as required by the law of the time. Onan "spilled his seed on the ground," so God killed him as well. (Genesis 38:1-10) Traditional Judaism has interpreted this story to prohibit the wasting or "spilling" of a man's seed, prohibiting masturbation. Many sages extend this to prohibit any sexual activity where a man doesn't climax within his wife's womb, although other sources permit this activity if performed only occasionally and without impeding efforts toward procreation.

Tzni'ut—Modesty

Tzni'ut, or "modesty," is of high value in Judaism. Judaism disapproves of excessiveness and showy displays, opting instead for moderation and humility.

The idea of tzni'ut most often extends to issues concerning displays of sexuality. While Judaism doesn't view sex as a sin, it also doesn't promote ostentatious displays of sexuality in public. For Orthodox Jews, this means a strict code of appropriate dress, especially for women. Many Orthodox Jews consider the display of a woman's body to transgress rules of tzni'ut requiring women to cover their legs to below their ankles, their arms to their wrists, and their neckline to above their clavicle. Other Orthodox and traditional Jews have similar requirements, although they may not be quite as strict.

Many Jews have rejected the strict rules of tzni'ut for dress, allowing men and women to wear the current fashions. Like almost every society, Jews maintain a sense of decorum—what is appropriate for the beach wouldn't suffice for the synagogue or a fancy restaurant. However, the clothing patterns of many Jews are indistinguishable from those of the surrounding nations and peoples.

The Least You Need to Know

- Sex is not a sin in Judaism, but an important part of human life.
- Judaism sees the primary purpose of sex to be procreation, but doesn't minimize its importance for pleasure and part of a happy marital relationship.
- Judaism especially approves sex on Shabbat, but disapproves of sex in certain relationships or without consent.
- Traditional Jews observe the laws of niddah, refraining from sex during a woman's menstrual period and the days following.
- Many Jews abide by the rules of tzni'ut (modesty), adopting codes for appropriate dress.

The Child's Space

A midrash teaches that when God decided to give the Torah to the Jewish people at Mount Sinai, God said to them, "I am prepared to give you the Torah. Before I do, present to me the people who will assure that you will study and keep the Torah, and then I will give it to you."

The people said, "The merit of our ancestors will assure that we will do this with the Torah."

God said, "Your ancestors are not sufficient to give that assurance. Bring Me someone else who will provide enough assurance, and I will give you the Torah."

The people said, "Our prophets will assure that we will study and keep the Torah."

God said, "Your prophets are not sufficient to give that assurance. Bring Me someone else who will provide enough assurance, and I will give you the Torah."

The people said, "Our children will assure that we will study and keep the Torah."

God said, "Your children are sufficient to give enough assurance. For their sake, I will give you the Torah." (Song of Songs Rabbah 1:24)

In This Chapter

- The importance of becoming parents
- Obligations of Jewish parents to their children
- Finding a name for a Jewish child
- Special cases of Jews who don't have children
- Honoring fathers and mothers

Judaism considers having children one of the greatest joys and blessings in life. The Talmud teaches that "childhood is a garland of roses" that brings joy and sweetness to the child, the community, and the child's parents. (Talmud Bavli, Shabbat 152a) Consequently, raising children becomes one of the most important aspects of Jewish life.

The Mitzvah of Having Children

The very first mitzvah God gave to the first human beings, Adam and Eve, was *P'ru ur'vu*— "Be fruitful and multiply." This has been interpreted in different ways. The great sages of the Mishnah, Hillel, and Shammai, agreed that each couple should have at least two children, although Shammai taught each couple should have at least two sons, while Hillel finds the obligation complete if the couple has a son and a daughter. (Mishnah, Yevamot 6:6)

A midrash illustrates the Jewish value of having and caring for children. It tells of an old man who specified in his will, "My son will receive nothing until he acts like a fool." This confused everyone, so they went to a great sage, Rabbi Joshua ben Korcha, for an explanation. When they arrived at the great sage's home, they found the teacher crawling on his hands and knees, a reed in his mouth, being pulled along by his baby son, truly acting like a fool. They then understood what the old man meant by his will. (Psalms Rabbah 92:13)

WORDS OF WISDOM

"Far kinder tsereist men a velt—For your children's sake you would tear the world apart."—Yiddish proverb

Jews from different movements hold varied understandings of the commandment to be fruitful and multiply. Some Orthodox communities hold that this mitzvah means every couple should have as many children as they can. For these communities, the more children in a household, the more the household is blessed. Other Jews, particularly those in the non-Orthodox movements, understand the mitzvah to mean they should have children, but they may choose to limit or control their family size.

The difference among the movements plays out in the opinions about birth control and abortion. The details of each movement's view on these subjects are quite nuanced and beyond the scope of this book. The non-Orthodox movements generally permit a broader use of birth control under more circumstances than the Orthodox.

However, even many Orthodox communities allow birth control in certain cases such as preventing the birth of a child with dangerous deformities, recognizing when the couple can't economically care for more children, or acting to stop when having a child would be a hazard to the mother's physical or mental health. This derives from a section of the Talmud allowing birth control for minors, pregnant women, and nursing women. (Talmud Bavli, Yevamot 12b) The different movements similarly diverge on abortion, with all permitting it under certain circumstances involving the imperiled health of the mother. (Mishnah, Oholot 7:7)

Choosing a Name

One of the greatest gifts Jews give their children is a name. In the Jewish tradition, a name conveys identity and connection to the family and the entire Jewish people. Pirkei Avot teaches that, "Rabbi Shimon said, 'There are three crowns: the crown of Torah, the crown of priesthood, and the crown of kingship. But the crown of a good name is superior to them all.'" (Mishnah, Pirkei Avot 4:17)

Traditionally, every Jew receives a special name that may or may not correspond to the name he or she uses every day. This name is used for ritual purposes and events, such as calling that person to the Torah for an aliyah or for composing the ketubah at a wedding. This name is given in Hebrew, Yiddish, or Ladino regardless of the language of the country in which the child lives.

Ashkenazic and Sephardic Jews have different traditions involving the selection of the first, and if they desire, middle name of their children. Many Ashkenazic Jews follow the custom of naming their children after a relative who has died, often a grandparent. The child keeps alive the memory of the deceased and preserves the honor of the deceased relative's name.

According to this custom, it's an insult to name a child after a living relative, because if the accepted practice is to name a child after a deceased relative, the act of naming after a living relative is equivalent to wishing the death of the relative. Others believe that if a child shares the same name as a living older relative, the Angel of Death might get confused when coming for the older relative and accidentally take the child in his or her place. Sephardic Jews have the opposite custom, often naming their children after living relatives, especially grandparents, as an honor.

Parents don't always give their children the identical name as the relative they choose to honor. Some use a different name with the same initial sound or letter. Others choose not to follow this custom of naming after a relative at all, opting instead to choose the name of a favored and admired Biblical figure, a name describing something about the child, or a name they happen to like.

The second part of a Jewish name follows a pattern connecting the child to his or her family. The name chosen by the parents is followed by the word *ben,* meaning "son," or *bat,* meaning "daughter." The name concludes with the father's name. A Jewish name therefore would be something like *Shlomo ben David*—Solomon, son of David.

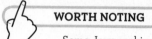

Some Jews seeking gender equality today add the mother's name as well as the father's. Such a name might be *Shlomo ben David v'Sarah*—Solomon, son of David and Sarah.

Obligations of Parents to Children

The Talmud tells the story of Choni the Circle-Maker. Choni came across a man planting a carob tree. He asked the man how long the tree would take to reach maturity. The man replied that it would take 70 years, but he planted it for children. Choni ridiculed the man, but then suddenly became dizzy and realized 70 years had passed. He saw the man's descendants and appreciated how the man had ensured the future by his care. (Talmud Bali, Ta'anit 23a)

Jewish parents generally take the mitzvah of caring for their children very seriously. The Talmud specifies that fathers have the responsibility to their sons of circumcision, redemption, teaching Torah, acquiring a wife, and teaching a craft. The Talmud adds that some authorities hold a father also must teach his son how to swim. (Talmud Bavli, Kiddushin 29a)

The responsibility to provide an education in Torah is a particularly important one. Every Jewish daily worship service includes the words from Deuteronomy 11:19, which reminds parents to "teach Torah to their children, speaking of them at home and when travelling." A parent must also be a good example and take care in how he or she behaves around a child because "children will speak in the marketplace the way parents speak to them." (Talmud Bavli, Sukkah 56b)

Blessing of the Children

Jews traditionally add a blessing of the children to the festive and spiritual family Shabbat evening meal. Blessing the children creates a warm and loving atmosphere, bringing the family together and creating special memories for the children that they often give to their own children when they become parents.

The parents' blessing of their daughters invokes the merit of the Matriarchs of the Jewish people, expressing the hope that "God may help you to be like the Matriarchs of the Jewish people—Sarah, Rebecca, Rachel, and Leah." The blessing for sons actually recalls Jacob's blessing of his grandsons and Joseph's sons, Ephraim and Menasheh. Jewish tradition teaches that Ephraim and Menasheh preserved the traditions of the Israelites when they lived in Egypt, just as Jewish parents hope their sons will continue Jewish life, learning, and tradition as well.

Childlessness

Jewish tradition is very aware that some couples, for one reason or another, don't have children. Like marriage, Judaism views having children as an ideal that not everyone can meet. People who don't have children aren't viewed as bad in the eyes of Judaism. Instead, Judaism gives special consideration to cases where a couple cannot or doesn't have children.

Infertility

About 10 percent of all couples today can't get pregnant without medical assistance, and some can't even with the help. Judaism offers a way for these people to fulfill the mitzvah of *p'ru ur'vu*— "be fruitful and multiply." (Genesis 1:28)

The root of this opportunity is found in the beginning of the third chapter of Numbers. The chapter begins, "These are the generations of Aaron and Moses on the day God spoke with Moses on Mount Sinai." The Torah lists all of Aaron's sons, but doesn't mention Gershom and Eliezer, Moses' sons. The Talmud explains this omission by saying that Gershom and Eliezer didn't study Torah, but Moses took great care to ensure that Aaron's sons did. As a result, the Talmud states that anyone who teaches his friend's sons the Torah is considered by the text as if he had sired them. (Talmud Bavli, Sanhedrin 19b) A commentary to the *Shuchan Aruch* called *Chochmat Shlomo,* written by Rabbi Shlomo Kluger, explicitly states that "by teaching Torah to others, one might thereby fulfill the obligation to be fruitful and multiply."

A couple therefore can fulfill this mitzvah even if they personally can't or don't have their own children. They may teach Torah to other children, or support a school, community, or teacher that teaches the children. These acts satisfy the obligation by ensuring the legacy, spirituality, and continuity of the Jewish people.

Yibbum—Levirate Marriage

The Torah specially considers the circumstances of when a husband dies before he and his wife have children. It contains a procedure called *yibbum,* or levirate marriage. In some such situations, depending on a number of specific technicalities, the brother of the deceased husband has the obligation to marry the widow and have a child with her. This provides the widow with an heir, which may have great importance for her protection. If the two don't want this marriage, they may perform a ritual called *halitzah,* in which the widow removes her brother-in-law's shoe and spits on the ground as they both say ritual words. This symbolic humiliation for the brother-in-law's failure to perform his obligation removes the requirement of what could be a very awkward situation. (Deuteronomy 25:5-10)

Most people in the non-Orthodox movements, and many even in the Orthodox movements, don't follow the practice of yibbum and halitzah at all. Even among communities that still follow these rules, there's far more halitzah than yibbum today.

In Return, Honoring Parents

Judaism obligates children to honor their parents in return for bringing them into the world and caring for them. The fifth of the Ten Commandments teaches Jews to "honor your father and your mother, that your days may be long in the land that Adonai your God gives to you." (Exodus 20:12; Deuteronomy 5:16) The Torah directly connects the fear or respect of parents with the ability to be a holy people. (Leviticus 19:1-3)

According to the Talmud, children give this honor to their parents by showing concern for their position and dignity, following their instructions, and giving them respect. Children ordinarily must not stand or sit in their parent's place, oppose them publicly, or contradict their words. When they grow old, children must give them food and drink, keep them clothed and cover them, and help them when they go to and from their home. (Talmud Bavli, Kiddushin 31b)

 ASK THE RABBI

How does a child show honor to a parent who is doing something wrong or immoral? The Shulchan Aruch says the child shouldn't tell the parent he or she is wrong, but should study Torah with them. Showing the parent the text that exposes the wrongness of the behavior preserves the child's honor for the parent as opposed to shaming him or her. (Shuchan Aruch, Yoreh De'ah 241:6)

A child may disobey his or her parent in a limited set of circumstances. If a parent tells his or her child to violate a rule of the Torah such as doing something that would make the child ritually impure, the child may not do what the parent says. (Talmud Bavli, Yevamot 6a) Maimonides extended this rule to include not only commandments in the Written Law, but also anything found in the Oral Law. (Mishneh Torah, Hilchot Mamrim 6:12) A child may also disobey the parents by leaving the home against their wishes to receive a better Jewish education than he might otherwise receive, or if the parent wants the child to marry someone who the child doesn't want as his or her spouse. (Shulchan Aruch, Yoreh De'ah 240:25)

Mamzerim

A child may receive a special status called *mamzer* if the child is born from an incestuous act, adultery by a woman, or if his or her parents are themselves *mamzerim* (the plural of mamzer). (Mishnah, Yevamot 4:13) This status doesn't make the child a complete social outcast, and the community still generally treats him or her with respect. The important effect of this status is that the mamzer can't marry a "nonmamzer" Jew.

The Reform and Reconstructionist movements, and many in the Conservative movement, don't consider mamzer status an impediment to a Jew marrying anyone he or she might want. Some Conservative and Orthodox communities still consider these laws to apply.

The Least You Need to Know

- Having children is an important mitzvah in Judaism. The first mitzvah God gave to the people was "be fruitful and multiply."
- Parents have the responsibility of caring for their children, which traditionally includes circumcision, redemption, teaching Torah, acquiring a wife, and teaching a craft.
- Even if a couple doesn't or can't have children, they may fulfill the mitzvah of "be fruitful and multiply" by helping the children of others learn Torah.
- Children must honor their parents in accordance with the fifth of the Ten Commandments.

The Jewish Community

Jews don't live only within their homes. Their call to be a people means they must congregate together and share their lives with each other. As a popular Jewish folk song says, "How good and joyous it is for brothers (and sisters) to reside together!" This part considers the aspects of Jewish community.

Chapter 23 describes the center of the Jewish community, the synagogue, and its functions. Chapter 24 explains the purpose, ideas, and practices behind Jewish prayer. Chapter 25 speaks about other customs Jews share, including clothing, symbols, and other activities.

Communal Jewish Space: Synagogues

The Talmud contains a parable about a group of people travelling across the sea on a small boat. Each person rows their oar as they struggle against the current and waves. Suddenly, one rower stops and takes a drill out of his bag. He begins to drill a hole under his seat. The others cry out in alarm:

> "What are you doing?" they ask.
>
> "What does it matter to you?" said the first. "I am just drilling a hole under my own seat."
>
> "They protested, "You will make the water come into the boat, and we'll all drown!" (Leviticus Rabbah 4:6)

For centuries, the "boat" of the Jewish community has been the synagogue. The synagogue has been where people have experienced Jewish life and learning with one another. Ancient authorities such as Josephus and the *Targum* trace the synagogue back to Moses, and although this is certainly historically inaccurate, it illustrates just how long the synagogue has been the center of Jewish communal life. As we read in the Tanach, "Thus says Adonai: Although I have removed [the people] far off among the nations, and although

I have scattered them across the countries, yet I have been to them as a little sanctuary in the countries where they have come." (Ezekiel 11:16)

Community is essential in Judaism. Hillel enjoins the Jews in the Mishnah, "Do not separate yourself from the community." (Pirkei Avot 2:4) What does a synagogue do to keep the Jewish community together? What are they like? What do they contain? This chapter will address these questions.

The Three Roles of the Synagogue

The synagogue is a holy place to the Jewish community. It's dedicated to holy works, but exactly what this means varies depending on the values and decisions of the rabbi and the community. The Talmud says the synagogue should not be a place for levity or idle chatter. (Talmud Bavli, Megillah 28a) Some congregations therefore have strict rules for their use.

Some traditional communities will not allow weddings to take place in their synagogues because of the levity and cavorting that happens at some celebrations. Other communities will rent their synagogues to outside non-Jewish groups, or even share space with non-Jewish congregations. It all depends upon the community and what it feels falls within the bounds of holiness and respect.

 ASK THE RABBI

Why do some Jewish congregations call themselves a "synagogue" and others a "temple"? And what's a shul? Most traditional communities use the word synagogue instead of temple to avoid confusion of their community center with the Temple in Jerusalem. To them, there can be only one Temple. Reform congregations don't hope to rebuild the Temple, so they call their congregations temples. *Shul* is the Yiddish word for synagogue.

Different synagogues involve themselves in a variety of different activities. Some engage in community relations and represent the Jewish community within the general community. Some have soup kitchens and other community services. Staff and facilities also vary, depending on the size and resources of the congregation. Some have administrators and large staffs, including specialized educators, teachers, and youth workers. Others have a very small staff.

Regardless of these differences, all synagogues from all branches of Judaism serve three main purposes. Each is a Beit Tefillah, a Beit Midrash, and a Beit Knesset.

Beit Tefillah—House of Prayer

A synagogue is a *Beit Tefillah*—a House of Prayer—where Jews congregate to pray to God during Shabbat and the holy days. A synagogue is a standing home for the minyon, which we'll discuss in Chapter 24. Communal prayer is necessary according to one tradition because God might be able to disregard an individual's prayers, but God can't ignore the prayers of an entire community. (Talmud Bavli, Berachot 8a) The synagogue as Beit Tefillah provides a home for this communal prayer.

Beit Midrash—House of Study

A synagogue is a *Beit Midrash*—a House of Study—where Jews can gather to delve into the sacred texts. The Mishnah tells us, "If two people sit together and study Torah, then the Divine Presence resides with them." (Mishnah, Pirkei Avot 3:3) This teaches Jews that they should not study alone, but always have at least one partner. It's through discussion and the exchange of ideas and interpretations that one finds wisdom. As a Beit Midrash, the synagogue provides a natural gathering place for this study to take place by providing teachers, books, and a shared space for Jews to meet and study, and by making a main part of its facility and mission to be a religious school. One opinion even states that a scholar is not permitted to live in a town without a synagogue. (Talmud Bavli, Sanhedrin 17b)

 WORDS OF WISDOM

"Anyone who studies in a synagogue will not easily forget (the teachings)."—Talmud Yirushalmi, Berachot 5:1

Beit Knesset—House of Meeting

The final classical role of a synagogue is it's a *Beit Knesset*—a House of Meeting. The great sage Hillel taught that Jews should not separate themselves from the community. (Mishnah, Pirkei Avot 2:4) Moses is called the greatest prophet ever because he knew God *panim el panim*—"face to face." This models the ideal kind of relationship for all Jewish people today. They are at their best when they see each other, hear each other, and experience life together. This can happen only if they have a place to gather, which the synagogue provides.

What You Will See in the Synagogue

Synagogues come in all sizes. Some are small and modest, while others are grand structures. You can find them designed according to just about every style of architecture from Moorish to Modern. You won't see synagogues with the classic features of the houses of worship of other religions such as steeples, bell towers, and minarets. Aside from that, just about anything is possible.

Many synagogues contain the usual rooms you might expect to find in any house of worship—classrooms, kitchens, activity rooms, and offices. However, there are some features unique to the synagogue, most often found in the central room used for worship—the sanctuary.

The Bimah

The Bimah is the area in the sanctuary from which the leader conducts the worship service. *Bimah* simply means "platform" or "stage." Some *bimot* (the plural of bimah) are large and high, while others are small and barely lifted from the floor.

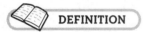

DEFINITION

A **bimah** is the stage or platform in the sanctuary from which the service leaders conduct the worship service. Jews don't ever call this area an altar.

Traditional synagogues often place their bimah in the middle of the sanctuary. Many congregations from the non-Orthodox movements place their bimah along the wall at one end of the room. Usually, it's placed so the congregation faces east, allowing them to easily pray toward Jerusalem as tradition requires. Some congregations don't follow this rule and orient their sanctuaries in a different direction.

A bimah in a synagogue in Tzfat.

The Aron Kodesh

The central feature of the bimah is the *aron kodesh*—the holy ark. The Torah scrolls are kept in the aron kodesh along with any other sacred Scriptural documents the congregation may own, such as the Scroll of Esther read on Purim.

The aron kodesh often has doors that the congregation opens only for worship services or to access the Torah scrolls for study. A curtain called a *parochet* hangs between the doors and the Torah scrolls. During the service, the parochet usually remains closed. The congregation must rise when the parochet opens, as a sign of respect. Some synagogues don't use a curtain for a parochet but some other barrier less substantial than the main ark doors, such as a second set of doors made from glass.

The aron kodesh often has a verse from Jewish tradition prominently displayed for the worshippers. A common verse used for this is "*Da lifnei mi atah omeid*—Know before Whom you stand," which appears in the plural in the Talmud Bavli in Berachot 28b.

The Torah Scroll

The aron kodesh's primary purpose is to hold at least one *sefer Torah, or* Torah scroll. A sefer Torah is the entire Torah written on animal skins sewn together and wrapped around two poles called *atzei chayyim*—"the trees of life." The first skin with the beginning of the Torah is attached to one pole and the last skin with the end is attached to the other. The skins can roll back and forth so the Hebrew text becomes visible when the reader parts the atzei chayyim. Many synagogues have more than one Torah scroll in their ark, which helps a great deal when a holy day requires the reading of a different part of the Torah than the weekly portion. It's much more difficult to roll a sefer Torah to the proper place than to open a book to the correct page.

 WORTH NOTING

Many synagogues have a Holocaust Torah scroll in their ark. The Nazis preserved these scrolls even as they destroyed the Jewish communities of Europe, planning to open a museum to show their pride over their destruction of the Jews. Synagogues hold these scrolls in trust as especially revered objects in memory of those who died.

Jews retained the ancient method of producing *sifrei Torah* (the plural of sefer Torah) with animal skins on scrolls as part of their maintenance as sacred unchanging records of the words Moses received at Mount Sinai. The reading of the Torah takes place in the synagogue with great ceremony and fanfare. Using a book instead of a scroll wouldn't create the same feeling.

A special skilled artisan and scholar called a *sofer* (scribe) constructs and writes a sefer Torah in the same way they've done for centuries. A sofer receives intense training on the shapes of the letters, proper spacing, production of the materials, and construction of the sefer Torah. A sofer must be a knowledgeable, active, and pious Jew, although the standard for this varies among different Orthodox and non-Orthodox communities.

The sofer writes the Torah on treated skins from a young animal to have the smoothest, cleanest surface possible. He uses a quill and special black ink. He can't make an error in the writing, so he copies the words from another source instead of relying on his memory. If he does make an error, he may erase and fix it, unless the error is made in the name of God. If that happens, the entire skin must be buried like any scroll that has too many errors or has become too worn to use.

Yads used to help the Torah reader keep the proper place while reading from the Torah,
and preventing fingers from touching and dissolving the ink.

A sofer also reviews existing Torah scrolls to ensure the letters have not faded or flaked away. Natural oil from fingers eventually dissolves the ink, so Torah readers use a pointer called a *yad* to keep their place while reading. The yad may be made of almost any material, and often takes the shape of a small hand. Nevertheless, even the most cared-for Torah wears over the years, and the letters eventually fade and need a sofer to repair them.

ASK THE RABBI

How does a sofer know that a letter needs repair? Soferim vary in their methods, but one once told me he shows the letter to a young student first learning the Hebrew alphabet. If the student can't easily read the letter, it needs repair.

A sefer Torah has a cover made of cloth, linen, or other fine material. It often has a breastplate that commonly looks like those worn by the High Priest in the Temple, including an *urim v'tumim*. The sefer Torah commonly has a crown called a *keter* that covers the top of both atzei chayyim, or a finial over each *eitz chayyim* (the singular of atzei chayyim) called a *rimon*. The crowns represent God's sovereignty over the world and the Jewish people as demonstrated by the gift of the Torah. Each keter or rimon often has bells. As a sign of respect, a Jew should always face the Torah when the parochet is open or the Torah has been removed from the aron kodesh. The bells ensure that you can hear where the Torah is even if you can't see it so you never turn your back on it.

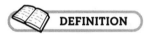

DEFINITION

Urim v'tumim is a set of 12 jewels, one for each of the tribes of Israel, which the High Priest of the Temple wore on his breastplate. Legend says that light reflected from the jewels would provide answers to questions for the Priest and the people.

A Sephardic congregation often has its sefer Torah encased in a wooden casing that opens and stands upright when it's time to read from it. Other scrolls rest on a table while read.

The last of the 613 mitzvot is the commandment to write a sefer Torah at least once during a lifetime. Many do this through donations to help purchase a scroll for a synagogue.

The Ner Tamid: Eternal Light

Synagogues have a light above the ark that always remains lit. This *ner tamid* (eternal light) represents the Presence of God in the sanctuary and among the Jewish people, particularly as it appears over the Torah. Some synagogues still use oil for their ner tamid. Others use an electric light, and many of these synagogues have back-up battery systems to guard against the light going out during a power failure. A contemporary trend is to use solar energy to keep the ner tamid burning.

The Menorah

Exodus 25:31-40 describes a seven-branched candelabrum called a menorah placed in the Tabernacle. The menorah brought the mystical number seven into the Tabernacle, and reminded the Israelites of Shabbat. Many synagogues today have a menorah or an artistic representation of the menorah in their sanctuaries. Some Orthodox synagogues purposely don't have a menorah to prevent the confusion of their current place of worship with either the Tabernacle or the Temple, which also had a menorah.

The Mechitzah

Traditional Orthodox and some Conservative synagogues separate men and women during prayer as described in Chapter 21. Some synagogues achieve this by keeping women on another level in the sanctuary, usually in a balcony. Others have a barrier between the men's and women's sections called a *mechitzah*. There's a tremendous amount of variation among *mechitzot* (the plural of mechitzah) among congregations. Some separate the women from the men by creating a separate section for them toward the rear of the sanctuary. Some divide the sanctuary through the middle. Some mechitzot are solid, high barriers that prevent anyone on one side seeing people on the other. Some are latticework or lower in height, so a separation is provided while maintaining a sense of connection among everyone in the sanctuary.

Some synagogues today still use the mechitzah but in a way that attempts to respect diverse religious sensibilities. They use two mechitzot to create three sections—one for men only, one for women only, and one for mixed seating. The Reform Movement prioritizes gender egalitarianism, so you will not find a mechitza in use in a Reform synagogue.

Other Items

You may find a variety of other items in the sanctuary depending on the community. Some sanctuaries have the flags of the State of Israel and the nation in which the synagogue is located. Others have a representation of the Ten Commandments, which may have originally been placed in sanctuaries as a compromise once the sages removed their recitation from the liturgy. Some sanctuaries have lists of names of people who have died on plaques as a way to honor the departed. Often, lights designate those for whom *Yahrzeit* is being observed that week.

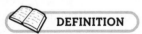 **DEFINITION**

Yahrzeit is the observance of the anniversary of a person's death.

Different congregations respond in varying ways to one of the Ten Commandments that prohibits inclusion of graven images. Some don't have any pictures or representations of any living creatures at all. Others say the commandment applies only to pictures of God or people, and therefore their sanctuaries may contain depictions of animals. Some communities feel the commandment forbids only pictures of animals used in pagan rituals. Some contain figures that aren't quite human beings, but something that suggests a human image. I once saw stained glass in a sanctuary that appeared to show the hands of the High Priest as he made a blessing, but on close examination, the hands had only three fingers. This artist was able to convey the idea without technically violating the commandment. Still other congregations apply the rule only to images of God and do allow pictures of animals or people.

The Jewish Clergy

Synagogues are led by both lay leaders and clergy. The balance depends on the congregation and the movement of Judaism to which it belongs. The Orthodox and Conservative synagogues are likely to give more authority to the clergy. Reform and Reconstructionist congregations are more apt to share authority between the clergy and a lay board of trustees.

Each synagogue engages its own clergy independently, especially in the non-Orthodox movements. The clergy and the trustees both agree to abide by a code of ethics and treat each other with respect. Clergy must represent the values of the community and Judaism. They must be good and moral people, learned in Judaism and worthy of having the honor of leadership in the synagogue.

The Rabbi

The term *rabbi* means "my teacher." The word first came into use during the time of the Mishnah. This term describes the primary function of the rabbi. It's his or her role to teach the community about Judaism and build the congregants' understanding of the texts, values, and practices of the religion. The knowledge and respect given to the rabbi by the congregation also entitles him or her to certain prerogatives. The rabbi is *mara d'atra*—the master of the community—which gives them a large amount of say over what are the proper bounds of conduct and teaching within the synagogue. They may serve on a *beit din* (religious court), and act as *shaliach tzibur* (service leader) and *m'sader kiddushin* (marriage officiant). Often rabbis have a large role in the administration of the synagogue.

People become rabbis after intense study and training. In the past, after a student had immersed himself in learning the texts, the student's rabbi would place his hands on the student in a ceremony called *s'micha*, which would designate the student as a rabbi. This ceremony reflected how Moses passed the mantle of leadership over to the Israelites to Joshua in Numbers 27:18-23. Many Orthodox Jews don't use that term today, believing it to be an honor available only in times gone by. Some of the other movements and communities still use the term.

ASK THE RABBI

Can Jewish clergy marry and have children? Can women be clergy? Clergy in all movements may marry and have children. Indeed, they are encouraged to do so, reflecting Judaism's value of family and procreation. Women may become clergy in all movements except Orthodox Judaism.

Many Orthodox Jews study and become rabbis even if they don't act as rabbis in their daily occupation. It's an honor to become a rabbi, and this reflects their achievement of knowledge of the halachah and the texts. The other movements have professionalized the rabbinate, requiring a course of study in a seminary modeled after a modern academic institution.

The Cantor

Many synagogues employ another clergy person called a cantor or *hazzan*. Initially, *hazzanim* (the plural of hazzan) were responsible for many aspects of the synagogue from music and conduct of the worship services to cleaning and maintaining the facilities. Over time, the latter functions stopped being a particular role for the hazzan, and music, leading worship services, and teaching children became their primary roles.

The rules for family and gender follow the same patterns as those for the rabbis in each of the movements. Like rabbis, the non-Orthodox movements have professionalized the study and requirements to become a cantor. Unlike rabbis, however, many knowledgeable and musically talented people call themselves cantors or cantorial soloists and act in that role in many synagogues without the formal training. Depending on the community, you may have an ordained or invested cantor, or the cantor may not have earned this honor from a seminary.

Synagogue Membership

Every Jew is entitled to become a member of a synagogue. The only way a community may remove a person from synagogue membership is if they misbehave in their personal conduct or otherwise act in a manner contrary to the values of the community. Even so, this removal is always temporary, and the congregant can rejoin the community after appropriate *teshuvah*, or repentance.

It's a mitzvah to support a synagogue through participation in all its endeavors and through financial contributions. Synagogues maintain different systems to enable them to survive economically. Some ask for a set fee or dues payment from each member. Others ask each to pay their fair share to the community based on what the community deems is fair. More synagogues today rely entirely on free-will offerings than in the past. Every synagogue fundraises in addition to collecting dues. No synagogue collects money during worship services as some houses of worship in other religions do. Traditionally, Jews don't carry or handle money on Shabbat, so this practice never came to be used in synagogues, even in Reform congregations.

Any synagogue that follows the values of Judaism will be understanding of an individual's financial circumstances. They won't turn anyone away for the inability to pay the set dues or even any amount at all. At their best, synagogues act with compassion, and make it easy for anyone to become part of the community regardless of how much they contribute financially. Congregants recognize the needs of maintaining a synagogue, and support the holy work of the congregation as best they are able.

The Least You Need to Know

- A synagogue serves three primary functions. It's a Beit Tefillah (House of Prayer), Beit Midrash (House of Study), and Beit Knesset (House of Meeting).
- The center of the synagogue is the ark in the sanctuary where the congregation keeps their Torah scrolls. A Torah scroll is made of animal skins attached to two wooden poles, and is produced the same way books were prior to the development of the printing press.
- The two types of Jewish clergy are the rabbi (teacher, community leader) and the cantor (musical leader).
- Jews become members of synagogues through their affiliation with and support of the institution. Synagogues maintain themselves financially in different ways, but anyone may join regardless of financial means.

Sing Unto God!
Jewish Prayer

The Midrash tells the story of a general who approached a pious Jew in prayer. The general tried to greet the Jew, but the Jew didn't acknowledge him, choosing instead to complete his prayers.

When the Jew finally looked at the general, the general said, "I could have killed you with my sword!"

The Jew replied, "If you were addressing a king of flesh and blood, and a friend came to greet you, what would have happened if you ignored the king and spoke to your friend?"

The general said, "The king would kill me for my disrespect."

The Jew replied, "How much the more so that I continue my prayers even when you approach. For if this is what a worldly king would do, imagine what would happen if I interrupted my prayers to the King of kings for you?" (Talmud Bavli, Berachot 30b)

Prayer is a serious and important matter in Judaism. Prayer is an essential part of Jewish practice, enriching Jewish life and enhancing the spirituality of the Jewish people.

In This Chapter

- The reasons why Jews pray
- When is the time for prayer?
- The balance between intention and structure
- Different types of blessings
- The basic outline of a service

The Purpose of Prayer

Judaism describes many reasons for prayer. Prayer serves many needs, and different Jews at the same worship service may receive different benefits from prayer. A Jewish worship service is designed to meet all of these needs simultaneously. They allow the worshipper to receive spiritual comfort, support, and enrichment at different times in the same service, sometimes even giving these gifts to the worshipper all at once. Prayer also serves needs beyond a formal worship service, as it may become a significant part of a Jew's life outside the synagogue.

Communication and Petition to God

Like most religions, Jews pray to connect with God. Prayer allows Jews an opportunity to express praise and appreciation to God for all the blessings they're privileged to have in their lives. Prayer also gives Jews the chance to ask God for further blessings, especially in times of need.

Prayer in Judaism delves much deeper than concern with material needs. Jews explore the spiritual realm through prayer, seeking understanding of God and the universe God created. Prayer allows Jews to ask questions about life, receive comfort, learn about their place in the world, and gain as much of an understanding about God as a human being can. Along with study, prayer is often a major spiritual experience in Jewish life.

Another important function of prayer is to bind the Jewish community together. There are times when a Jew prays or says a blessing alone; however, Judaism views regular prayer as a communal experience. The halachah requires Jews to attend a *minyon*—a gathering of Jews to pray that must include at least 10 people 13 years old or older.

The requirement of 10 people for a minyon arises from the story of Sodom and Gomorrah, when Abraham argues with God about saving the cities for the righteous people. He begins by asking if God will spare the cities if God finds 50 righteous men there. God agrees. Abraham continues to ask God to reduce this number, stopping when he reaches 10 people. This proves that even 10 righteous people comprise a complete community. (Genesis 18:17-33)

This communal function develops familiarity and friendships, and helps continue Jewish life with the idea that Jews are stronger when they're together than when they live apart.

When and Where Jews Pray

Prayer is an activity that both finds its home within the synagogue and transcends the synagogue walls. Set worship services have an important role in Judaism, but a Jew may pray outside the synagogue when the need or occasion to do so arises. Judaism says the more *brachot* ("blessings") a Jew says, the better off are both the reciter of the prayer and the world.

WORTH NOTING

Many brachot begin *"Baruch ata Adonai, Eloheinu Melech haolam—*Blessed are You, Adonai our God, King of the Universe ...." The blessing then praises God or acknowledges the mitzvah the Jew is performing.

Three Times Daily

Traditionally, a male Jew 13 years old and older has the obligation to pray with the community three times daily—morning, noon, and evening. Some communities combine the noon and evening services, beginning before sunset, doing both services consecutively and ending after sunset, thus fulfilling the obligation.

Some communities hold services in the synagogues at each required time. Other synagogues have a daily service either in the morning or evening, leaving the individual to find another place to worship at a different time. Some synagogues don't hold any daily services at all.

It's not uncommon to see Jews gathering for one of the required services wherever they may be when the time for prayer arrives, particularly in places where many Jews live. Virtually any room or open space may qualify as a suitable place for worship if 10 men can be found for the minyon. It's not uncommon to find a minyon gathering in a public space or market in Israel, or on a flight on the national airline of the Jewish state, El Al.

Blessings over Food

Through prayer, Jews honor God as the Creator of the world and the Provider of sustenance. Jews therefore give thanks to God for their food both before and after they eat.

The most common *brachah* ("blessing") Jews recite before eating is called *HaMotzi*. This one-sentence blessing thanks God for "bringing forth bread from the earth," and is said before eating meals or snacks that include bread. If the meal doesn't include bread, there are other formulations of the appropriate brachah, including a blessing when eating fruit that grows on trees and foods that grow in soil, and a general blessing when eating or drinking anything that doesn't fall into these categories.

ASK THE RABBI

How big does the meal or item have to be to require a Jew to say a blessing before eating it? The sages say a blessing must be said if a Jew eats anything at least as big as a *kezayit*, or the size of an olive. Generally, this is understood to be equivalent to one ounce, although some authorities say it means something larger.

Jews say a longer blessing after eating, called *Birkat HaMazon.* This blessing includes several paragraphs praising God for providing the food, thanking God for the Covenant and the Torah, and asking for further blessings from God. The traditional version of Birkat HaMazon includes a plea for the return to Israel. It also includes special paragraphs for different holy days and occasions, including Shabbat and weddings.

Mee Shebeirach

There are a variety of prayers that begin with the Hebrew words *Mee Shebeirach* …. These words, and those that follow, mean "May the One who blessed our ancestors, Abraham, Isaac, and Jacob …." The formulation petitions God to remember the merit of our patriarchs and matriarchs, and grant a blessing upon a person or persons for whom the prayer is said.

A Mee Shebeirach prayer may be said for many different types of people. Often it is used to ask God for a blessing upon someone at a pivotal lifecycle event. A Mee Shebeirach prayer is said for a baby at a brit milah, and for a wedding couple at an aufruf—a blessing before the ceremony. Often the rabbi will say a Mee Shebeirach for someone who has done an aliyah—the blessing for the Torah reading at a worship service described in a later section.

Perhaps the most common use of a Mee Shebeirach prayer is for healing. Such a prayer may be said during a worship service, in a hospital at a patient's bedside, or any time the need arises to ask God for strength and healing. Usually, one person says this prayer for another. In many congregations, the leader offers the worshippers the opportunity to say the names of those in need of healing, and a version of the prayer is spoken or sung.

Blessings for Special Occasions

There are a variety of blessings Jews may say for special occasions. For example, Jews say the *Shehechiyanu* at any joyous time, such as a festival, celebration, or happy life cycle event. This blessing thanks God "for giving us life, for sustaining us, and for enabling us to reach this season."

In contrast, there's a special blessing called *Birkat HaGomeil* that Jews say after surviving a dangerous situation or an illness, or upon reaching a destination safely after a journey. Unlike the joyfulness of the Shehechiyanu, Birkat HaGomeil expresses relief and subdued gratitude for God's favor in allowing the person to overcome his or her ordeal.

Additionally, Judaism has a number of blessings appropriate for times when a Jew sees or hears something that reflects God's glory or power, or that causes awe or fear in the perceiver. These include blessings when someone sees or hears:

- a rainbow

- the ocean

- lightning

- thunder

- beautiful flowers or other vegetation

- a secular king

- a Torah scholar

- fragrances

- earthquakes or comets

- a destroyed synagogue

- a restored synagogue

- 600,000 Jews together

How Jews Pray

A Jewish worship service has a distinctive character. It uses Hebrew, chanting, and melodies that Jews have experienced for centuries. More than that, a worship service wraps theological ideas and values around forms, texts, and practices that create an atmosphere unique to the Jewish people.

Keva and Kavanah

Two competing concerns in Jewish worship are *keva* and *kavanah*. Keva are the fixed prayers Jews say in a worship service. Since the time of the Talmud, the sages have prescribed certain prayers for worshippers to say as part of the service. These fixed prayers praise and petition God for the blessings God may provide. The sages believed that Jews should always include certain requests and thanks in their prayers, so they wrote out the words of the prayers and set them in a logical order. Over time, some prayers were added and others were amended, and differences in the prayers arose among the various movements in Judaism. However, almost every Jewish worship service in all the movements contains keva, a core set of prayers required for the particular time of day, week, or year on which the worship service is held.

In many ways, kavanah is the opposite of keva. Kavanah is the intention experienced by the worshipper while reciting a prayer. Kavanah is the emotional aspect of prayer, describing the feeling of the worshipper and the meaning the worshipper senses in his or her heart during prayer. A worshipper may experience kavanah while reciting the keva of a prayer, but kavanah doesn't rely upon the precise words of a prayer. Kavanah is the sentiment of comfort, consolation, or celebration a worshipper feels during prayer. It's what makes prayer more than "going through the motions." Kavanah might spur a worshipper to say a personal prayer in his or her heart, or to pray with greater vigor.

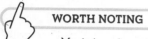

WORTH NOTING

Music is an important part of creating kavanah during Jewish worship. Whether traditional chants and melodies, or the modern melodies favored by some congregations, music helps set the mood and makes prayer meaningful for the worshippers.

A story about the Chassidic master, the Baal Shem Tov, describes the value of kavanah. A father brings his young son to synagogue on Rosh HaShanah. The boy stands among the men, listening to their chanting of the prayers, and wants to join with them. However, the boy doesn't know the words or the chants the men recite, and he's too intimidated to ask.

Wanting to pray, the boy reaches into his pocket and takes out a flute. He begins to play a melody that the prayers of the men had moved him to produce.

All the men stop praying and look at the boy in shock. A musical instrument is not allowed to be played in traditional prayer, and certainly not on the sacred day of Rosh HaShanah! And how can this boy have the audacity to disturb the prayers of these holy men! The boy's father is embarrassed, and hurries to stop his son's flute playing.

The Baal Shem Tov, who happens to be in the synagogue, stops the man and urges the boy to keep playing. "This boy prays from the heart (kavanah) in the way that he knows. His prayers allow all of ours to reach heaven!"

Even though the static nature of keva and the emotional and flexible nature of kavanah are contradictory, they're both necessary in a Jewish worship service. Without keva, the service would feel chaotic and disjointed, filled with uncertainty about the relationship between God and the worshippers, and potentially missing important aspects of Jewish thought, like the Covenant and praise for the Torah. Without kavanah, Jewish prayer would become words without meaning, a rote and unfulfilling exercise that doesn't fill the worshipper with love for God. An ideal Jewish worship service balances the keva and the kavanah to produce an orderly, intellectually stimulating, emotionally fulfilling Jewish experience.

A Traditional Service

A traditional Jewish worship service has a unique atmosphere and cadence. A *shaliach tziboor,* or "leader of the congregation" stands near the ark or the eastern wall of the sanctuary. The shaliach tziboor may be the cantor or rabbi, but often is a learned member of the community or guest given this honor. The shaliach tziboor leads the prayers, but doesn't say every word out loud.

Sometimes each person says the prayers softly to himself. At other times the entire community joins together. The shaliach tziboor leads the communal prayers, and chants lines more loudly at various times so that everyone knows about where in the service they should be during the private recitations.

The worshippers repeat many prayers during a traditional Jewish worship service, sometimes saying the prayers softly and privately at their own pace, then joining together to do a section of the service as a community. The repetition most often occurs for the *amidah* section of the service, described later. Some of the repetition occurs to ensure that everyone says the prayers correctly, and so that even those who don't know the prayers may fully participate. According to Jewish tradition, if a person says "amen" to the blessing said by the shaliach tziboor, he's credited as if he said the entire prayer himself. Another set of repetitions on Shabbat, festivals, and Rosh Chodesh called *Mussaf* occurs in remembrance of the additional sacrifice at the Temple made on those days in ancient times.

Music plays a large role in a traditional Jewish worship service. The worshippers chant or sing most of the sacred prayers and texts. However, there aren't any musical instruments in a traditional service. This is because instruments were used in worship at the Temple, and their absence reflects mourning for the great loss of this central place of worship. The sages also feared musical instruments would confuse Jewish worship with pagan Hellenistic worship practices that used this accompaniment, and forbade their presence in Jewish services to avoid confusion and potential intermingling of prayers and ideas.

While an ordinary daily traditional worship service tends to be short, services for Shabbat and holy days can last three or more hours. In some congregations, not everyone participates in every part of the service, and much socializing, conversation, and private study occurs in the sanctuary while the service proceeds. The layout of the space set aside for prayer sometimes reflects how the community prays. Some traditional sanctuaries have fixed seating and rows of chairs. Others have chairs haphazardly placed throughout the room, and some have no seating at all.

A traditional service may appear beautifully chaotic, with worshippers in every space and corner, bowing and praying privately in their own prayer called *davening,* then joining together with the entire community. People may be praying alongside other people chatting, and there's a spiritual atmosphere of community and connection with God and each other throughout the room.

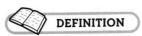 **DEFINITION**

Davening is the Yiddish word meaning "praying," a form of Jewish worship involving praying during the service with great kavanah, also including bowing and swaying while reciting the prayers.

Decorum in Reform

Worship was one of the primary focuses of the early Reform Jews. They looked at traditional worship and felt it was too chaotic, incomprehensible, and undignified. They compared Jewish services with those they saw in Christian churches, and found they preferred the latter. They decided to reform the worship service to reflect their preferences, and institute what they considered proper decorum for their prayer.

Some of the reforms involved the layout of their sanctuaries. Instead of an open space with people milling about or praying in their own space, they opted for fixed seating. They built ornate synagogues with magnificent prayer spaces, attempting to reflect God's glory. They eliminated separate seating for men and women, choosing to seat families together.

Other reforms involved the style of the service. The Reformers greatly reduced the amount of Hebrew, practically eliminating use of the language in some congregations. They made this change because their members no longer understood Hebrew, and they felt that comprehension was more important than keeping the original language. The worshippers listened to the rabbi or cantor, or joined together to read in English, eliminating most of the private davening of the traditional service. They added an edifying sermon by the rabbi. As they no longer mourned the loss of the Temple, they restored the use of musical instruments in worship, especially using the popular instrument of the day, the organ.

They made some changes to the words of the prayers as well, to reflect their theology and aesthetic. They eliminated most of the repetitions, as well as references to returning to Israel, the Messiah, and resurrection.

 ASK THE RABBI

> What about worship in the other movements? The Conservative, Reconstructionist, and Renewal movements often combine traditional practices with changes developed by the Reform movement. For example, worshippers may prefer more Hebrew and independent prayer, but sit in fixed and mixed seating.

More recently, the Reform movement has curbed some of its more dramatic worship changes, returning to a greater use of Hebrew and more traditional verbiage. Musical instruments remain in use, but pianos and guitars have generally replaced organs. Reform services today have more of a traditional feel, while maintaining many of the changes favored by the early Reformers.

Common Jewish Prayers

A Jewish worship service is a complex configuration of blessings, prayers, and practices. The service developed over centuries of debates and decisions over proper content and wording of each prayer. Over time, the appropriate sages or authorities opted to add prayers and entire sections to the service. The sages and authorities generally didn't delete when they made additions, leading to lengthy worship services, particularly on Shabbat and holy days.

Consequently, a complete exploration of the prayers in a Jewish worship service far exceeds the scope of this book. However, a brief description of the main sections of the service will aid the understanding of Judaism.

Beginning the Service

Ironically, much of the development of the beginning sections of Jewish worship services occurred much later than the development of the other service sections. After the other sections were established, the sages realized it was difficult for worshippers to jump immediately into these important prayers. They added introductory prayers and meditations to build kavanah and prepare the worshippers for the primary sections to come.

This was the particular motivation for the addition of *Kabbalat Shabbat,* or "the welcoming of Shabbat." The Kabbalists added this section at the beginning of the Friday evening service to begin Shabbat with joy, singing, and praise to God. This spiritual "warm-up" to the service includes several psalms. Its highlight is *Lecha Dodi,* a poem the worshippers sing to welcome Shabbat like a bride. Worshippers rise and face the door as they sing the last verse, bowing to welcome the Sabbath bride.

The morning blessings ("*Birkot HaShachar*") that begin a service vary slightly among congregations. Generally, they begin with *Mah Tovu,* the blessing given by Bilaam upon seeing the Israelites in Numbers 24. The morning blessings also include thanks to God for giving us pure souls, appreciation for health and working bodies, psalms, and a blessing for the study of Torah.

> **WORTH NOTING**
>
> A form of a prayer called the Kaddish often separates sections of the service. This Aramaic prayer praises God, and is used when completing a course of study or when someone dies, as described in Chapter 17. The shorter version of this prayer used to separate service sections is called the "*hetzi Kaddish,*" or "partial Kaddish."

The introductory section of the service leads to a bridge to the next section called the *Barchu.* The Barchu is a call to worship. The *shaliach tziboor* says the first line: "*Barchu et Adonai hamvorach!*—Praise to Adonai, to whom our praise is due." The congregation responds: "*Barchu Adonai hamvorach l'olam vaeid!*—Praise to Adonai, to whom our praise is due forever!" In a sense, the leader asks the congregation if they're ready to pray, and the congregation responds affirmatively. The leader repeats the second line, as if to say, "Let us proceed," and the next section of the service begins.

The *Sh'mah* and Her Blessings

The central prayer of the next section of the service is the Sh'mah, described in Chapter 1 as the central formulation of the Jewish belief in One God, from Deuteronomy 6:4. The Sh'mah recited in the service also includes further verses from Deuteronomy 6:5-9 and 11:13-17, and Numbers 15:37-41, called the *V'ahavta*. This prayer calls upon Jews to love Adonai with all their hearts, souls, and might. It also contains several important commandments, such as teaching Torah to Jewish children and keeping Torah in mind at all times. The sages interpret some of the verses of the V'ahavta to require Jews to wear a *tallit* and *tefillin*, described in Chapter 25, and affix mezuzot on doorposts, as described in Chapter 19.

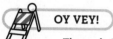 **OY VEY!**

The early Reform movement rejected the use of the tallit, so it deleted these verses from the V'ahavta. It's important to realize that different congregations within and among the different movements may include variations in their prayers.

Three blessings surround the Sh'mah and V'ahavta, invoking the three primary roles of God according to Jewish thought. The first two appear before the Sh'mah, praising God for creation and for revealing the Torah. There are different forms of these blessings in the morning and evening prayers due to their appropriateness for the time of day and as a result of disagreements among the sages. The third blessing appears after the V'ahavta, praising God for redemption. This blessing includes the *Mee Chamocha*, the song the Israelites sang after passing through the Red Sea to safety following the Exodus from Egypt.

The evening service adds a fourth blessing called the *Hashkiveinu*. This blessing asks God to safely preserve our lives, especially through our sleep during the night.

Petitionary Prayers

The next section of the service is the primary petitionary section of the service. It has three traditional names. The first is the *tefillah*, which simply means "prayers." The second is *amidah*, meaning "standing," describing the posture of the congregants when they recite this section. The third is the *shmoneh esrei*, which means "eighteen," reflecting the tradition that this section contains eighteen prayers.

The tefillah draws upon the image of God as a sovereign ruler and king. Its structure casts God as the monarch and the worshippers as subjects approaching the heavenly court to request favor from God. Traditionally, a worshipper beginning the tefillah takes three steps forward and bows, just as someone would approach a king. The first three blessings comprise the information a petitioner would tell the king. The first, the *avot*, refers to Abraham, Isaac, and Jacob, reminding

God that the worshipper is a descendant of these luminaries and that God has a relationship and obligation to the worshipper. The second blessing is the *givurot*, which praises God for God's might and power. The third blessing invokes the holiness of this moment.

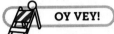 **OY VEY!**

Many non-Orthodox congregations have added the Matriarchs Sarah, Rebecca, Rachel, and Leah, to the avot, to demonstrate equal appreciation for women's contributions to Judaism.

The final three blessings of the tefillah similarly reflect how a petitioner would depart from a king. The first of the final three blessings is *avodah*, expressing the hope that God will grant the worshipper's petitionary prayers and restore the Temple. The next blessing is *modim*, expressing thanks to God for God's favor. The final blessing is a prayer for peace. The worshipper then takes three steps backward and bows, just as one would depart from a king.

On a normal weekday, the worshipper asks God to grant the community needed gifts. These are

- Wisdom
- Repentance
- Forgiveness
- Redemption
- Healing
- Fulfillment of material needs
- Return to Israel
- Justice
- Protection from heretics
- Reward for the righteous and scholars
- Restoration of Jerusalem
- The Mashiach
- Hearing of prayers

ASK THE RABBI

I count 3 prayers at the beginning, 13 in the middle, and 3 at the end. That's 19. Why is this section called the *shmoneh esrei* ("eighteen")? Scholars believe this section once contained 18 prayers, but the sages added an additional prayer. By that time, the name shmoneh esrei had become so familiar that they didn't change it. Also, 18 is a mystical number in Judaism, as the word spelled by the letters is *chai,* or "life."

On Shabbat and holy days, work is forbidden. It would be unseemly to ask God to work and give the people gifts on these days. Consequently, the tefillah omits all the intermediate petitionary prayers in these services, replacing them all with a general praise to God for the glory of the day.

The non-Orthodox movements may alter these prayers slightly to reflect their unique theologies. For example, the Reform movement removes the longing for a return to Israel and speaks of a Messianic Age instead of the Mashiach.

Reading Scripture

The tradition of reading Scripture in public traces back to Ezra the Scribe in the Book of Nehemiah. Chapter 8 of the book tells how Ezra read the Law in public for the people following the return from the Babylonian exile. Jews have read Scripture in public as part of their worship since then.

Scripture isn't read at every service. It's read on Shabbat and holy days during morning and afternoon services. It's also read on Mondays and Thursdays, as these traditionally were market days in the ancient world. The gathering of people led to the extra inclusion in the service and the opportunity to have everyone hear and learn from the text.

The primary Scriptural reading for an ordinary Shabbat and weekday comes from a designated Torah portion of the week, or "*parashah.*" A parashah consists of several chapters of the Torah. Congregations read the first parashah, *Bereshit,* on the Shabbat following the holiday of *Simchat Torah.* They continue each week in the order of the chapters in the Torah, progressing from Genesis to the end of Deuteronomy, until the end of the Torah is reached before Simchat Torah, and the cycle immediately begins again.

Some congregations read the entire parashah on Shabbat. Others follow a triennial cycle, reading the first third in year one, the second third in year two, and the final third in year three. Other congregations read a selection for the parashah. Whatever system the congregation employs, almost every Jewish congregation in the world reads for the same parashah on every Shabbat.

Holy days have special Torah portions designated for reading, stepping away from the chronological parashah cycle. These selections usually mention the holy day or consider a theme of the celebration or commemoration.

The Scriptural readings on Shabbat, festival days, and fast days also include a *"Haftarah."* The Haftarah is a portion from the Prophets connected by subject to the Torah portion of the time of the year. Like the Torah parashah, the Haftarah is set in the Jewish calendar for each week.

There are different theories as to why the sages included the reading of a Haftarah. Some say it was added to include each of the three parts of the Tanach in the service, as the Torah reading covered the first part and the prayers contained selections from the third part, the Writings. Others believe communities added the Haftarah during a time when the secular authorities prohibited the reading of the Torah. The link of the Haftarah to the Torah portion reminded the community of the appropriate reading for the week even if they couldn't hear it during the service.

A traditional, ornate siddur (Jewish prayer book).

The Torah reading occurs with great fanfare during the service. There are many prayers sung as the prayer leaders remove the Torah scroll from the ark. A congregant is given the honor of carrying the Torah throughout the congregation in a special procession called the hakafah. Jews traditionally touch their *tzitzit* (tallit fringes, discussed in Chapter 25) or *siddurim* (prayer books) to the Torah and give them a kiss as a sign of respect. The Torah reading is divided into sections called *aliyot,* and someone is called to the bimah for each *aliyah* (the singular of aliyot) to say a blessing before and after the reading.

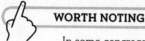

In some congregations, the first and second aliyot are given to a *kohein*, the descendant of someone from the Temple priesthood, and a Levite, a descendant from the Tribe of Levi, who had the honor of caring for the Temple.

After the Torah reading, two people are called forward for honors. One honor is *hagbah*, a person who lifts the Torah scroll with one rod in each hand, holding the rods apart and showing the congregation the text. After this, the second honored person, the *gelilah*, dresses the Torah, replacing the cover, yad, crowns, and breastplate.

Ending the Service

The service ends with two prayers. The *alienu* expresses the hope for the Mashiach or Messianic Age. The final prayer of the service is the Kaddish Yatom, the prayer that praises God for life, but is used to remember those who have died, discussed in Chapter 19. Many congregations end the service with a song.

Jewish Meditation

Jews have used several meditative practices at different times in their history. The Kabbalists would use visioning of God and the *sephirot* as part of their worship practices. In more recent times, some Jews have applied modern and Eastern meditative techniques to Jewish ideas, including mantras and guided experiences. Although many communities still retain the traditional forms of prayers, a strong community of Jewish meditators has added a new dimension to Jewish prayer.

The Least You Need to Know

- Prayer is an important aspect of Judaism, allowing Jews to petition and communicate with God, gain an understanding of the universe, and gather as a community.
- Jews traditionally gather for prayer three times daily. However, there are many opportunities for Jews to pray or say a blessing.
- A Jewish worship service combines fixed prayers and individual intentions, called keva and kavanah.
- Some Jews use meditative techniques in their prayers.

Symbols, Clothes, and a Sacred Space

This chapter considers aspects of Judaism that weave into the everyday fabric of Jewish life. For example, as in all cultures that people are proud to be a member of, Jews often wear cultural symbols and clothing. Some symbols or articles of clothing have profound religious or personal meaning for the wearer. Whether it's a piece of jewelry handed down through the generations or a T-shirt addressing a contemporary issue, Jews choose to share their identity in a variety of ways, the most common of which we'll explore in this chapter.

We'll also consider another very sacred and important practice in the Jewish tradition—the mikvah. The mikvah provides a way to receive spiritual cleansing and return to holiness. The mikvah isn't necessarily part of a synagogue and it's not found in a Jewish home, but it's an institution that many Jews make a part of their regular lives and routines.

In This Chapter

- Emblems of Jewishness and Judaism
- Clothes and accessories that make the Jew
- Special attire for Orthodox Jews
- The mikvah—a spiritual cleansing

Some Symbols of Judaism

There are several symbols that Jews identify as having meaning to them, or representing their thoughts, culture, or people. Some have their origin in the Tanach or religious practice. Others derive from culture or superstition. As you'll see, the most common Jewish symbol today, the *Magen David,* has no certain origin at all.

These symbols appear in many places. Sometimes, synagogues depict them in their artwork and decorations of their sanctuaries. They appear on documents, maps, papers, and other writings. Jewelry and ritual objects also often incorporate these symbols, and Jews wear and use them with pride and a sense of connection with their history and tradition that the symbols convey.

Menorah

The oldest identifiable Jewish symbol is the *menorah,* a seven-branched candelabra. The Tanach details a menorah for placement and use in the Tabernacle, which later became the model for The Temple in Jerusalem. (Exodus 25:30-40, 37:17-24)

> **WORTH NOTING**
>
> A midrash teaches that the description of the menorah in the Torah so confused Moses that God had to construct it for him. (Numbers Rabbah 15:4)

The seven branches most likely represent the seven days of creation, and reflect the mystical meaning that number has in Judaism. Another theory about the seven branches is the possibility that they represent the seven worlds of the solar system known in the ancient world. Some claim the menorah represents the fragrant moriah plant whose branches look like a menorah when pressed flat. This ties the symbol of the menorah to the beauty and fertility of Israel. Later in Jewish history, the Kabbalists believed that the seven branches represented the seven lower *sefirot,* the aspects of God according to Kabbalah considered in Chapter 6.

The Arch of Titus in Rome contains one of the oldest pictures of a menorah. The Arch depicts Romans carrying the menorah from the Temple as a prize from the war against the rebellious Jews of Jerusalem. In modern times, the State of Israel uses the menorah as a symbol on its coins and documents. A large menorah sits outside the *Knesset,* the Israeli parliament.

The fact that this Jewish symbol has survived through so many millennia gives it deep meaning to Jews. The menorah represents the light of God and Jewish tradition, and the belief that Jews will continue to survive and persevere over every obstacle or challenge.

The Magen David

The *Magen David* is a six-pointed star comprised of two overlapping triangles, one pointed upward and the other downward. Sometimes called the "Jewish Star" or "Star of David," Magen David actually means "The Shield of David." According to legend, King David had a mystical shield that protected him from harm during battle, and this star received the name "Magen David" at some time in history.

The irony of this name is that there's no evidence King David ever used this symbol. Older descriptions of David's shield say it was inscribed with one of the names of God or a menorah, but never a six-pointed star. Moreover, there are very few images of a six-pointed star in ancient synagogues, and those that exist might just be decorations instead of symbols of meaning for Judaism or the Jewish people.

Nevertheless, the Magen David became the symbol of Judaism, equivalent in use to the cross in Christianity and the crescent in Islam. This occurred only after a long process. The flag of the Jewish community of Prague in 1354 contained a six-pointed star, and the ghetto walls of Vienna in the seventeenth century used a six-pointed star to designate the Jewish side. French Jews used a six-pointed star to represent their community following the French Revolution. The Magen David likely solidified its universal acceptance as the Jewish symbol after the early Zionists chose it for the Jewish State. Theodor Herzl eventually approved this symbol because it was well known among Jews, and it contained no inherent religious meaning.

The true origin and meaning of the Magen David is lost to history. Some say one triangle represents the male and the other the female. Others say one triangle represents fire and the other water. The Jewish philosopher Franz Rosensweig based his description of Judaism around the six points of the star in his book *The Star of Redemption,* saying they represented the main points of Judaism: Redemption, Revelation, Creation, God, Human Beings, and the Universe.

However one interprets the symbol, the Magen David has become the most recognizable symbol of Judaism today. Its inclusion as the central figure on the Israeli flag solidifies its place as the "logo" of the Jewish people.

Hamsa

Like many Mediterranean cultures, Judaism has the symbol of an inverted hand as part of its culture. In Judaism, this symbol is called a *hamsa,* and Jews see it as a means to ward off the "Evil Eye," a force that causes misfortune in Jewish superstition. The hamsa represents the hand of God reaching out to protect its owner. It's also sometimes called "the hand of Miriam," perhaps adhering to the pattern of Christianity and Islam that attribute the symbol to Mary and Fatima.

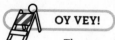

OY VEY!

The root of hamsa comes from the Hebrew word for "five," representing the five fingers of a hand. However, it's not unusual to find a hamsa with six fingers to ensure it doesn't violate the Jewish prohibition against making graven images of people.

Tree of Life

Jewish liturgy calls the Torah "The Tree of Life." It says the Torah is "a Tree of Life to all who hold fast to it, and all its supporters are happy." Consequently, some Jewish artwork and jewelry literally depicts a tree meant to represent the Torah.

Pomegranate

The pomegranate is another Jewish symbol that finds its origin in the Tanach. A pomegranate is one of the seven items illustrating the bounty and beauty of The Promised Land. (Deuteronomy 8:8)

This symbol has a deeper meaning than just the prosperity and abundance of Israel. The Talmud explains that each pomegranate has 613 seeds, one for each of the mitzvot in Judaism. While the connection is more metaphorical than biologically correct, the symbol of the pomegranate gains deep spiritual meaning through this association.

Some Torah scrolls have two crowns, one on each rod holding the scroll, called *rimmonim*, the Hebrew word for pomegranates. These silver ornaments, often including a bulbous shape like a pomegranate, connect the ideas of God's sovereignty, creative power, and mitzvah in one set of objects.

Lion of Judah

The final common symbol in Judaism is a lion, which the Torah connects to the tribe of Judah. Jacob blessed each of his sons as he lay dying, and he compared Judah to a lion. (Genesis 49:9-10) Judah became the sole remaining tribe following the Babylonian exile, and may have used the lion as its symbol. Later generations used the lion motif to demonstrate Jewish strength, both physical and spiritual, including the animal in art and ritual objects.

Dress for Jewish Success

Throughout history, Jews have tended to wear the same kinds of clothing as those in the surrounding nations. This clothing proved to be the best suited for the climate and the most available, so there was no need to develop a separate mode of dress. However, there are a few items of apparel unique to Jews that contain religious meaning or reflect Jewish values.

Yarmulke

Yarmulke is a Yiddish word referring to a cloth or knit head covering Jewish men wear as a sign of respect to God. The Hebrew word for yarmulke is *kippah.* Yarmulkes come in all different shapes and sizes, from smaller knitted circles to broad caps that cover most of the wearer's head. The traditional yarmulke is usually black or dark blue in color, but today they're made in all different colors and designs. An Orthodox or Conservative woman may also cover her head, but instead of a yarmulke she would use lace, a handkerchief, or a hat.

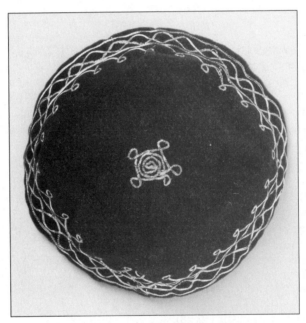

Traditional blue velvet yarmulke with silver design.

Many traditional Jewish men wear the yarmulke from the time they rise to the time they go to sleep, with the exception of when they bathe. Other Jews wear the yarmulke only during Jewish study or prayer. Initially, the Reform Movement criticized wearing the yarmulke, claiming it obstructed true religious observance. Many Reform congregations even prohibited people from wearing them at services. In more recent times, the yarmulke has gained greater acceptance among Reform Jews, and they are available to everyone who comes to services.

Many Jews today believe that wearing a yarmulke is one of the 613 mitzvot, required by the traditional halachah equally as keeping kosher or observing the holy days. In reality, wearing the yarmulke isn't required by the halachah at all. It's a custom that developed over time, and has come to be viewed as essential by traditional Jews. Despite this value for the head covering, wearing a yarmulke isn't a commandment.

Tallit and Tefillin

The Tanach prescribes in Numbers 15:37-41 a special garment for Jewish men to wear called a *tallit* in Hebrew and *tallis* in Yiddish. A tallit is a four-cornered garment with wound and knotted fringes on each corner. The fringes, called the *tzitzit*, are the most important part of the tallit. As the Torah explains, the tallit wearer sees the tzitzit, and this reminds the wearer to perform the mitzvot.

Tallit on left, with chanukkiah, yarmulke, and Jewish book.

WORDS OF WISDOM

"God spoke to Moses, saying, 'Speak to the children of Israel and tell them to put fringes (tzitzit) on their garments throughout the generations ... that you might look upon it, and remember all God's commandments and do them ....'"–Numbers 15:37-39

There are two types of *tallitim* (the plural of tallit). The first is the *tallit katan* (small tallit), also sometimes called *arba kanfot* (four corners). This tallit is a thin garment with fringes worn by a man under his shirt. Some men tuck the fringes inside their clothing, while others allow the fringes to hang over their waists in full view. Most of the men who wear this form of tallit are Orthodox.

The second form of tallit is a four-cornered shawl with tzitzit worn over the shoulders during prayer in morning and afternoon services and at the *Kol Nidrei* service that occurs on the evening of Yom Kippur. These tallitim come in all sizes. The tzitzit described in the Torah has a blue thread, so many of these tallitim today are white with blue stripes. Many artists and tallit makers today depart from the traditional appearance of the garment, and use all kinds of colors and designs for their tallitim.

 ASK THE RABBI

I've seen a tallit with black stripes instead of blue. Why? Most Jews agree that the exact shade of blue of the stripes used in ancient times remains unknown. To avoid wearing an incorrect color, but to keep the traditional appearance of the tallit, some Jews wear a garment with black stripes instead of blue.

Jews sometimes cover their heads with the tallit during prayer at times requiring intense concentration, such as during the recitation of the Sh'mah. Some Jews also touch the tzitzit to the Torah scroll during the *hakafah* or before and after reciting an aliyah, and kiss the tzitzit as a sign of respect.

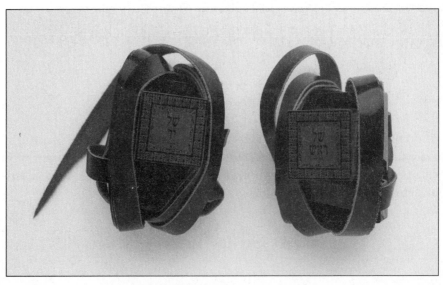

Tefillin with straps wound around them.

Traditional Jewish men also often wear ritual objects called *tefillin* during weekday morning services and on the afternoon of Tisha Be'Av. In English, these objects are referred to as phylacteries. Tefillin are black boxes with leather straps. They come in sets of two: one worn around the forehead, and the other wrapped around the wearer's nonmaster forearm. The boxes have four chambers, each containing parchment written by a sofer with one of four texts: Exodus 13:1-10, Exodus 13:11-16, Deuteronomy 6:4-9, and Deuteronomy 11:13-21.

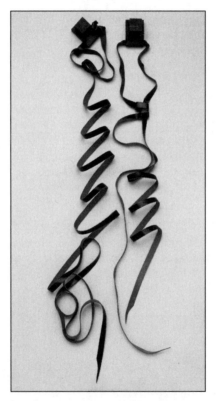

Tefillin with straps unwound.

The tefillin are a literal enactment of words from these texts that say, "Bind (these words) as a sign upon your hand; let them be a symbol before your eyes." The transformation of these verses into a tangible, worn object resulted from Rabbinic interpretation, and has become standard practice in traditional Judaism.

WORTH NOTING

In traditional Judaism, only men wear the yarmulke, tallit, and tefillin. This is because only men have the responsibility for the formal daily prayer, and the Tanach prohibits a woman from wearing a man's clothing. However, many non-Orthodox women have begun to wear these items, and the tallitim and yarmulkes they wear may have nontraditional designs.

Like the yarmulke, the Reform Movement initially rejected the wearing of the tallit and tefillin. More recently, Reform communities have embraced wearing the tallit. Some Reform Jews also wear tefillin, although that has not yet received the same widespread use in Reform synagogues as the yarmulke and tallit.

A Jewish man praying while wearing tallit and tefillin.

Kittel

A kittel is a special white robe worn by traditional Jewish men during Yom Kippur and at their weddings. Some Jewish men also are buried in their kittel. The white of the garment represents the spiritual purity needed at these special times.

Orthodox Dress

Many Orthodox Jews wear clothing that conforms to their ideas of *tzni'ut* (modesty). This clothing avoids flamboyance, reflecting the concern that fancy or loud clothing only serves as an expression of vanity. Consequently, men wear simple black suits with white shirts, and possibly a dark tie. Women also dress conservatively, although many communities permit a wider latitude of colors and styles. However, women must abide by tzni'ut rules that reflect sexual modesty. Married women can't allow their natural hair to show, and some wear wigs, because their hair would be sexually attractive to men. The women also must wear a blouse that doesn't show their skin below their necks, and other clothing that covers their arms to their wrists and their legs to their ankles.

Chassidic Jewish men often wear distinctive clothing influenced by the attire of the Polish nobility of the sixteenth century and later. They often wear long black coats and black hats. Some of the hats contain fur. Each Chassidic sect has its particular mode of dress, and a Jew familiar with this community often can identify the Chassid's sect by the cut and color of the clothing or the shape and composition of the hat.

Dressing for Services

Different congregations have different expectations for dress at worship services. Some congregations encourage casual dress. Other communities have sanctuaries filled with men in suits and women in beautiful dresses and jewelry as part of the expression of *hiddur mitzvah,* beautifying the performance of the commandment of worship and observance, especially during Shabbat, the High Holy Days, and festivals.

If you plan to attend a Jewish worship service, it's appropriate and advantageous to call the synagogue prior to the holy day and ask them about expectations for dress. You might receive an answer that "anything nice is appropriate," which may be true in that no one will comment to you or refuse you entry for what you're wearing, but it also might not reflect the true expectations and mores of the community. You might want to ask for examples of what congregants typically wear to services to give you a clearer idea of how you should dress.

Mikvah—The Ritual Bath

Jewish laws have been concerned with spiritual and ritual purity since Talmudic times. Some acts or conditions make a Jew ritually or spiritually pure, while others make a Jew impure. If a Jew becomes ritually impure or otherwise needs to affirm his or her purity, one way he or she may do this is through a visit to the mikvah.

A mikvah is a ritual bath. It's not a bath for physical cleanliness, but for spiritual renewal and ritualizing a change in status. The waters of a mikvah convey holiness and renewal.

Rules for a Mikvah

Any flowing natural body of water may serve as a mikvah. However, people often live in places without an appropriate ocean, river, or stream. Communities therefore may construct a special bath for use as a mikvah.

The primary rule for a mikvah is that a percentage of the water in the pool for each immersion must be naturally collected and guided into the pool. Often the community designs the mikvah to collect water from rain falling upon the building's roof, and creates a path for it to flow into the pool without being touched by a human being. The halachah deems this equivalent to a natural body of water, allowing the construction of a kosher mikvah.

When Jews Go to the Mikvah

One of the primary uses of the mikvah is for *niddah*—the ritual purification of a woman after menstruation as described in Chapter 21. Immersion into the mikvah restores the woman's purity, allowing physical contact with her husband to resume.

The other primary use of the mikvah is for conversion. Conversion to Judaism is a significant change in status requiring a ritual and method of spiritual transformation to holiness. The waters of the mikvah provide this spiritual change.

Other occasions also call for the use of the mikvah. Some men use the mikvah after a nocturnal emission or prior to the High Holy Days. Brides and grooms sometimes visit the mikvah prior to their weddings. In modern times, some Jews go to the mikvah after recovery from illness, prior to a holy day or Shabbat, or when confronting any change in their lives.

 **WORTH NOTING**

Some students visit the mikvah prior to their ordination as a rabbi or cantor.

Taking the Plunge

A person arriving at the mikvah first must wash completely before entering the actual ritual bath. He or she must cleanse himself or herself of every speck of dirt, taking care to ensure there is nothing under the fingernails. All makeup, jewelry, and nail polish must be removed. Physical cleanliness and taking care to ensure the mikvah's waters remain pure comes before the spiritual cleansing.

A person enters the mikvah entirely naked and alone. If the person to be immersed is a child, a parent may accompany him or her. Some immersions require at least one witness. If that's the case, only someone of the same gender may serve as a witness who actually views the immersion. If a rabbi or a person of a different gender serves as a witness, he or she remains behind a door or screen and witnesses the immersion by listening and hearing the water splash.

The person entering the mikvah must go under the water three times. Each time, he or she must allow the water to flow entirely around his or her body, keeping his or her arms and legs away from pressing against each other or any other part of the body. Prior to immersion, the person entering the mikvah recites a blessing or the Sh'mah. After the three submersions, the person exits the mikvah spiritually and ritually renewed.

The Least You Need to Know

- The most common symbol of Judaism today is the six-pointed star called the Magen David. Other symbols throughout Jewish history include the menorah, hamsa, Tree of Life, pomegranate, and Lion of Judah.

- Traditional Jewish men wear a head covering called a yarmulke or kippah. They wear a prayer shawl called a tallit and leather boxes with straps called tefillin during some worship services.

- Orthodox Jews dress modestly, often in subdued colors and fashions or in black. Orthodox women generally must dress modestly without showing much of their skin below their necks, or above their wrists and ankles.

- Many Jews visit a ritual bath called a mikvah to mark a change of status or to restore spiritual purity.

Comparisons and Questions

I have described the important aspects of Judaism. The final part of your journey to understanding Judaism presents and answers some remaining questions.

Chapter 26 compares Judaism and Christianity so that you may gain an understanding of how they differ, and also the many ways they are similar. Chapter 27 provides 20 common questions about Judaism and their answers for easy reference.

Judaism and Christianity: Where We Differ

The history of the relationship between Judaism and Christianity is long and complex. Judaism and Christianity have a "mother-daughter" relationship, as Christianity sprang forth from Judaism. However, the two philosophies quickly diverged. The early Christian Church had to decide whether being Jewish was a prerequisite to becoming a Christian, as both some Jews and some Gentiles claimed Christianity in the decades following Jesus' death. Ultimately, the early Christians decided Gentiles could be Christians, further separating themselves from Judaism.

Over time, greater philosophical and theological differences arose. Christians and Jews often lived next to each other, but that didn't mean the relationship was always positive. Mutual suspicion prevailed, and anti-Semitism rooted in verses in the Book of Matthew imposing responsibility for Jesus' death and other misunderstandings that sometimes led to discrimination and even violence.

Thankfully, we live in a much different world today. The general relationship between Jews and Christians is positive and respectful, and there have been significant strides in interfaith dialogue, understanding, and cooperation over the last 50 years. Differences remain, and sometimes there are

In This Chapter

- Similarities between the religions
- Jesus as viewed by the Jewish people
- Differences in the views of sin
- Christianity's divergence from the Jewish idea of mitzvah
- The afterlife in the two religions

significant disagreements about ideas and actions. However, through the lens of history, it may be that the relationship between Jews and Christians has never been better.

Having a Respectful Dialogue

Judaism and Christianity share far more similarities than differences. Nevertheless, in order to really understand Judaism, especially in North America and Europe, it's important to consider the differences between the two faiths. The majority religion in many of the nations where Jews live is Christian. A respectful comparison of the two religions often leads to a greater understanding among Christians as to exactly what Judaism is and why Jews maintain their distinctive beliefs and practices.

There are several difficulties inherent in such a discussion, especially in a basic overview like this chapter. First, the only way to discuss the differences between Judaism and Christianity in one chapter is to generalize about both. There are nuances in theology and practice for both that are important to know, but a deeper examination falls beyond the scope of this book.

Second, a comparison in a limited chapter like this must set aside differences between the various sects and movements of the religions. For example, Catholicism has important differences with Protestantism, and Orthodox Judaism has important differences with Reform, but our limited discussion cannot cover many of these important distinctions.

Third, and most important, too often a comparison of religions leads to offense. Saying one religion differs from another doesn't mean that one is wrong or that its beliefs are unreasonable. It only means that one holds a certain set of beliefs, and the other holds another set of beliefs. I have spoken to many Christian groups, and I always tell them the same thing: by learning about each other and understanding how we differ, we enhance peace. Knowledge, respect, and understanding don't lead to agreement, but if we approach each other with open hearts, we find friendship and build a kinder world. The discussion that follows intends to help build that understanding.

Similarities Between Two Great Religions

At their core, Judaism and Christianity share many of the same ideas and values. Both religions are monotheistic faiths, even though they hold important differences in exactly what that means. Both believe God rewards good behavior and punishes wrongful behavior. The adherents of both religions have the potential for redemption through repentance.

Both religions call for many of the same moral behaviors of their adherents. Both require helping the poor and less privileged through tzedakah or charity. Worship is an important aspect of regular life for both Jews and Christians.

Many of the most important teachings of both religions either are identical or very similar. Both Judaism and Christianity ask their adherents to "love your neighbor as yourself," with Judaism finding this mitzvah in Leviticus 19:18 and Christians finding it in several places in their Scripture, including Mark 12:31. Jesus taught that one should "do unto others as you would have others do unto you" (Matthew 7:12), while Rabbi Hillel taught Jews the similar rule that "what is hateful to you, do not do to your fellow." (Talmud Bavli, Shabbat 31a)

Christians adopt much of Tanach as part of their holy Scripture. They call these texts by a different name, the Old Testament, but they're largely identical. Depending on the sect of Christianity, the Old Testament contains some books that Jews didn't include in their Bible, such as Tobit, Judith, and Maccabees. Some versions of the Christian Old Testament also present the books in a different order, or include other minor differences such as different numberings of verses or psalms.

 ASK THE RABBI

Why don't Jews use the term "Old Testament"? Many Jews consider this term a misnomer. "Old" implies that the Scripture has been replaced by something "New," and Jews don't believe there is any more holy Scripture beyond what they've adopted. "Testament" means "testimony" or "witnessing," appropriate for Christianity as the Gospels are witnesses to Jesus' role and life. The Tanach is more than a witnessing to Jews. Finally, Jews like and have always used the name Tanach for their Scripture, and respectfully see no reason to change their terminology to match Christian nomenclature.

Although most of the Tanach matches the Christian Old Testament, there are some very important differences that reflect the different theological interpretations. For example, in the Book of Isaiah, the text tells of King Ahaz's reluctance to fight a battle. Isaiah responds by saying that a child will be born with the name Immanuel, meaning "God is with you," as a sign that the king should fight the battle. (Isaiah 7:14)

Some of the Christian versions of the Old Testament read that the mother of this child will be a "virgin," and some Christians understand the meaning of the name to foretell the coming of Jesus. However, the Tanach uses the Hebrew word *almah* to describe this child's mother. Almah means a young woman who hasn't had a child, but doesn't necessarily mean virgin. This slight difference in understanding and translation of one word leads to very significant theological meanings. It shows how the two religions can have virtually identical Scriptures, but still draw very different beliefs from them.

The Primary Difference: Views of Jesus

The primary difference between Judaism and Christianity is the two religions' perspectives of Jesus. Christianity considers Jesus to have the highest importance in its religion. Judaism doesn't give Jesus any role at all in its beliefs. The different views occur at many levels of understanding about Jesus.

The Jewish View of Jesus as Divine

Christians hold that Jesus has a special aspect of divinity. For many, Jesus is part of a Holy Trinity, the one and only Son of God. Some believe Jesus was God incarnate who came to Earth as a human being to understand and experience human life, and ultimately, to suffer and die as a means to save human souls from their sins. This is an important theology too complex to completely describe here. The important point is that many of these Christian beliefs depend on Jesus having a unique divine aspect that no other human being has ever had.

Judaism disagrees that Jesus had any special divine aspect. This belief arises both from Jewish ideas about God and from Jewish ideas about human beings.

 WORDS OF WISDOM

"We cannot conceive Christianity without Jesus …. For Judaism, God is the only ideal of absolute perfection, and [God] only must be kept always before the eye of man's inner consciousness …."

—Ahad Ha-am, *Jewish and Christian Ethics* (1873)

As we learned in Chapter 1, Judaism's primary statement of faith is the Sh'mah, which says, "Hear Israel, Adonai is Your God, Adonai is One." Jewish thought through the centuries, as described by Maimonides, has expressed that this means God is singular, unique, and incorporeal. God isn't divided into separate parts of aspects, because this would lessen God from the all-powerful entity envisioned in the Jewish idea of monotheism.

Clearly, these ideas conflict with the notion of a human being with a special and unique divine aspect such as Christianity extends to Jesus. Giving God a physical body contradicts the Jewish idea of God's incorporeity, and dividing God between a "Father" and a "Son" departs from the Jewish idea of God's unity. Moreover, any sort of understanding of God as a human being challenges the Jewish idea of God's uniqueness.

The idea of one person having a special aspect of divinity also conflicts with Judaism's idea of human beings. Judaism says God created all human beings b'tzelem Elohim—in God's image. This requires everyone to have an aspect of divinity within them, understood by Judaism to be the soul and the breath of life God gives to everyone.

The Midrash also teaches that God created everyone through one man and woman, so that no one would say one person is greater or has a greater lineage than another. All these beliefs contravene the idea of one person as a special divine entity with human form, as required by the Christian idea of Jesus.

WORTH NOTING

One of the manifestations of the difference between Jewish and Christian views of Jesus may be seen in artwork and decorations in places of worship. Jews believe the prohibition against "graven images" in the Ten Commandments forbids any physical representation of God. Such a representation is also hindered by the Jewish belief that God has no body. In contrast, Christian artwork and church adornment includes paintings and statues depicting both God and Jesus.

The Jewish View of Jesus as Messiah

Christianity generally calls Jesus "the Messiah." The word comes from the Hebrew word *Mashiach,* and the word *Christ* derives from the word meaning "anointed one" in Greek, the same meaning as Mashiach. There are different views within Christianity as to what Jesus' role as Messiah means. However, they generally include the idea of a spiritual figure who has a role in "saving souls," and has mystical and amazing abilities, such as the capacity to walk on water or turn one loaf of bread and one fish into enough to feed a multitude.

The Jewish view of Mashiach is worldlier, and even political. In Judaism, the Mashiach is the King of Israel who will restore the Israelite Kingdom, including the reestablishment of the Temple in Jerusalem. The Mashiach isn't a divine figure with extraordinary abilities, but a Jewish ruler who will rule when God brings a qualitative change to the world, instituting universal peace, harmony, and prosperity.

From the Jewish perspective, Jesus was not the Mashiach because he didn't meet these definitional criteria held by Judaism. He wasn't the anointed King of a Jewish state in Israel, and he didn't regain independence from the Romans. His presence on Earth didn't bring peace, harmony, and prosperity. He simply didn't do what Jews believe the Mashiach would do.

OY VEY!

The idea of the "second coming" of Jesus doesn't change the Jewish position that Jesus isn't the Mashiach. Even though both religions envision a future time when either Jesus or the Mashiach will establish himself on Earth, the role each religion gives to its chosen figure differs. Moreover, the Christian belief that Jesus will return to be the Messiah isn't enough to convince Jews that Jesus will be the Mashiach they foresee.

The Jewish View of Jesus as Prophet or Teacher

Many Christians see Jesus fulfilling two other roles: a prophet and a teacher. Judaism doesn't accept Jesus as a prophet, nor does it accept Jesus as a teacher of Judaism.

Judaism provides a very specific role for a prophet. A prophet generally acts as the spokesperson for God, warning a specific people to turn from their evil ways toward God. Although Jews later study the words of the prophets and apply their teachings to current life, a Jewish prophet has a particular purpose for the society in which he preaches. For example, Jeremiah is concerned with the Kingdom of Judah prior to the Babylonian exile, and Jonah is called as a prophet to aid the people of Ninevah.

Christianity portrays Jesus as having a far greater universal and eternal emphasis than the prophets recognized by Judaism. Even Moses, who the Tanach calls the greatest prophet ever (Deuteronomy 34:10), doesn't have such a role for Jews. The Christian view of Jesus so exceeds the Jewish view of a prophet that it removes him from qualification for that role in Judaism.

Judaism doesn't give the prophets any special divine status the way Christianity views Jesus. Prophets in Judaism only serve as spokesmen for God. They aren't saviors, and they generally don't perform miracles. In contrast, the Tanach disapproves of people who seek to assert their status as a prophet through the performance of miracles, cautioning Jews to disregard this effort and reject the claimant. (Deuteronomy 13:2-6)

Additionally, the sages of Jesus' time had already declared the age of prophecy to have passed. The canonization of the second part of the Tanach, the Prophets, had long been completed, and the prophets had already handed the authority to interpret the Torah to the rabbis. (Mishnah, Pirkei Avot 1:1) Jesus' actions, role in Christianity, and time in which he lived all preclude Judaism from accepting him as a prophet.

Judaism takes a similar view toward seeing Jesus as a teacher of Judaism. The Gospels present Jesus as teaching many worthy ideas, with some identical or substantially similar to those found in Judaism. However, this actually argues against Judaism accepting Jesus as a great or revolutionary teacher of Judaism. Jews have no need to accept Jesus as a teacher of Jewish ideas because they already have their own teachers.

There are many people throughout history who have taught ideas and values similar to those found in Judaism. This doesn't make any of them necessarily part of Jewish teaching. Moreover, a person's status as a Jew, such as that held by Jesus, doesn't mean he is accepted as a great or innovative teacher of Judaism.

Judaism and some forms of Christianity take very different views of proselytization. Some Christians believe themselves obligated to introduce people to Jesus and Christian ideas with the goal of having them become Christian. Most Jews reject proselytization, and Jews even traditionally attempt to dissuade perspective converts three times.

More importantly, Jews have a realistic concern that if they recognize Jesus as a great teacher of Judaism, there will be undesirable results. Some of Jesus' important teachings, or those attributed to Jesus by his later followers, contradict essential tenets of Judaism. Jews also realistically fear the acceptance of Jesus as a teacher of Judaism will lead some to believe that Jews accept these teachings, or accept other perspectives of the role of Jesus such as Jesus being divine or the Mashiach.

The spiritual Christian perspective of Jesus, necessary in Christianity for a full appreciation of Christian theology, in effect removes him from consideration as either a prophet or teacher in Judaism.

Philosophical Differences

Beyond the different understandings of Jesus, Judaism and Christianity vary about some important philosophical concepts. The two great religions have much in common, but also have significant disagreements on some basic principles about life.

These differences as a whole create a disagreement between some Christians and Jews. Some Christians believe Jesus' arrival on Earth voided the Jewish Covenant with God and replaced it with a New Covenant. The idea that Christianity and Christian beliefs effectively replace Judaism is called *supersessionism.* Jews emphatically reject the idea of supercessionism, firmly holding to their beliefs and teachings as valid and still meaningful to them.

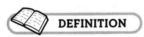

DEFINITION

Supersessionism is the belief that Christianity replaces Judaism, and the Christian idea of the Covenant through Jesus replaces the Covenant made by the Israelites at Mount Sinai. Jews firmly reject this idea.

The Role of Sin

Many sects of Christianity hold the idea of sin as central to their philosophy. These sects believe everyone is born with sin, which they view as a serious deficiency for a human being. Sin is a bad thing that needs to be removed from one's soul.

The way a person removes sin in these forms of Christianity is through Jesus. Christianity holds Jesus as the only person born without sin, and believes God sent him to Earth to die for the sins of human beings. The Christian view of the Messiah gives Jesus the spiritual role of acting as an intermediary between human beings and God. Christians can relate to God through Jesus, and Jesus can save a person's soul if that person adopts this belief as his or her own. As Jesus says in John 4:16, "I am the truth and the life. No one comes to the Father but through me."

Judaism takes a very different perspective on sin, repentance, and a person's relationship with God. In Judaism, people are not born with sin. The Jewish morning prayers say that, "The soul that You have given me is pure." Judaism also believes that sin is equivalent to failing to follow the mitzvot, or "missing the mark." While not following the mitzvot certainly isn't desirable, it isn't necessarily as blameworthy or corrupting as expressed in some forms of Christianity. Judaism recognizes that everyone misses the mark during their lives, and the appropriate response is to repent through the process of teshuvah.

The concept of teshuvah significantly diverges from the idea of repentance through Jesus. Teshuvah is a personal process. If a person sins against God, he or she must direct their prayers and pleas directly to God. Judaism doesn't find an intermediary such as Jesus required or beneficial to a person's relationship with God. Judaism often speaks of a "personal God," holding the ideal to be a direct relationship between an individual and the Divine. In Judaism, the role of sin and how a Jew spiritually cleanses the sin varies significantly from Christianity.

Views of the Law

Judaism regards the mitzvot very highly. A Jew's role in the Covenant with God is to follow the 613 mitzvot in life as best he or she is able. These detailed laws cover every aspect of life, including dress, relationships, food, morality, and worship. A Jew becomes holy by following the mitzvot.

Christianity takes a sharply different view of the mitzvot. Matthew 22:37-40 says "Love the Lord your God with all your heart, with all your soul and with all your mind ….and love your neighbor as yourself. All the Law and the Prophets hang on these two commandments." Jesus says, "I am the way and the truth and the life" in John 14:6. Later writers understand these and other statements by Jesus in the Gospels to mean that following the mitzvot is no longer necessary. The way to holiness is through acceptance of Jesus and following his teachings, not through the specific acts required by the Torah and the Oral Law. By adopting this philosophy, Christianity made one of its greatest divergences from Judaism.

Views of the Afterlife

Some forms of Christianity have a very detailed idea of the afterlife. They see heaven as a place of eternal reward, and hell as a place of eternal punishment. A person's destination after death depends upon the moral quality of the life he or she lived on Earth.

As we saw in Chapter 18, Jews have a different perspective on what happens after death. Most Jewish thought is vague in comparison to Christianity, leaving more questions than answers. The roles of sin, reward, and punishment are also less clear and less emphasized in Judaism than in some forms of Christianity.

> **WORTH NOTING**
>
> Judaism believes non-Jews will have a place in *olam haba*—the world to come—if they follow the seven Noahide laws: belief in one God in their own way, having courts of law, not stealing, not committing adultery, not worshipping idols, not eating a live animal, and not cursing God. Some Christians believe non-Christians may go to heaven after death, while others believe the only way to this reward is through acceptance of Jesus.

Some of these differences are a matter of emphasis. Some forms of Christianity greatly accentuate what happens after death, and view the entire purpose of life on Earth as preparation for what comes afterward. Judaism focuses its theology and teachings on what Jews should do on Earth during life, leaving what happens afterward as unknowable. This is another example of two great religions holding beautiful yet divergent views.

The Least You Need to Know

- Judaism and Christianity share many values, and have a great deal in common with each other.
- Judaism doesn't accept Jesus as a special divine figure, the Messiah, a prophet, or a teacher of Judaism.
- Judaism and Christianity differ in their views of the role of sin, including whether a person is born with sin and how a person renews himself after sinning.
- Christianity significantly diverged from Judaism by replacing performance of the mitzvot with belief and faith in Jesus.
- Judaism emphasizes life on Earth and performance of the mitzvot, while some forms of Christianity place a greater emphasize on the afterlife. Judaism says little specifically about the afterlife, while some forms of Christianity have well-developed descriptions of it.

Twenty Questions

Judaism is a tradition that values questions. The Talmud may be viewed as a collection of discussions about the answers to questions that spawn yet further questioning. It's a never-ending process.

This chapter considers questions that haven't been addressed in the previous chapters of this book. Some address very serious topics, while others are fun and/or Jewish trivia. All are questions I have been asked by students or people curious about Judaism. Many of the answers illustrate important lessons about Judaism.

In This Chapter

- Questions about the Jewish people
- Biblical queries
- Theological mysteries
- Cultural conundrums

Questions About the Jewish People and History

Some questions that arise are inquiries about how Jews developed as a people, or who Jews are today.

The Population Question

How many Jews are living in the world today?

There are approximately 14 million Jews in the world today. About six million live in Israel, and another six million live in North America. Most of the remaining Jewish population lives in Europe, especially the United Kingdom, France, Russia, and Germany. Australia, Brazil, and Argentina also have Jewish communities approaching or exceeding 100,000 Jews.

These figures demonstrate the impact of the Holocaust upon the Jewish people. Six million Jews were killed in the Holocaust, which is more than 40 percent of today's Jewish population. When Jews also consider the loss of the children, grandchildren, and great-grandchildren these victims would have had, they recognize the further devastation of the Nazis' efforts. This realization also causes Jews to be especially concerned about the safety of every Jewish life.

The Jewish Majority Question

Have Jews ever been the majority, or has Judaism ever been the national religion, of any nation besides Israel?

It's possible that there has been one country besides ancient and modern Israel that has either had a majority of Jews or adopted Judaism as the official religion. This country is Khazar, a nation formed in western Turkey between the Black Sea and the Caspian Sea between the seventh and eleventh centuries. There are few sources about this country, and scholars debate about exactly what happened there. It seems that many religions operated in the area during its history. However, there is evidence that Judaism held a significant, or even a primary, place in the country through at least some of its history. At some point, the ruling class seems to have converted to Judaism. Judah HaLevi, a Spanish Jewish philosopher, wrote a treatise called "The Kuzari" around 1140 C.E. describing a debate between a rabbi and a pagan. Other documents also support the presence of Judaism in this state.

The importance of this question is less about Khazar, and more about what it says about Judaism. As a major religion with such a long history, it's remarkable that so few nations have had either a majority of Jews or accepted Judaism as its primary religion. It's also remarkable that despite the lack of support and strength other religions have gained from becoming the majority culture or practice, Judaism continues to exist and is considered to be a major religion in the world.

The Mashiach Question

Has any Jew after Jesus claimed to be the Mashiach?

The most notable claimant to the title of Mashiach was a man named Sabbatai Tzvi. Sabbatai Tzvi lived in Turkey and throughout the Middle East. He was a charismatic rabbi and adherent to the Kabbalah.

Sabbatai Tzvi managed to convince thousands of Jews that he was the Mashiach. He found a self-proclaimed prophet named Nathan who supported his claims. Many Jews throughout the Middle East and Europe accepted him as the Mashiach, while others rejected his claims.

Sabbatai Tzvi's career as potential Mashiach came to a climax with the Turkish Sultan in 1666. The Sultan, concerned about Sabbatai Tzvi's growing influence and power, captured him and convinced him to convert to Islam. Tzvi's conversion basically ended his influence among the Jews, and most of his followers abandoned him.

Sabbatai Tzvi had a significant influence upon later generations. His dramatic fall from respect and his quick conversion away from Judaism made later generations of Jews much more wary of claims by anyone to be the Mashiach. Jews have required much more proof before following someone who claims this role, as authorities have cautioned Jews against following someone "lest he proves to be another Sabbatai Tzvi."

One leader who may be viewed to have transcended these concerns is the Lubavitch Chassidic Rebbe Menachem Mendel Schneerson. Rebbe Schneerson was a man of great charisma and scholarship. He never explicitly claimed to be the Mashiach, but many of his followers hold him in such high esteem, even after his death, that they consider him to be the Mashiach.

The Loyalty Question

If there were a war between Israel and the United States, for whom would Jews fight?

Most Jews strongly dislike this question for three reasons. First, the United States and Israel are long-time friends and allies. Israel is the only democracy in the Middle East, and the two nations share many values. Israel is an important resource of technological and bio-medical innovation, and the idea that these two nations would act against their interests, values, and national interests makes no sense to Jews.

American Jews also dislike this question because it implies that they might be disloyal, or at best, not completely American. They note that Irish Americans aren't asked the same question about Ireland, or Italian Americans about Italy, and so on. They wonder why they should be singled out for the doubt implicit in this question.

Third, American Jews remain aware of the treatment of Japanese Americans before and during World War II. They worry that the tensions or international situation of a given moment might cause Jews to suffer the same discrimination as the Japanese Americans. When they also consider the experience of the Holocaust, where long-time Jewish citizens of Germany had their loyalty to their nation questioned as one of the first steps of the Holocaust, this question raises fear and concern.

Nevertheless, it's a question that many Jews are asked in one way or another, and although it may offend or raise worries, it must be answered. Many Jews feel a special bond with Israel, but this bond wouldn't necessarily cause a Jew to support Israel over the United States were a conflict to arise. Most likely, some Jews would support the United States, some would support Israel, and many would seek to stay neutral or find reconciliation between the two nations. American Jews cherish both countries and their values, and so they endeavor to ensure that they never will need to take sides between the two.

The Jewish Success Question

Why are Jews so successful, more successful than other people?

Bill Gates. Donald Trump. Steven Hawking. Every President of the United States. There are many successful people who aren't Jewish. In truth, there are far more successful non-Jews than there are successful Jews. There are also many Jews who aren't successful or rich, disproving the stereotype that some hold about Jews.

One of the reasons some claim Jews are so successful is the simple truth that differences stand out. If there's an industry where most of its leaders are Christian, but a minority are Jews, then the Jews attract attention. Another possible reason why Jews seem more successful than others is historical. Jews weren't allowed to own land or join guilds for decades in Europe, so they were drawn to professions Christians weren't allowed to do like banking and moneylending for interest. They also used their connections with other Jews to become successful merchants. This led several Jews to notably gain success in business, which influenced how some people viewed all Jews.

If Jews are indeed so successful, much of this may result from their culture of learning. For centuries, Jews valued education and study of Talmud, devoting great resources to this task. This value for the highest education came to apply to secular studies as well when Jews were allowed to pursue these paths, leading to success by some in law, business, and the sciences.

Many Jews have enjoyed success, and many haven't. There are still many more successful people who aren't Jews than successful people who are Jews. The Jewish hope is that all people will experience success, and will have enough resources to support themselves and their families in peace and happiness.

Questions About the Bible

The Tanach provides important stories, laws, poetry, and history for the Jewish people. However, the Tanach also leaves many subjects open to interpretation, especially how some of its teachings apply today.

The Tribes Question

What are the Twelve Tribes of Israel? What is the "lost tribe?"

The Twelve Tribes of Israel is a division of the Jews from Biblical times. Each of the tribes received individual recognition and representation, but also had to provide their own sacrifices and participation in the army. The Book of Numbers begins with a census of the tribes, noting the number of males older than 20 years old in each tribe fit to go to war.

The sons of Jacob provide the basis for the divisions of the tribes. This leads to some dispute concerning exactly which sons are the forefathers of the tribes. Some of the sons of Jacob have a tribe in every counting, including:

- Asher

- Benjamin

- Dan

- Gad

- Issachar

- Judah

- Naphtali

- Reuben

- Simeon

- Zebulun

The difficulty arises from the special status of Levi and Joseph. The tribe of Levi is given the responsibility for caring for the Tabernacle, and later, the Temple. Consequently, they receive no land grant in Israel, and they don't have to send soldiers to the army. (Numbers 1:47-49) As a result, some lists of the tribes include Levi and some don't.

Joseph is the only son of Jacob never counted as a tribe. Instead, Joseph's sons, Menasseh and Ephraim, receive this status because Jacob gave them each a special blessing before he died just as he did with his own sons. If Levi isn't counted as a tribe, Menasseh and Ephraim each count as a full tribe, completing the twelve. If Levi is counted as a tribe, Menasseh and Ephraim are called "half-tribes" in consideration of their relationship with Joseph, allowing the number of tribes to remain twelve.

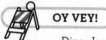

OY VEY!

Dina, Jacob's only daughter, never is counted as the foremother of one of the twelve tribes.

The idea of the Lost Tribe of Israel arises from what happened after the first exile in 586 B.C.E. When the Israelites returned and rebuilt the Temple, the northern tribes didn't reconstitute as political entities, and an Israelite government didn't control their land. Only the southern kingdom of Judah was restored, absorbing some of the adjacent small tribes' land and reinstituting the authority of the Levites over the Temple. Several legends arose about what happened to the tribes that didn't return, leading to several fanciful stories about a "Lost Tribe." More likely and realistically, they either joined with Judah, became assimilated in Babylonia, or were absorbed by the Jewish community there.

The Tribes Today Question

Do Jews identify themselves by their tribe today?

Only one significant aspect of the idea of the tribes remains today. Some Jews still trace their lineage to the tribe of Levi, and they receive special honors in some synagogues. A descendant of the family of the High Priest, called a *kohein,* receives the honor of the first aliyah in many traditional synagogues. An ordinary *Levite* receives the honor of the second aliyah. A Levite also doesn't have to redeem his first son from Temple service, as they're already irrevocably committed to their tribe.

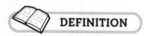

DEFINITION

A **Levite** is a descendant of the tribe of Levi, the tribe with the special responsibility to care for the Tabernacle and the Temple. A **kohein** is a member of the tribe of Levi who is also a descendant of the family of the high priest of the Temple.

The Levites also have some obligations that impose some restrictions upon them. For example, a Levite must maintain the pure lineage of his family, so he can't marry a divorcee.

Anyone who is not a kohein or Levite simply identifies himself or herself as an "Israelite." The other tribal identifications have been lost to time.

The Reform Movement, influenced by the democratic ideas of the Enlightenment, rejected the idea of any status passed through the tribes or lineage.

The Sacrifices Question

Where do Jews perform the sacrifices described in the Bible?

Jews don't do sacrifices today as part of their worship. The only location where Jews performed sacrifices was at the Temple in Jerusalem that the Romans destroyed in 70 C.E. Since then, Jews have replaced the sacrifice of animals with prayer. There is also an understanding by some that the Shabbat table where the family gathers for the Friday evening celebratory meal has replaced the Temple alter.

A related question might be whether Jews would ever perform sacrifices again as part of their worship. Some Jews imagine that if the Temple were ever rebuilt, sacrifices would return. There are even a few small groups of Jews that are preparing for that day, trying to breed the perfect red heifer Numbers describes as necessary for sacrifices. (Numbers 19:2-3)

Most Jews take a different view, believing the time for sacrifices has long passed. The great medieval scholar Maimonides explained that God knew the Israelites needed sacrifices as their form of worship after their Exodus from Egypt. The Israelites had seen the Egyptians using sacrifice as worship to their many deities, and assumed that God also preferred this mode of worship.

God commanded the Israelites to perform sacrifices at the Temple, but to direct the sacrifices to God instead of the Egyptian or pagan gods. This command constituted an improvement, and a step toward weaning the Israelites away from idolatry, while not forcing too many changes upon them that they weren't prepared to do. Maimonides concluded that, by the time of his life, the Jews had outgrown the need for sacrifices and would never adopt this mode of worship again.

The Slavery Question

Do Jews believe in slavery? Slavery is described in the Bible.

Modern Jews don't believe in slavery. Everything belongs to God, and all human beings are created in God's image. Judaism holds freedom as a high value. The idea of slavery contradicts these important Jewish values.

It's also important to recognize that the slavery described in the Tanach greatly differs from the slavery envisioned by many in the United States today. When Americans think of slavery, they generally imagine the antebellum south, where Caucasians owned and sold Africans as property. The slave owners controlled every aspect of the slaves' lives.

The system described in the Tanach more resembles an indentured servitude, where one person becomes the servant of another. This status didn't rely on race or nationality—an Israelite could find himself or herself in this status just as easily as someone from another people. These indentured servants also had rights. Some could marry and have their own property. This status also was temporary for some, as some automatically received their freedom in their seventh year in servitude, and their families could redeem others.

The Moses Question

If Moses was so great, why wasn't he allowed into the Promised Land?

The story in the Torah that answers this question is found in Chapter 20 of the Book of Numbers. After Miriam dies, the people start complaining that they have no water. God tells Moses to speak to a rock, and water will spring forth. Moses gathers the people and says, "Shall we give you water out of this rock?" He then strikes it twice with his staff, and water comes forth. However, God tells Moses and Aaron, "Because you didn't believe in Me, to make My name holy in the eyes of the children of Israel, therefore you shall not bring this people into the land that I am giving to them." (Numbers 20:12)

The sages have found many possible explanations for this punishment. One is that Moses disobeyed God's command. He struck the rock instead of speaking to it. Another is that Moses acted in anger, proving that he wasn't worthy of entering the land and leading the people any farther than the desert. Yet another is that Moses used the term "we" in speaking to the people, seeming to take personal credit for the miracle instead of giving all the credit to God.

Finally, Moses struck the rock twice. Why did he strike it a second time? Didn't he believe the first strike would be enough? One possibility is that Moses had no faith that the first strike would work. He doubted God, so he hit the rock again, proving that he didn't have complete faith in God, just like the Israelites when they built the Golden Calf. Like the Israelites, he wasn't allowed to enter the Promised Land for his failure of faith.

Moses' punishment leads to an important lesson for Jews. The Torah says there never was, nor will be, a prophet as great as Moses. (Deuteronomy 34:10-12) Jews consider him the greatest teacher and leader ever in Jewish history. Yet Moses also is imperfect, and doesn't receive everything he wants. The location of his grave remains unknown, so he doesn't even receive a shrine or veneration after his death. This teaches Jews that they are all only flesh and blood, and that the only perfect being is God. No human being, no matter how great, is perfect and worthy of worship.

The Lost Ark Question

What happened to the Ark of the Covenant?

The Ark of the Covenant was a receptacle built by Bezazel as part of the Tabernacle. It was a box made of acacia wood and covered in pure gold. People carried it on two poles that fit through rings on its bottom. Its cover was also made of pure gold and had two winged cherubim facing each other on it. The Ark carried both sets of tablets received at Mount Sinai: the first set that Moses broke, and the second complete set Moses brought down from the mountain.

The fate of the Ark remains unknown. It disappeared after the destruction of the First Temple in 586 B.C.E. Some claim the Babylonians captured it, but that seems less likely because there's no record of it among other lists of items taken by the Babylonians. Some claim it was hidden, possibly by King Josiah, but there's no clear evidence of this either. It's possible the Ark was destroyed.

> **WORTH NOTING**
>
> The Ark was the central artifact sought in the classic movie *Raiders of the Lost Ark*. There's no evidence to support that the Ark ever was located where the movie claimed, and certainly the end of the movie is pure fiction.

Questions About Theology

Theological issues spawn many questions as Jews delve into the mysteries of heaven.

The Angels Question

Do Jews believe in angels?

Angels play a significant role in the Tanach. One of the most important stories of Abraham's life is the Akeidah, the episode where God orders Abraham to sacrifice his son Isaac as a test of faith. Abraham accepts God's command, but an angel calls to him from heaven at the last moment, stopping him from completing the sacrifice.

The prophet Isaiah envisions angels as part of the heavenly court honoring God. He describes angels standing as if they had one leg, raising their voices in praise to God. They say, "Holy, holy, holy is the God of Hosts; the whole earth is God's glory!" (Isaiah 6:3) The power of these words and this image prompted the sages to include them as part of an important prayer in the morning and afternoon tefillah, the kedushah.

There is no word for angel in Hebrew. Instead, these heavenly creatures are called *melachim Adonai*—"messengers of God." This reflects their important role as heavenly beings that convey important messages from God to human beings.

The Midrash contains many references to angels, and angels remain a part of Kabbalistic and Jewish mystical thought. Many Jews today believe angels exist as beings in heaven with God, and they may either proclaim God's will or protect people in need.

Some sages throughout Jewish history have expressed concerns or doubts about angels. For these sages, the idea of a cadre of heavenly beings with powers contradicts the notion of one unique God. The Reform Movement initially rejected the existence of angels. Although some Reform Jews have moderated their position as Reform has recently turned more to tradition and mysticism, the doubt of angels in the movement remains intact. It's safe to say that today, some Jews believe in angels, and some don't.

The Satan Question

Do Jews believe in Satan?

The idea of Satan exists within Jewish thought, but this idea is very different from the Satan described in other religions.

Some religions describe Satan as an evil force or entity, counterbalancing God's goodness. Some cast Satan in the role of tempter, encouraging human beings to sin, or trying to obtain their souls.

Satan has a very different role in Judaism. Satan isn't a countervailing force to God. Jewish thought says God is omnipotent and unique—there can't be another equivalent or opposing force. In Judaism, everything comes from God, including everything Jews consider good or bad.

Instead, Satan is an angel, just like any other angel. However, Satan usually plays the role of "doubter of humanity's goodness," or "humanity's prosecuting attorney in the heavenly court." For example, the Midrash notes that the Akeidah story begins with the words "After these things …." The sages naturally ask, "After what things?" The Midrash answers that Satan went to God and challenged Abraham's faith, saying that if tested, Abraham would abandon God for his own desires. God responded by testing Abraham with the command to sacrifice Isaac.

Satan plays a similar role in the Book of Job. Satan claims that Job, a man who had everything, would give up his faith in God if he encountered misfortune. God responds by inflicting terrible losses upon the man—the death of his family, the loss of his wealth, and illness. Despite urging from his companions to give up his faith in God, Job remains patient and endures his suffering. God eventually restores Job's blessings, and humanity again proves Satan's doubts to be incorrect.

Satan doesn't have a large role in Judaism. Whether a Jew believes in Satan's existence largely depends on his or her view of angels and if he or she believes the Tanach literally or allegorically. Nevertheless, Satan does have a place in Jewish thought.

Questions About Religion

Judaism's religious practices are an intrinsic part of its teachings. Often, these teachings are compared to other religions.

The Observance Question

Are Orthodox Jews "more Jewish" than other Jews?

Judaism considers every Jew just as Jewish as every other Jew. The details of an individual's practice don't affect a person's status as a Jew. Jewish tradition says once a person is a Jew, that person is always a Jew.

Orthodox Jewish practice tends to be stricter and more rigorous than other Jews. Some Jews call the Orthodox "more observant" than others, or even call the Orthodox "observant" as opposed to others. Other Jews reject this claim, saying a non-Orthodox Jew may be "observant" according to the practices of his or her community, but this is simply different from the Orthodox due to their perspectives and beliefs. To these Jews, calling the Orthodox "observant" and implying that the non-Orthodox Jews are not "observant" doesn't fairly describe their commitment to Judaism.

The Jewish Pope Question

Is there a hierarchy among rabbis, like a Jewish pope?

There is no formal hierarchy among rabbis. Every rabbi is *mara d'atra* of his or her congregation, meaning that he or she is "master of the area." As mara d'atra, the rabbi has the authority to determine all questions of Jewish law and practice for the community. Another rabbi can't enter the community and overrule the community's rabbi. Rabbis of great scholarship and renown may influence an individual rabbi with their teachings, but the ultimate authority remains with the community's rabbi.

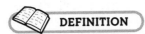 **DEFINITION**

Mara d'atra literally means "master of the area," the authority given to the rabbi of a community to make decisions concerning Jewish law and its application for his or her community.

Some communities alter this rule to an extent. Each Chassidic community adopts one rabbi as their leader, called their *rebbe.* The rebbe has greater authority over the community and other rabbis within it than most rabbis in non-Chassidic communities.

Some countries select a chief rabbi, including Israel. In fact, Israel has two chief rabbis, one for the Ashkenazic Jews and one for the Sephardic Jews. These rabbis have a greater authority over matters affecting national policy and have significant influence over the rabbis in their state. However, each individual rabbi still maintains his or her status as mara d'atra of his or her own congregation even if the country has a chief rabbi.

The Judaism/Islam Question

What are the similarities and differences between Judaism and Islam?

There are many similarities between Judaism and Islam. If Judaism and Christianity have a "mother-daughter" relationship as noted in Chapter 26, Judaism and Islam may be said to have a "grandmother-granddaughter" relationship, since Islam recognizes Jesus as a prophet and has been influenced by both Judaism and Christianity.

Judaism and Islam both view their ancient origins with one of the sons of Abraham. Judaism traces its lineage through Abraham's son Isaac, while Islam traces its lineage through Abraham's son Ishmael. The word "Islam" itself reflects a shared heritage. The root of the word Islam is the same as the Hebrew word "shalom," meaning peace, wholeness, and completeness.

Both great religions have a Holy Scripture, with Jews adhering to the Tanach and Muslims to the Koran. These Scriptures contain many similar teachings and stories, although there might be some differences between those teachings. For example, the Torah teaches that Abraham took his son Isaac to Mount Moriah to be sacrificed to God, while the Koran teaches that Abraham took Ishmael. Nevertheless, many of the laws and practices that emerge from these Scriptures are very similar, as both religions require circumcision of their males, have similar dietary laws in the kashrut and halal systems, and have lunar calendars.

Despite the similarities, there are significant differences between Judaism and Islam. Islam accepts Mohammed as the primary Prophet of God, and Judaism doesn't. This means the Islamic holy cities of Mecca and Medina hold no special significance for Judaism, and the holy days of Islam set forth in the Koran or relating to Mohammed's life aren't observed by Jews. Notably, Islam also accepts Jesus as a prophet, while Judaism doesn't.

Islam has a concept called jihad that Judaism doesn't have. Jihad means "struggle" or "striving," and commonly means contending against outside influences that might alter or pull a Muslim away from Islam. Often, jihad is an inner struggle and a peaceful and spiritual effort, although some interpret it to apply to outer forces to be fought in any way possible if necessary to preserve the sanctity of Islam. Judaism has no equivalent concept to jihad, and the only striving in Judaism is to gain knowledge and an understanding of God.

Another difference between Judaism and Islam involves the idea and effect of reformation. Many scholars and journalists have noted that Judaism, as well as Christianity, was greatly influenced by the Western ideas of the Enlightenment. These caused both Judaism and Christianity to experience a liberalizing reformation, and a greater openness to pluralism. These challenges affected both those who wanted major reforms, as well as those who didn't. Some have suggested that Islam hasn't experienced a liberalizing reformation in the same way or to the same extent. This creates differences in outlook about modern influences such as feminism and pluralism among many Muslims and Jews.

The Christmas Tree Question

Do Jews have Christmas trees in their homes?

Most Jews don't have Christmas trees in their homes. For most Jews, Christmas is a holiday that belongs to Christians, and its celebration not only would be contrary to Jewish practice, but also would potentially offend Christians. A Jew can't keep the religious practices of Christmas that contradict Judaism, and removing these important elements of the holiday might upset religious Christians.

Some Jews have Christmas trees. They might have Christian spouses or relatives, and they have the trees so their relatives may celebrate and enjoy their holiday. Other Jews view Christmas as a national, secular holiday, or simply like the colorful tree. Although this practice has no basis in Judaism, and actually contradicts important Jewish ideals, some Jews do it anyway.

Questions About Jewish Culture

Jewish culture is a deep subject that spans many centuries and locations throughout the world. It's understandable that there would still be some questions about Jewish culture remaining to answer.

The Jewish Music Question

Is there any special Jewish music?

There are a few particular forms of Jewish music. Hazzanim and congregations chant prayers and Scripture according to a set melody, called *nusach*. Nusach varies based on the particular day of the service, such as whether it's Shabbat or a holy day. There are also variations that arose in different geographical locations.

Another special Jewish musical form is the *nigun*. A nigun is a melody without words, but sung with repetitive syllables with no contextual meaning. For example, the only "word" in a nigun may be "lai" sung over and over. A popular nigun is "Bim Bam," where Jews on Shabbat sing these syllables in different patterns over and over, until they finally sing "Shabbat Shalom!" The melodies set a mood, making real words unnecessary.

Klezmer music is a well-known form of Jewish music. Klezmer reflects the Eastern European origin of many Jews, and consists of upbeat melodies played with violins, clarinets, piano, and brass.

There's also a genre of modern Israeli, Jewish folk, and Jewish rock music. This music has similarities to other cultures' modern music, but is distinguished by its composition in Hebrew and its frequent incorporation of Jewish and Biblical themes.

The Jewish Superstition Question

Are there any Jewish superstitions?

Several Jewish superstitions have developed over the centuries. Not all Jews adhere to these superstitions, but they are strong enough within Jewish culture that it isn't surprising to suddenly find a non-observant Jew to become very concerned with one of them.

Some of the Jewish superstitions are concerned with warding off the "evil eye." The evil eye is the ability to look maliciously at someone and cause him or her misfortune. Some Jews wear a positive Jewish symbol around their necks to protect themselves from the evil eye, such as a mezuzah, a *chai* (the Hebrew word for "life"), or a hamsa.

There are a variety of other superstitions meant to protect life or guard against misfortune. It's a Jewish superstition to not bring any baby items into the house of a pregnant woman until the baby is born lest they bring in the evil eye and bring misfortune to the child. Sometimes a Jew will spit or fake spitting three times when hearing either good or bad news to defend against a change from good fortune or further misfortune. Some Jews put salt in their pockets or in corners of their homes to protect against evil spirits. Others wear a metal pin while traveling to ensure a safe voyage. Jews will often close an open book or chew on a thread when repairing a garment for luck.

The Jewish Athletes Question

Who are some of the greatest Jewish sports heroes?

Whenever considering the many Jewish sports heroes, the list begins with Mark Spitz. Mark Spitz was an American swimmer who won seven gold medals at the 1972 Olympic Games in Munich. He held the record for most gold medals at a single games until Michael Phelps won eight in 2008. Spitz's accomplishment meant something extra special for Jews because of the murder of eleven Israeli Olympic athletes at the same games.

Other notable and well-known Jewish sports heroes include:

- Amy Alcott—winner of 29 tournaments in the LPGA

- Max Baer—heavyweight boxing champion who wore a Star of David on his trunks

- Hank Greenberg—Detroit Tigers slugging first baseman

- Sarah Hughes—Olympic gold medal figure skating champion

- Sid Luckman—American football quarterback and Hall of Fame member

- Sandy Koufax—legendary baseball starting pitcher who wouldn't play on Yom Kippur

- Aly Raisman—Olympic gold medalist in gymnastics

- Dick Savitt—Wimbledon and Australian Open tennis champion

Glossary

Adonai   "My Lord," one of the more common Jewish names for God.

afikomen   The Greek word for dessert.

agunot   Anchored women; women whose husbands refuse to give a *get,* or document for Jewish divorce, and who consequently can't remarry.

aliyah   Going up; a Jew's immigration in Israel.

arba'ah minim   Four species; a term for *lulav* and *etrog,* symbols used on Sukkot.

aron kodesh   Holy ark; a storage place for the Torah scrolls and other holy documents in the sanctuary of the synagogue.

Aseret HaDibrot   The Ten Statements or The Ten Words found in Exodus 20 and Deuteronomy; the Hebrew term for the Ten Commandments.

Ashkenazic   An ethnic division of Jews who lived in Europe from France through Russia.

atzei chayyim   Trees of life; the two poles on which the Torah scroll is wound.

aufruf   Aliyah and blessing for a wedding couple prior to the wedding ceremony.

Aveenu Malkeinu   Our Father, Our King; a special prayer for Rosh HaShanah celebrating God's kingship over the world.

baal tashchit   The requirement that Jews don't needlessly destroy or waste any of the world's resources.

bar/bat mitzvah   Son/daughter of the commandments; someone obligated to follow Jewish law applied to all Jews when they reach the age of 13 or when they convert to Judaism if older than 13. Also refers to the celebration of a child reaching this age.

bat   Daughter or daughter of.

bedeken   The veiling ceremony of the bride prior to a wedding.

Beit Din   A court of three learned Jews, often rabbis, who determine questions of Jewish law and acceptance of converts.

Beit Knesset   House of Meeting; one of three traditional names for a synagogue.

Beit Midrash   House of Study; another of the three traditional names for a synagogue.

Beit Tefillah   House of Prayer; another of the three traditional names for a synagogue.

ben/bar   Son or son of.

Beta Yisrael   A community of Jews from Ethiopia.

bikur cholim   The mitzvah of visiting the sick.

bimah   A stage in the sanctuary of a synagogue.

Birkat HaMazon   The blessing recited after eating, giving thanks to God.

brachah   A blessing.

brit ba   A ceremony for girls called a Covenant for a Daughter or brit chayyim, Covenant of Life.

brit milah   A Covenant of Circumcision.

b'tzelem Elohim   In God's image.

cantor   English word for *hazzan*; a clergy person who chants prayers at worship service and teaches Scriptural reading.

chameitz   Leavened food prohibited on Pesach.

chanukkiah   The nine-branched candelabra used during Chanukkah.

charoset   A spread of apples, nuts, wine, and spices eaten at Pesach Seder representing the mortar used by the Israelite slaves in Egypt.

Chassidim   Members of Chassidic Judaism, an ultra-Orthodox division of Jews.

chavurot   Friends; groups of families who join together for spiritual worship and other Jewish experiences without the formality of synagogue.

cheshbon nefesh   An accounting of the soul; a contemplation and assessment of behavior in the past year performed during Ten Days of Repentance.

chevre kadisha   Holy society; a group of people who care for the body after death.

chol amoeid   The intermediate days of the festivals of Pesach and Sukkot, as distinguished from the first and last days of the festival for which there are greater observances and requirements and an abstention from work.

Chumash   A book with text of Torah, commentaries, and possibly translations.

chuppah   The canopy placed over the bride and groom at a wedding ceremony.

davening   An intense prayer form characterized by deep concentration, swaying, and bowing while reciting words.

Diaspora   A term for the spread of Jews from Israel following the destruction of the Second Temple; anywhere Jews live except Israel.

drash   Creative interpretations and understanding of the text.

dreidel   A four-sided top with a letter on each side that stands for a Hebrew word. In Israel, the letters are nun, gimmel, hey, and pey, which stand for *"Nes gadol hayah po—*A great miracle happened here." In the Diaspora, the pey is replaced by a *shin,* representing the word *sham,* which means "there."

d'var Torah   The words of Torah, a teaching or lesson.

Eil malei rachamin   Prayer that describes how God, in mercy, takes the departed into the "shelter of God's wings," protecting those who have died.

eiruv   An unbroken barrier or enclosure that allows Jews to carry items while remaining within the borders, to keep the requirement for Shabbat.

eitz chayyim   The singular of atzei chayyim.

erev   Evening; the beginning night of a festival or a holy day.

Essenes   A strict ascetic sect concerned with purity that separated itself from Temple worship in ancient Israel at the beginning of the Common Era.

etrog   Citrus fruit used on Sukkot.

fleishig   Meat.

gefilte fish   Traditional Ashkenazic fish meatball of carp and other white fish.

gelilah   The honor of dressing the Torah scroll with the mantle, breastplate, yad, and crowns during the Torah service.

gelt   Coins given to children on the fifth day of Chanukkah; manufacturers make gold and silver foil-covered chocolates in the shape of coins that are accepted as gelt.

gemilut chasadim   Acts of loving kindness that help someone in need.

ger   Someone who converts to Judaism.

glatt kosher   A strict form of kashrut requiring the animals used for food to have unblemished lungs and other additional requirements.

Green Line   The line that established territorial possessions following the 1949 armistice between Israel and its neighbors.

groggers   Loud noisemakers used on Purim.

Haftarah   A reading from the Prophets during worship services on Shabbat and other holy days.

hagbah   The honor of lifting Torah and showing text to congregation during the Torah service.

Haggadah   Telling the story; the book used to tell the story of the Israelites' exodus from Egypt and containing the prayers and procedures of the Pesach Seder.

hakafah   The procession of the Torah through the congregation during the Torah service.

halachah   The way or the path; the set of mitzvot traditional Judaism says each Jew must follow in accordance with the Covenant.

Hallel   A group of Psalms praising God recited as part of festival services.

hamentashin   Triangular-shaped filled cookies served on Purim.

HaMotzi   A blessing recited before eating any meal with grain.

hatafat dam brit   A ritual drawing of a drop of blood from already an circumcised man seeking to convert to Judaism to make his circumcision considered as a sign of the Jewish Covenant.

Havdalah   A ceremony marking the end of Shabbat that prepares Jews to re-enter everyday life.

hazzan   See *cantor.*

heksher   The seal used by rabbinical authority to certify food is kosher to that authority's standard.

hesped   A speech telling about the deceased and giving honor to him or her at a funeral.

hiddur mitzvah   Beautifying a commandment; doing a mitzvah in a special way or adding beauty to an act to increase God's glory.

Israelites   A term used for people who would become Jews from the time of Jacob and Egyptian slavery through the destruction of the Second Temple.

Jew   A person who is accepted as part of the people descended through the patriarchs and matriarchs described in Genesis.

Kabbalah Jewish mysticism largely developed in Tzfat in the sixteenth century conceiving of God as the ascending sefirot a Jew may come to comprehend through prayer, study, and meditation.

Kabbalat Shabbat Welcoming Shabbat; the initial part of Friday evening service beginning Shabbat with song and psalms.

kaddish A prayer praising God used in different forms at the end of studying a book or lesson and at the conclusion of a section of the worship service.

Kaddish Yatom The prayer said to praise God for the gift of life.

kaparot A ritual involving slaughter of a chicken as a means of achieving repentance on Yom Kippur.

kareit Biblical punishment of separation from the community.

karpas Greens used at Pesach Seder to represent springtime.

kashrut Jewish dietary laws.

Kavod HaMeit Honoring the dead; a value embodied in Jewish death rituals.

kedushah Holiness.

keriah The tearing of clothes or a ribbon upon hearing of a relative's death or prior to the funeral.

keter A crown found on the Torah scroll.

ketubah A document containing the terms of marriage.

keva Fixed prayers of a worship service.

kiddush The blessing over the fruit of the vine.

kinyan Acquisition; refers to the traditional act of a man acquiring his wife at a marriage.

kisei Eliyahu The chair of Elijah; the chair where a child is placed during brit milah.

kittel A white robe worn by men during Yom Kippur.

Knesset The Israeli parliament.

k'nish A potato- or spinach-filled delicacy.

kohein A descendant of the High Priests of the Temple.

kol isha Voice of a women; referring to the idea that a woman's voice will distract a man from his obligatory devotions to God if heard during prayer.

Kol Nidrei The evening service of Yom Kippur.

Kristallnacht   Night of Broken Glass; the night of a large Nazi pogrom in Germany on November 9, 1938.

kvatter/kvatterin   An honored relative who brings a baby into brit milah and acts as a godparent.

Ladino   A Sephardic language combining Hebrew and Spanish.

lashon ha-ra   Evil speech.

latkes   Potato and onion pancakes traditionally eaten on Chanukkah.

Law of Return   A law in Israel giving any Jew and many of a Jew's relatives the right to immigrate to Israel.

Lecha Dodi   A liturgical poem written by Kabbalistic scholar and author Rabbi Shlomo HaLevi Alkabetz that welcomes Shabbat every Friday evening. It was added to the liturgy in 1584 C.E.

L'shanah tovah tikateivu   "May you be inscribed for a good year."

lulav   A ritual object for Sukkot whose three branches come from the palm, myrtle, and willow trees.

luni-solar calendar   A calendar based on both the moon and the sun.

maror   Bitter herbs representing the bitterness of slavery eaten at a Pesach Seder.

Marrano Jews   Jews who pretended to convert to Christianity in the Middle Ages to avoid the Inquisition.

mashgiach   A rabbi who supervises restaurant or food producers to ensure food is kosher.

Mashiach   Annointed King of Israel, viewed by tradition as the person who will bring peace and prosperity to the entire world.

matzah   Unleavened bread eaten at Pesach.

mechitza   The barrier between the men's and women's sections in the sanctuary.

megillah   A scroll containing a book of the Tanach.

menorah   Any multiple branched candelabrum used for Jewish religious purposes. A seven-branched menorah is described in the Tanach and found in many synagogues. A special nine-branched menorah called a chanukkiah is used on Chanukkah.

mentsch   Someone who helps others and improves the world; a good person.

menuchah   Rest.

mesader kiddushin   The officiant at a Jewish wedding.

mezuzah   A scroll containing prayers affixed to doorposts of Jewish homes.

mikdash me'at   The small sanctuary; term for Shabbat dining table.

mikvah   A ritual purifying bath.

milchig   Dairy food.

minyon   Ten adult Jews required to hold a full worship service. In traditional Judaism, only men are counted in a minyon.

mishloach manot   Baskets of food given to the elderly and poor on Purim.

mitzvah   Commandment; good deed.

mitzvot   The plural of mitzvah.

mizrach   A decoration placed on an eastern wall to identify the direction to face toward Jerusalem during prayer.

mohel   A person who performs a circumcision.

monotheism   The idea that there is one and only one God; first realized by Abraham.

nefesh   Soul.

Neilah   The final worship service of Yom Kippur.

ner tamid   The eternal light representing God's presence in the sanctuary of a synagogue.

nichum aveilim   Comforting the mourners; a value in Jewish death rituals and practices.

niddah   The time of a woman's menstrual period, a time when the halachah forbids any sexual contact to occur.

olam haba   The world to come; a time of peace and prosperity brought by the Mashiach in which all Jews will be resurrected.

omer   The counting of the days between the second day of Pesach and Shavuot.

oneg   Joy.

onen   The seven relatives obligated for mourning rituals: the father, mother, son, daughter, sister, brother, and spouse of the deceased.

Oral Law   Mitzvot and their details and interpretations determined by the rabbis and sages over centuries derived by implication, study, and questioning of Scripture.

pareve   Food that may be eaten with either milk or meat according to the laws of kashrut.

parochet   A curtain covering the Torah scrolls in the ark.

pekuach nefesh   Primacy of life; the idea that the preservation of life supersedes every other mitzvah.

Pharisees   A class of scholars who believed in an evolving set of mitzvot and worship practices in ancient Israel at the beginning of the Common Era. Led by Yochanan ben Zakkai, the Pharisees were the forerunners of the rabbis in the Talmudic era.

pidyon haben   The redemption of the firstborn son.

pitom   A stem of an etrog.

pogrom   An organized riot against Jews.

polytheism   The idea that there are many gods, each with his or her own powers or dominion.

Promised Land   An area in the fertile crescent along the western shore of the Mediterranean Sea to about the Jordan River that God pledged to the Israelites as a homeland according to Jewish belief.

pshat   The plain meaning of the text.

rabbi   My teacher; the primary Jewish clergyperson.

remez   Hints about what the text might mean.

rimon   A pomegranate; the crown over a single rod of the Torah scroll.

Saduccees   The wealthy aristocratic class, including the priesthood, in ancient Israel at the beginning of the Common Era.

sandak   An honored person who holds a baby at a Brit milah.

Sanhedrin   The ancient rabbinic court of Talmudic times.

schmaltz   Chicken fat used as a spread.

Seder   "Order"; a Pesach ritualized meal that tells the Exodus story.

sefer Torah   The Torah scroll composed of animal skins with the text written upon it, sewn together and wrapped around two poles.

sefirot   Spheres representing an aspect of God in Kabbalistic theology.

selichot   Petitions for forgiveness from God; name for a service usually held the Saturday evening before Rosh HaShanah.

Sephardic   The ethnic division of Jews originating in Spain, Africa, and the Middle East.

seudah   A feast; a special meal.

shadchan   A matchmaker.

shaliach tziboor   The worship service leader.

shalom   Peace and completeness; shalom is also used to say hello and goodbye, expressing the hope that people feel peace and completeness when they meet and when they depart from each other.

shalom bayit   Peace in the home.

shalosh seudah   "Third meal" eaten on Shabbat afternoon following the practice of adding joy to Shabbat in Talmudic times when people usually ate only two meals a day.

shamas   The helper candle on the channukkiah, which is used to light the others.

she'eilah   A question sent to higher rabbinic authority about question of Jewish law that the authority answers.

Shehechiyanu   A prayer that thanks God for giving us life, sustaining us, and enabling us to reach this time.

shelosh regalim   The three pilgrimage festivals of Pesach, Shavuot, and Sukkot when ancient Israelites brought sacrifices to the Temple.

sheloshim   The 30-day period of mourning following death.

Sheol   The shadowy netherworld where people go when they die according to Biblical philosophy.

sheva brachot   The seven special blessings recited at a wedding ceremony.

shiva   The period of mourning following a funeral, usually lasting seven days.

Sh'mah   A prayer said in every Jewish worship service proclaiming the existence and Oneness of God.

shochet   A butcher who slaughters animals according to the laws of kashrut.

shofar   A ram's horn blown on the High Holy Days.

shofet   A judge.

shtetls   The rural Jewish communities of Eastern Europe.

shul   Yiddish for synagogue.

siddur   A prayer book.

simcha   A joyous occasion.

sinat hinam   Baseless hatred; the cause of the destruction of the Second Temple according to traditional Judaism.

s'micha   The laying on of hands by a teacher, designating a student as a rabbi.

sod   Secrets found in the text only through skill after intense study and understanding.

sofer   A scribe who writes the Torah scroll and other religious and Scriptural documents.

sufganiyot   Jelly doughnuts, traditionally eaten for Chanukkah.

sukkah   A booth representing the tents of the Israelites in the desert and the temporary shelters Jews used to construct near their fields during harvest.

synagogue   A term from the Greek meaning "place of gathering" used to refer to a Jewish house of worship besides the temple.

tallit   A four-cornered prayer shawl with fringes the Torah commands Jews to wear.

tashlich   A casting of bread on waters representing the casting away of sins during Days of Repentance.

tefillin   Phylacteries; leather boxes worn around the head and arm in accordance with interpretation of Torah.

Temple   The central place of worship in Jerusalem where sacrifices occurred in accordance with the Book of Leviticus. The First Temple built by King Solomon was destroyed in 586 B.C.E., and a second was built shortly afterward. The Second Temple was destroyed in 70 C.E. The term "temple" is also used to refer to the house of worship in Reform and part of Conservative Judaism.

tenaim   The conditions of marriage.

teshuvah   Return; repentance.

Tetragrammaton   A four-letter name for God in Hebrew spelled "yod-hey-vav-hey" found in Scripture but pronounced as "Adonai." See also *Yahweh*.

te'udat ger   A certificate of conversion to Judaism.

tikkun olam   Repair of the world.

tish   A gathering of men with the groom prior to the wedding ceremony.

Torah   Literally means "teaching." It's the first part of the Hebrew Bible consisting of the Five Books of Moses. Also used to refer to all Jewish learning.

treif   Nonkosher food.

tza'ar baalei chayyim   The protection of cruelty to animals.

tzadik   A righteous person.

tzedakah   Righteous acts; charity.

tzitzit   Fringes on a tallit that remind the wearer to do mitzvot.

tzni'ut   Modesty.

Unetaneh Tokef   A Rosh HaShanah prayer that speaks of mortality and God's judgment.

urim v'tumim   The breastplate of the High Priest at the Temple.

ushpizim   Guests who visit a sukkah.

vidu'i   A confession of the sins we have committed.

Western Wall   The last remaining wall of the Temple Mount in Jerusalem, considered the holiest site in Judaism due to its proximity to the Temple altar. Also called the Wailing Wall because Jews would cry there in mourning for the loss of the Temple.

Written Law   A mitzvot found in the actual written statements in Scripture.

yad   A pointer often shaped like a hand used by a Torah reader to keep place while reading text.

Yahrzeit   The observance of the anniversary of a person's death.

Yahrzeit Candle   A candle lit on the anniversary of a relative's death.

Yahweh   The ancient pronunciation of the Tetragrammaton as believed by many scholars.

Yamim Nora'im   Days of Awe; the 10 days between Rosh HaShanah and Yom Kippur.

Yavneh   A town in ancient Israel where Yochanan ben Zakkai and the Pharisees from the School of Hillel began to compile the Mishnah.

yetzer ra   The appetites, ambition, and the drive for sex.

yetzer tov   The noble and spiritual aspects of a human being, including the desire to live a holy life, study Torah, and perform unselfish and caring acts.

Yizkor   The remembrance of those who have died.

Zealots   Rebels against Roman rule in ancient Israel at the beginning of the Common Era. Some committed suicide at the fort at Masada.

Zionism   The aspiration to create and sustain a Jewish state in the Holy Land.

Sages and Sources

The following is a listing of historical figures, scholars, rabbis, and texts cited in this book.

Aaron   Moses' brother who went with Moses to demand that Pharaoh let the Israelite slaves go free. Aaron became the first High Priest of the Israelites, and his descendants constituted the priesthood for hundreds of years afterward.

Abraham   The first person to recognize the truth of monotheism and the first of the patriarchs. Abraham had his name changed from Avram to show that God was with him. Abraham's story is found in the Book of Genesis. His name is Avraham in Hebrew.

Akiva, Rabbi   A Talmudic sage of the late first to early second century C.E. who contributed to the Mishnah.

Alkabetz, Rabbi Shlomo Halevi (1505–1576 C.E.)   A Kabbalistic teacher and poet who lived in Safed. He's noted for his composition of *Lecha Dodi*, "Come My Beloved," a poem sung to welcome the Sabbath on Friday evenings.

Apocrypha   Books of similar nature and contemporaneous to the Tanach but not canonized.

Avot deRabbi Natan   A collection of Midrash and Mishnah composed between 700–900 C.E. largely focusing upon Pirkei Avot.

Baal Shem Tov (1698–1760 C.E.)   The name given to Rabbi Yisroel ben Eliezer, meaning "Master of the Good Name"; founder of Chassidism.

Balfour, Secretary Lord Alfred James (1848–1940 C.E.)   The English Foreign Secretary who wrote a letter in 1917 titled "The Balfour Declaration" expressing British support for a Jewish state in Palestine.

ben Judah, Rabbi Gershom (960–1040 C.E.)   Scholar of Talmud and Halacha in France, noted for his *Cherem d'Rabbeinu Hershom*, which ended the practice of polygamy in most of Judaism.

Caro, Rabbi Joseph (1488–1575 C.E.)   The author of the great code of Jewish law, the Shulchan Aruch.

Dreyfus, Captain Alfred (1859–1935 C.E.)   An officer in the French army framed for treason due to his Jewishness; Dreyfus's trial motivated Theodor Herzl to begin modern Zionism.

Frank, Anne (1929–1945 C.E.)   A Jewish teenager who hid with her family from the Nazis in an attic in Amsterdam; she wrote a diary of her experience that is a highly regarded memoir of the Holocaust.

Gemara   One of main sections of the Talmud containing interpretations of the Tanach and Mishnah, legal arguments and Midrashim.

Halevi, Judah (1075–1141 C.E.)   A Spanish Jewish poet and philosopher.

Herzl, Theodor (1860–1904 C.E.)   The founder of modern political Zionism.

Hillel (first century B.C.E.–first century C.E.)   A great scholar of the early Talmudic period whose opinion was usually adopted as the halachah. He became the *nasi,* or patriarch, of the great Rabbinic Court called the Sanhedrin.

Ibn Ezra, Abraham (1089–1164 C.E.)   A Spanish Jewish philosopher, commentator, and linguist.

Isaac   Abraham's son; the second of the patriarchs whose story is told in the Book of Genesis. His name is Yitzchak in Hebrew.

Jacob   The third of the patriarchs whose story is told in Genesis. Jacob's twelve sons become the forefathers of the tribes of Israel. Jacob wrestled with a man considered to be an angel, which allowed Jacob to gain an understanding of himself and God at a critical time in his life. As a result, Jacob received the name Yisrael—the one who struggles with God—which is applied to Jews throughout history.

Kagan, Rabbi Yisroel Meir (1838–1933 C.E.)   A nineteenth-century Polish rabbi who wrote an ethics book addressing hateful speech.

Kaplan, Rabbi Mordecai (1881–1983 C.E.)   A teacher and philosopher whose definition of Judaism as a civilization centered around "God and the Torah; Israel" became the foundation of the Reconstructionist Movement.

Ketuvim   "The Writings"; the third part of the Tanach.

Kluger, Rabbi Shlomo (1788–1869 C.E.)   A Polish commentator and author.

Luria, Rabbi Isaac (1534–1572 C.E.)   A Kabbalistic rabbi and teacher in Tzfat, one of the founding thinkers of contemporary Jewish mysticism.

Maimonides (1135–1204 C.E.)   Also known as Rabbi Moses ben Maimon, which becomes the acrostic "Rambam." A rabbi, philosopher, and commentator known for his *Mishneh Torah,* a codification of all the rules of the Talmud, and *The Guide for the Perplexed,* a philosophical treatise. Maimonides was also a renowned physician.

Mekhilta d'Rabbi Ishmael   An early commentary on selected portions of the Torah attributed (probably incorrectly) to Rabbi Ishmael.

Mendelssohn, Moses (1729–1786 C.E.)   A German Jewish philosopher who was one of the first to attempt to adapt Enlightenment philosophies to Judaism.

Midrash Rabbah   The Great Midrash, consisting of classical aggadic Midrashim on texts of the Tanach. Each book is referred to by the name of the book in the Tanach it examines. For example, the collection on Genesis is called "Genesis Rabbah."

Mishnah   The first compilation of Jewish law following the Torah redacted from 180 to 220 C.E. forming part of the core of the Talmud.

Mishneh Torah   The code of Jewish law written by Maimonides between 1170 and 1180 C.E..

Moses   The greatest teacher and prophet in Judaism. Moses was raised in the Pharaoh's household in Egypt while the Israelites were enslaved. After killing an Egyptian taskmaster who was beating an Israelite slave, Moses ran away and became a shepherd. God called to Moses from a burning bush that was not consumed, and told him to return to Egypt to convince Pharaoh to let the Israelites go. Pharaoh finally agreed, and Moses led the Israelites to Mount Sinai, where he brought the Torah to the people. Moses led the people for 40 years through the desert to the Promised Land, but was not allowed to enter himself. He died on Mount Nebo.

Nachmanides (1194–1279 C.E.)   Rabbi Moses ben Nachman, also called by the acronym Ramban; a medieval Bible commentator and philosopher.

Nivi'im   "Prophets"; the second part of the Tanach.

Pirkei Avot   Sayings of the Fathers; a section of the Mishnah containing a series of ethical sayings and teachings.

Pisikta Rabbatai   A collection of classical aggadic Midrashim written toward the end of the Talmudic Era.

Rabbah (c. 270–c. 330 C.E.)   An early Talmudic sage and head of an academy at Pumbedita.

Ramban   *see* Nachmanides.

Rothschild, Meyer Amschel (1744–1812 C.E.)   A German Jewish banker who created a large international banking network unlike any that had existed previously; it exerted great influence in Europe for generations.

Sarah   Abraham's wife and the first of the matriarchs whose story is told in Genesis. Sarah had her name changed from Sarai to show God was always with her.

Shammai (first century B.C.E.–first century C.E.)   A great scholar of the early Talmudic period whose opinion was usually not adopted as the halachah when it conflicted with the rulings of his rival, Hillel.

Shulchan Aruch   "The Set Table"; the definitive code of Jewish law written by Joseph Caro in Tzfat in 1563.

Spinoza, Baruch (1632–1677 C.E.)   A Dutch Jewish philosopher who was excommunicated from the Jewish community because of his doubting of the Divine origins of the Biblical texts.

Suleiman (1494–1566 C.E.)   A sultan of the Ottoman Empire under whose governance the current walls of the Old City of Jerusalem were built.

Talmud Bavli   A great text of law, stories, and discussions comprising the core of rabbinic Judaism and the Oral Law. It is centered around the Mishnah and Gemara with several commentaries. The central part of the Talmud Bavli, which was developed between 200 and 600 C.E. in Babylonia and contains 63 tractates and thousands of pages.

Talmud Yirushalmi   A version of the Talmud developed in Palestine between 200 and 350 C.E. that's shorter than the Talmud Bavli, although there is significant overlap between the two. Also called the Jerusalem Talmud, although it wasn't developed in that city.

Tanach   The Jewish Bible; an acronym for three main parts of Bible—Torah, Nivi'im (Prophets), and Ketuvim (Writings).

Tanhuma   A collection of classical midrashim attributed to Rav Tanhuma.

Tosefot   Commentaries on the Talmud by Rashi's students.

Yochanan ben Zakkai (first century C.E.)   A Pharisee leader who was smuggled out of the Temple before its destruction and convinced Roman General Vespasian to allow him and his students to establish a school at Yavneh. At Yavnah, he and his students began to design a Judaism that could continue without its central feature, the Temple.

Zohar   "Radiance"; the primary text of Kabbalah.

For Further Reading

The following is a partial list of books and websites that were consulted for this book or that might be useful for further study of Judaism.

Books on Basic Judaism

Amsel, Nachum. *The Jewish Encyclopedia of Moral and Ethical Issues*. Northvale, New Jersey: Jason Aronson, Inc., 1996.

Kertzer, Rabbi Morris N., and Rabbi Lawrence A. Hoffman. *What Is a Jew?* New York: Simon & Schuster, 1996.

Kolatch, Alfred J. *The Jewish Book of Why*. Middle Village, New York: Jonathan David Publishers, 1981.

Telushkin, Rabbi Joseph. *Jewish Literacy*. New York: William Morrow, 2001.

Texts and Primary Sources

Bialik, Hayim Nahman, and Yehoshua Hana Ravnitsky. *The Book of Legends*. New York: Schocken Books, 1992.

Carasik, Michael, editor and translator. *The Commentators' Bible*. Philadelphia: Jewish Publication Society, 1985.

Freedman, Rabbi Dr. H., and Maurice Simon. *Midrash Rabbah*. London: Soncino Press, 1939.

Holt, Barry W., editor. *Back to the Sources: Reading the Classic Jewish Texts*. New York: Simon & Shuster, 1986.

Steinsaltz, Rabbi Adin, commentator. *The Talmud: The Steinsaltz Edition*. New York: Random House, 1989.

Talmud Bavli: The Schottenstein Edition. New York: Menorah Publications, 2009.

Tanakh: The Holy Scriptures. Philadelphia: The Jewish Publication Society, 1985.

Books on Jewish Milestones

Diamont, Anita. *The New Jewish Wedding.* New York: Simon & Schuster, 2001.

Knobel, Peter. *Gates of the Seasons.* New York: CCAR Press, 1986.

Lamm. Maurice. *The Jewish Way in Death and Mourning.* Middle Village, New York: Jonathan David Publishers, 2012.

———. *The Jewish Way in Love and Marriage.* Middle Village, New York: Jonathan David Publishers, 1991.

Maslin, Simeon J. *Gates of Mitzvah.* New York: CCAR Press, 1986.

Websites

www.aish.com   A general website with many articles on Judaism, primarily from an Orthodox perspective

www.chabad.org   The Orthodox (Chassidic) Movement's website, providing information, guidance, and information on programs and activities from that movement's perspective

www.conservativejudaism.org   The Conservative Movement's website, providing information, guidance, and information on programs and activities from that movement's perspective

www.jewfaq.org   An online Jewish encyclopedia answering frequently asked questions about Judaism from an Orthodox perspective

www.jewishrecon.org   The Reconstructionist Movement's website, providing information, guidance, and information on programs and activities from that movement's perspective

www.jewishvirtuallibrary.org   An online Jewish library that includes Jewish texts, provided by the American-Israeli Cooperative Enterprise, a nonprofit and nonpartisan organization to strengthen the U.S.-Israel relationship

www.MyJewishLearning.com   A transdenominational website of Jewish information and education

www.ou.org   The Orthodox Union website, providing information, guidance, and information on programs and activities from that movement's perspective

www.reformjudaism.org   The Reform Movement's website, providing information, guidance, and information on programs and activities from that movement's perspective

Index